MEMOI[RS]

OF

EXTRAORDINARY POPULAR DELUSIONS

AND THE

𝔐𝔞𝔡𝔫𝔢𝔰𝔰 𝔬𝔣 𝔠𝔯𝔬𝔴𝔡𝔰.

By CHARLES MACKAY, LL.D.

AUTHOR OF "EGERIA," "THE SALAMANDRINE," ETC.

ILLUSTRATED WITH NUMEROUS ENGRAVINGS.

N'en déplaise à ces fous nommés sages de Grèce,
En ce monde il n'est point de parfaite sagesse;
Tous les hommes sont fous, et malgré tours leurs soins
Ne diffèrent entre eux que du plus ou du moins.
BOILEAU.

VOL. II.

SECOND EDITION.

LONDON:

OFFICE OF THE NATIONAL ILLUSTRATED LIBRARY,

227 STRAND.

1852.

LONDON:

PRINTED BY LEVEY, ROBSON, AND FRANKLYN,

Great New Street, Fetter Lane.

CONTENTS.

꧁

THE CRUSADES.

THE WITCH MANIA.

THE SLOW POISONERS.

HAUNTED HOUSES.

POPULAR FOLLIES OF GREAT CITIES.

POPULAR ADMIRATION OF GREAT THIEVES.

DUELS AND ORDEALS.

RELICS.

LIST OF ENGRAVINGS IN VOL. II.

MEMOIRS

OF

EXTRAORDINARY POPULAR DELUSIONS.

THE CRUSADES.

They heard, and up they sprung upon the wing
Innumerable. As when the potent rod
Of Amram's son, in Egypt's evil day,
Waved round the coast, up call'd a pitchy cloud
Of locusts, warping on the eastern wind
That o'er the realm of impious Pharaoh hung
Like night, and darken'd all the realm of Nile,
So numberless were they. * * * *
All in a moment through the gloom were seen
Ten thousand banners rise into the air,
With orient colours waving. With them rose
A forest huge of spears ; and thronging helms
Appear'd, and serried shields, in thick array,
Of depth immeasurable. *Paradise Lost.*

EVERY age has its peculiar folly ; some scheme, project, or phantasy into which it plunges, spurred on either by the love of gain, the necessity of excitement, or the mere force of imitation. Failing in these, it has some madness, to which it is goaded by political or religious causes, or both combined. Every one of these causes influenced the Crusades, and conspired to render them the most extraordinary instance upon record of the extent to which popular enthusiasm can be carried. History in her solemn page informs us, that the Crusaders were but ignorant and savage men, that their motives were those of bigotry unmitigated, and that their pathway was one of blood and tears. Romance, on the other hand, dilates upon their piety and heroism, and portrays, in her most glowing and impassioned hues, their virtue and magnanimity, the imperishable honour they acquired for themselves, and the great services they rendered to Christianity. In the following pages we shall ransack the stores of both, to discover the true spirit that animated the motley multitude who took up arms in the service of the cross, leaving history to vouch for facts, but not disdaining the aid of contemporary poetry and romance, to throw light upon feelings, motives, and opinions.

In order to understand thoroughly the state of public feeling in Europe at the time when Peter the Hermit preached the holy war, it will be necessary to go back for many years anterior to that event. We must make acquaintance with the pilgrims of the eighth, ninth, and tenth centuries, and learn the tales they told of the dangers they had passed and the wonders they had seen. Pilgrimages to the Holy Land seem at first to have been undertaken by converted Jews, and by Christian devotees of lively imagination, pining with a natural curiosity to visit the scenes which of all others were most interesting in their eyes. The pious and the impious alike flocked to Jerusalem,— the one class to feast their sight on the scenes hallowed by the life and sufferings of their Lord, and the other, because it soon became a generally received opinion, that such a pilgrimage was sufficient to rub off the long score of sins, however atrocious. Another and very numerous class of pilgrims were the idle and roving, who visited Palestine then as the moderns visit Italy or Switzerland now, because it was the fashion, and because they might please their vanity by retailing, on their return, the adventures they had met with. But the really pious formed the great majority. Every year their numbers increased, until at last they became so numerous as to be called the "armies of the Lord." Full of enthusiasm, they set the dangers and difficulties of the way at defiance, and lingered with holy rapture on every scene described by the Evangelists. To them it was bliss indeed to drink the clear waters of the Jordan, or be baptised in the same stream where John had baptised the Saviour. They wandered with awe and pleasure in the purlieus of the Temple, on the solemn Mount of Olives, or the awful Calvary, where a God had bled for sinful men. To these pilgrims every object was precious. Relics were eagerly sought after ; flagons of water from Jordan, or panniers of mould from the hill of the Crucifixion, were brought home, and sold at extravagant prices to churches and monasteries. More apocryphal relics, such as the wood of the true cross, the tears of the Virgin Mary, the hems of her garments, the toe-nails and hair of the Apostles—even the tents that Paul had helped to manufacture—were exhibited for sale by the knavish in Palestine, and brought back to Europe "with wondrous cost and care." A grove of a hundred oaks would not have furnished all the wood sold in little morsels as remnants of the true cross; and the tears of Mary, if collected together, would have filled a cistern. .

For upwards of two hundred years the pilgrims met with no impediment in Palestine. The enlightened Haroun Al Reschid, and his more immediate successors, encouraged the stream which brought so much wealth into Syria, and treated the wayfarers with the utmost courtesy. The race of Fatemite caliphs,—who, although in other respects as tolerant, were more distressed for money, or more unscrupulous in obtaining it, than their predecessors of the house of Abbas,—imposed a tax of a bezant for each pilgrim that entered Jerusalem. This was a serious hardship upon the poorer sort, who had begged their weary way across Europe, and arrived at the bourne of all their hopes without a coin. A great outcry was immediately raised, but still the tax was rigorously levied. The pilgrims unable to pay were compelled to remain at the gate of the holy city until some rich devotee arriving with his train, paid the tax and let them in. Robert of Normandy, father of William the Conqueror, who, in common with many other nobles of the highest rank, undertook the pilgrimage, found on his arrival scores of pilgrims at the gate, anxiously expecting his coming to pay the tax for them. Upon no occasion was such a boon refused.

The sums drawn from this source were a mine of wealth to the Moslem governors of Palestine, imposed as the tax had been at a time when pilgrimages had become more numerous than ever. A strange idea had taken possession of the popular mind at the close of the tenth and commencement of the eleventh century. It was universally believed that the end of the world was at hand; that the thousand years of the Apocalypse were near completion, and that Jesus Christ would descend upon Jerusalem to judge mankind. All Christendom was in commotion. A panic terror seized upon the weak, the credulous, and the guilty, who in those days formed more than nineteen-twentieths of the population. Forsaking their homes, kindred, and occupation, they crowded to Jerusalem to await the coming of the Lord, lightened, as they imagined, of a load of sin by their weary pilgrimage. To increase the panic, the stars were observed to fall from heaven, earthquakes to shake the land, and violent hurricanes to blow down the forests. All these, and more especially the meteoric phenomena, were looked upon as the fore-runners of the approaching judgments. Not a meteor shot athwart the horizon that did not fill a district with alarm, and send away to Jerusalem a score of pilgrims, with staff in hand and wallet on their back, praying as they went for the remission of their sins. Men, women, and even children, trudged in droves to the holy city, in expectation of the day when the heavens would open, and the Son of God descend in his glory. This extraordinary delusion, while it aug-mented the numbers, increased also the hardships of the pilgrims. Beggars became so numerous on all the highways between the west of Europe and Constantinople, that the monks, the great almsgivers upon these occasions, would have brought starvation within sight of their own doors, if they had not economised their resources, and left the devotees to shift for themselves as they could. Hundreds of them were glad to subsist upon the berries that ripened by the road, who, before this great flux, might have shared the bread and flesh of the monasteries.

But this was not the greatest of their difficulties. On their arrival in Jerusalem they found that a sterner race had obtained possession of the Holy Land. The caliphs of Bagdad had been succeeded by the harsh Turks of the race of Seljook, who looked upon the pilgrims with contempt and aversion. The Turks of the eleventh century were more ferocious and less scrupulous than the Saracens of the tenth. They were annoyed at the immense number of pilgrims who overran the country, and still more so because they shewed no inten-tion of quitting it. The hourly expectation of the last judgment kept them waiting ; and the Turks, apprehensive of being at last driven from the soil by the swarms that were still arriving, heaped up diffi-culties in their way. Persecution of every kind awaited them. They were plundered, and beaten with stripes, and kept in suspense for months at the gates of Jerusalem, unable to pay the golden bezant that was to procure them admission.

When the first epidemic terror of the day of judgment began to subside, a few pilgrims ventured to return to Europe, their hearts big with indignation at the insults they had suffered. Every where as they passed they related to a sympathising auditory the wrongs of Christen-dom. Strange to say, even these recitals increased the mania for pil-grimage. The greater the dangers of the way, the fairer chance that sins of deep dye would be atoned for. Difficulty and suffering only height-ened the merit, and fresh hordes issued from every town and village, win favour in the sight of heaven by a visit to the holy sepulchre. Thus did things continue during the whole of the eleventh century.

. The train that was to explode so fearfully was now laid, and there wanted but the hand to apply the torch. At last the man appeared upon the scene. Like all who have ever achieved so great an end, Peter the Hermit was exactly suited to the age; neither behind it nor in advance of it; but acute enough to penetrate its mystery ere it was discovered by any other. Enthusiastic, chivalrous, bigoted, and, if not insane, not far removed from insanity, he was the very prototype of the time. True enthusiasm is always persevering and always eloquent, and these two qualities were united in no common degree in the person of this extraordinary preacher. He was a monk of Amiens, and ere he assumed the hood had served as a soldier. He is represented as having been ill-favoured and low in stature, but with an eye of surpassing brightness and intelligence. Having been seized with the mania of the age, he visited Jerusalem, and remained there till his blood boiled to see the cruel persecution heaped upon the devotees. On his return home he shook the world by the eloquent story of their wrongs.

Before entering into any further details of the marvellous results of his preaching, it will be advisable to cast a glance at the state of the mind of Europe, that we may understand all the better the causes of his success. First of all, there was the priesthood, which, exercising as it did the most conspicuous influence upon the fortunes of society, claims the largest share of attention. Religion was the ruling idea of that day, and the only civiliser capable of taming such wolves as then constituted the flock of the faithful. The clergy were all in all; and though they kept the popular mind in the most slavish subjection with regard to religious matters, they furnished it with the means of defence against all other oppression except their own. In the ecclesiastical ranks were concentrated all the true piety, all the learning, all the wisdom of the time; and, as a natural consequence, a great portion of power, which their very wisdom perpetually incited them to extend. The people knew nothing of kings and nobles, except in the way of injuries inflicted. The first ruled for, or more properly speaking against, the barons, and the barons only existed to brave the power of the kings, or to trample with their iron heels upon the neck of prostrate democracy. The latter had no friend but the clergy, and these, though they necessarily instilled the superstition from which they themselves were not exempt, yet taught the cheering doctrine that all men were equal in the sight of heaven. Thus, while Feudalism told them they had no rights in this world, Religion told them they had every right in the next. With this consolation they were for the time content, for political ideas had as yet taken no root. When the clergy, for other reasons, recommended the Crusade, the people joined in it with enthusiasm. The subject of Palestine filled all minds; the pilgrims' tales of two centuries warmed every imagination; and when their friends, their guides, and their instructors preached a war so much in accordance with their own prejudices and modes of thinking, the enthusiasm rose into a frenzy.

But while religion inspired the masses, another agent was at work upon the nobility. These were fierce and lawless; tainted with every vice, endowed with no virtue, and redeemed by one good quality alone, that of courage. The only religion they felt was the religion of fear. That and their overboiling turbulence alike combined to guide them to the Holy Land. Most of them had sins enough to answer for. They lived with their hand against every man, and with no law but their own passions. They set at defiance the secular power of the clergy; but their hearts quailed at the awful denunciations of the pulpit with regard to the life to come. War was the business and the delight of their existence; and when they were promised remission of all their sins upon the easy condition of following their favourite bent, it is not to be wondered at that they rushed with enthusiasm to the onslaught, and became as zealous in the service of the cross as the great majority of the people, who were swayed by more purely religious motives. Fanaticism and the love of battle alike impelled them to the war, while the kings and princes of Europe had still another motive for encouraging their zeal. Policy opened their eyes to the great advantages which would accrue to themselves by the absence of so many restless, intriguing, and bloodthirsty men, whose insolence it required more than the small power of royalty to restrain within due bounds. Thus every motive was favourable to the Crusades. Every class of society was alike incited to join or encourage the war: kings and the clergy by policy, the nobles by turbulence and the love of dominion, and the people by religious zeal and the concentrated enthusiasm of two centuries, skilfully directed by their only instructors.

It was in Palestine itself that Peter the Hermit first conceived the grand idea of rousing the powers of Christendom to rescue the Christians of the East from the thraldom of the Mussulmans, and the sepulchre of Jesus from the rude hands of the infidel. The subject engrossed his whole mind. Even in the visions of the night he was full of it. One dream made such an impression upon him, that he devoutly believed the Saviour of the world himself appeared before him, and promised him aid and protection in his holy undertaking. If his zeal had ever wavered before, this was sufficient to fix it for ever.

Peter, after he had performed all the penances and duties of his pilgrimage, demanded an interview with Simeon, the Patriarch of the Greek Church at Jerusalem. Though the latter was a heretic in Peter's eyes, yet he was still a Christian, and felt as acutely as himself for the persecutions heaped by the Turks upon the followers of Jesus. The good prelate entered fully into his views, and, at his suggestion, wrote letters to the pope, and to the most influential monarchs of Christendom, detailing the sorrows of the faithful, and urging them to take up arms in their defence. Peter was not a laggard in the work. Taking an affectionate farewell of the Patriarch, he returned in all haste to Italy. Pope Urban II. occupied the apostolic chair. It was at that time far from being an easy seat. His predecessor Gregory had bequeathed him a host of disputes with the Emperor Henry IV. of Germany, and he had converted Philip I. of France into an enemy by his strenuous opposition to an adulterous connexion formed by that monarch. So many dangers encompassed him, that the Vatican was no secure abode, and he had taken refuge in Apulia, under the protection of the renowned Robert Guiscard. Thither Peter appears to have followed him, though in what spot their meeting took place is not stated with any precision by ancient chroniclers or modern historians. Urban received him most kindly ; read, with tears in his eyes, the epistle from the Patriarch Simeon, and listened to the eloquent story of the Hermit with an attention which shewed how deeply he sympathised with the woes of the Christian Church. Enthusiasm is contagious ; and the pope appears to have caught it instantly from one whose zeal was so unbounded. Giving the Hermit full powers, he sent him abroad to preach the holy war to all the nations and potentates of Christendom. The Hermit preached, and countless thousands answered to his call. France, Germany, and Italy started at his voice, and prepared for the deliverance of Zion. One of the early historians of the Crusade, who was himself an eyewitness of the rapture of Europe,* describes the personal appearance of the Hermit at this time. He says, that there appeared to be something of divine in every thing which he said or did. The people so highly reverenced him, that they plucked hairs from the mane of his mule that they might keep them as relics. While preaching he wore in general a woollen tunic, with a dark-coloured mantle, which fell down to his heels. His arms and feet were bare ; and he ate neither flesh nor bread, supporting himself chiefly upon fish and wine. " He set out," says the chronicler, "from whence I know not; but we saw him passing through the towns and villages, preaching every where, and the people surrounding him in crowds, loading him with offerings, and celebrating his sanctity with such great praises, that I

* Guibert de Nogent.

never remember to have seen such honours bestowed upon any one."
Thus he went on, untired, inflexible, and full of devotion, communi-
cating his own madness to his hearers, until Europe was stirred from
its very depths.

While the Hermit was appealing with such signal success to the
people, the pope appealed with as much success to those who were to
become the chiefs and leaders of the expedition. His first step was to
call a council at Placentia, in the autumn of the year 1095. Here, in
the assembly of the clergy, the pope debated the grand scheme, and
gave audience to emissaries who had been sent from Constantinople
by the Emperor of the East, to detail the progress made by the Turks
in their design of establishing themselves in Europe.   The clergy
were of course unanimous in support of the Crusade ; and the council
separated, each individual member of it being empowered to preach it
to his people.

But Italy could not be expected to furnish all the aid required ;
and the pope crossed the Alps to inspire the fierce and powerful
nobility and chivalrous population of Gaul.   His boldness in entering
the territory, and placing himself in the power of his foe King Philip
of France, is not the least surprising feature of his mission.   Some
have imagined that cool policy alone actuated him ; while others
assert that it was mere zeal, as warm and as blind as that of Peter the
Hermit.   The latter opinion seems to be the true one.   Society did
not calculate the consequences of what it was doing.   Every man
seemed to act from impulse only ; and the pope, in throwing himself
into the heart of France, acted as much from impulse as the thousands who responded to his call. A council was eventually summoned
to meet him at Clermont, in Auvergne, to consider the state of the
Church, reform abuses, and above all, make preparations for the
war.   It was in the midst of an extremely cold winter, and the
ground was covered with snow. During seven days the council sat
with closed doors, while immense crowds from all parts of France
flocked into the town, in expectation that the pope himself would
address the people. All the towns and villages for miles around were
filled with the multitude ; even the fields were encumbered with
people, who, unable to procure lodging, pitched their tents under the
trees and by the way-side.   All the neighbourhood presented the
appearance of a vast camp.

During the seven days' deliberation, a sentence of excommunication was passed upon King Philip for adultery with Bertrade de
Montfort, Countess of Anjou, and for disobedience to the supreme
authority of the apostolic see. This bold step impressed the people
with reverence for so stern a Church, which in the discharge of its

duty shewed itself no respecter of persons. Their love and their fear were alike increased, and they were prepared to listen with more intense devotion to the preaching of so righteous and inflexible a pastor. The great square before the cathedral church of Clermont

THE CATHEDRAL OF CLERMONT.

became every instant more densely crowded as the hour drew nigh when the pope was to address the populace. Issuing from the church in his full canonicals, surrounded by his cardinals and bishops in all the splendour of Romish ecclesiastical costume, the pope stood before the populace on a high scaffolding erected for the occasion, and covered with scarlet cloth. A brilliant array of bishops and cardinals surrounded him; and among them, humbler in rank, but more important in the world's eye, the Hermit Peter, dressed in his simple and austere habiliments. Historians differ as to whether or not Peter addressed the crowd, but as all agree that he was present, it seems reasonable to suppose that he spoke. But it was the oration of the pope that was most important. As he lifted up his hands to ensure attention, every voice immediately became still. He began by detailing the miseries endured by their brethren in the Holy Land; how the plains of Palestine were desolated by the outrageous heathen, who with the sword and the firebrand carried wailing into the dwellings and flames into the possessions of the faithful; how Christian wives and daughters were defiled by pagan lust; how the altars of the true God were desecrated, and the relics of the saints trodden under foot. " You," continued the eloquent pontiff (and Urban II. was one of the most eloquent men of the day), " you, who hear me, and who have received the true faith, and been endowed by God with power, and strength, and greatness of soul,—whose ancestors have been the prop of Christendom, and whose kings have put a barrier against the progress of the infidel,—I call upon you to wipe off these impurities from the face of the earth, and lift your oppressed fellow-Christians from the depths into which they have been trampled. The sepulchre of Christ is possessed by the heathen, the sacred places dishonoured by their vileness. Oh, brave knights and faithful people ! offspring of invincible fathers ! ye will not degenerate from your ancient renown. Ye will not be restrained from embarking in this great cause by the tender ties of wife or little ones, but will remember the words of the Saviour of the world himself, ' Whosoever loves father and mother more than me is not worthy of me. Whosoever shall abandon for my name's sake his house, or his brethren, or his sisters, or his father, or his mother, or his wife, or his children, or his lands, shall receive a hundredfold, and shall inherit eternal life.'"

The warmth of the pontiff communicated itself to the crowd, and the enthusiasm of the people broke out several times ere he concluded his address. He went on to portray, not only the spiritual but the temporal advantages that would accrue to those who took up arms in the service of the cross. Palestine was, he said, a land flowing with milk and honey, and precious in the sight of God, as the scene of the grand events which had saved mankind. That land, he promised, should be divided among them. Moreover, they should have full pardon for all their offences, either against God or man. " Go, then," he added, " in expiation of your sins ; and go assured, that after this world shall have passed away, imperishable glory shall be yours in the world which is to come." The enthusiasm was no longer to be restrained, and loud shouts interrupted the speaker; the people exclaiming as if with one voice, " *Dieu le veult ! Dieu le veult !*" With great presence of mind Urban took advantage of the outburst, and as soon as silence was obtained, continued : " Dear brethren, to-day is shewn forth in you that which the Lord has said by his Evangelist, ' When two or three are gathered together in my name, there will I be in the midst of them to bless them.' If the Lord God had not been in your souls, you would not all have pronounced the same words ; or rather God himself pronounced them by your lips, for it was he that put them in your hearts. Be they, then, your war-cry in the combat, for those words came forth from God. Let the army of the Lord, when it rushes upon his enemies, shout but that one cry, ' *Dieu le veult ! Dieu le veult !*' Let whoever is inclined to devote himself to this holy cause make it a solemn engagement, and bear the cross of the Lord either on his breast or his brow till he set out ; and let him who is ready to begin his march place the holy emblem on his shoulders, in memory of that precept of our Saviour, ' He who does not take up his cross and follow me is not worthy of me.' "

The news of this council spread to the remotest parts of Europe in an incredibly short space of time. Long before the fleetest horseman could have brought the intelligence, it was known by the people in distant provinces; a fact which was considered as nothing less than supernatural. But the subject was in every body's mouth, and the minds of men were prepared for the result. The enthusiastic merely asserted what they wished, and the event tallied with their prediction. This was, however, quite enough in those days for a miracle, and as a miracle every one regarded it.

For several months after the Council of Clermont, France and Germany presented a singular spectacle. The pious, the fanatic, the needy, the dissolute, the young and the old, even women and children, and the halt and lame, enrolled themselves by hundreds. In every village the clergy were busied in keeping up the excitement, promising eternal rewards to those who assumed the red cross, and fulminating the most awful denunciations against all the worldly-minded who refused or even hesitated. Every debtor who joined the Crusade was freed by the papal edict from the claims of his creditors ; outlaws of every grade were made equal with the honest upon the same conditions. The property of those who went was placed under the protection of the Church, and St. Paul and St. Peter themselves were believed to descend from their high abode, to watch over the chattels of the absent pilgrims. Signs and portents were seen in the air, to increase the fervour of the multitude. An aurora-borealis of unusual brilliancy appeared, and thousands of the Crusaders came out to gaze upon it, prostrating themselves upon the earth in adoration. It was thought to be a sure prognostic of the interposition of the Most High, and a representation of his armies fighting with and overthrowing the infidels. Reports of wonders were every where rife. A monk had seen two gigantic warriors on horseback, the one representing a Christian and the other a Turk, fighting in the sky with flaming swords, the Christian of course overcoming the Paynim. Myriads of stars were said to have fallen from heaven, each representing the fall of a pagan foe. It was believed at the same time that the Emperor Charlemagne would rise from the grave, and lead on to victory the embattled armies of the Lord. A singular feature of the popular madness was the enthusiasm of the women. Every where they encouraged their lovers and husbands to forsake all things for the holy war. Many of them burned the sign of the cross upon their breasts and arms, and coloured the wound with a red dye, as a lasting memorial of their zeal. Others, still more zealous, impressed the mark by the same means upon the tender limbs of young children and infants at the breast.

Guibert de Nogent tells of a monk who made a large incision upon his forehead in the form of a cross, which he coloured with some powerful ingredient, telling the people that an angel had done it when he was asleep. This monk appears to have been more of a rogue than a fool, for he contrived to fare more sumptuously than any of his brother pilgrims, upon the strength of his sanctity. The Crusaders every where gave him presents of food and money, and he became quite fat ere he arrived at Jerusalem, notwithstanding the fatigues of the way. If he had acknowledged in the first place that he had made the wound himself, he would not have been thought more holy than his fellows; but the story of the angel was a clincher.

All those who had property of any description rushed to the mart to change it into hard cash. Lands and houses could be had for a quarter of their value, while arms and accoutrements of war rose in the same proportion. Corn, which had been excessively dear in anticipation of a year of scarcity, suddenly became plentiful; and such was the diminution in the value of provisions, that seven sheep were sold for five *deniers*.* The nobles mortgaged their estates for mere trifles to Jews and unbelievers, or conferred charters of immunity upon the towns and communes within their fiefs, for sums which, a few years previously, they would have rejected with disdain. The farmer endeavoured to sell his plough, and the artisan his tools, to purchase a sword for the deliverance of Jerusalem. Women disposed of their

* Guibert de Nogent.

trinkets for the same purpose. During the spring and summer of this year (1096) the roads teemed with Crusaders, all hastening to the towns and villages appointed as the rendezvous of the district. Some were on horseback, some in carts, and some came down the rivers in boats and rafts, bringing their wives and children, all eager to go to Jerusalem. Very few knew where Jerusalem was. Some thought it fifty thousand miles away, and others imagined that it was but a month's journey; while at sight of every town or castle the children exclaimed, "Is that Jerusalem? Is that the city?"* Parties of knights and nobles might be seen travelling eastward, and amusing themselves as they went with the knightly diversion of hawking, to lighten the fatigues of the way.

Guibert de Nogent, who did not write from hearsay, but from actual observation, says the enthusiasm was so contagious, that when any one heard the orders of the pontiff, he went instantly to solicit his neighbours and friends to join with him in "the way of God," for so they called the proposed expedition. The counts palatine were full of the desire to undertake the journey, and all the inferior knights were animated with the same zeal. Even the poor caught the flame so ardently, that no one paused to think of the inadequacy of his means, or to consider whether he ought to yield up his farm, his vineyard, or his fields. Each one set about selling his property at as low a price as if he had been held in some horrible captivity, and sought to pay his ransom without loss of time. Those who had not determined upon the journey joked and laughed at those who were thus disposing of their goods at such ruinous prices, prophesying that the expedition would be miserable and their return worse. But they held this language only for a day; the next they were suddenly seized with the same frenzy as the rest. Those who had been loudest in their jeers gave up all their property for a few crowns, and set out with those they had so laughed at a few hours before. In most cases the laugh was turned against them; for when it became known that a man was hesitating, his more zealous neighbours sent him a present of a knitting-needle or a distaff, to shew their contempt of him. There was no resisting this; so that the fear of ridicule contributed its fair contingent to the armies of the Lord.

Another effect of the Crusade was, the religious obedience with which it inspired the people and the nobility for that singular institution "The Truce of God." At the commencement of the eleventh century, the clergy of France, sympathising for the woes of the people, but unable to diminish them, by repressing the rapacity and insolence of the feudal chiefs, endeavoured to promote universal good-will by

* Guibert de Nogent.

the promulgation of the famous "Peace of God." All who conformed
to it bound themselves by oath not to take revenge for any injury,
not to enjoy the fruits of property usurped from others, nor to use
deadly weapons; in reward of which they would receive remission of
all their sins.   However benevolent the intention of this "Peace," it
led to nothing but perjury, and violence reigned as uncontrolled as
before.   In the year 1041, another attempt was made to soften the
angry passions of the semi-barbarous chiefs, and the "Truce of God"
was solemnly proclaimed.   The *truce* lasted from the Wednesday evening to the Monday morning of every week, in which interval it was
strictly forbidden to recur to violence on any pretext, or to seek
revenge for any injury.   It was impossible to civilise men by these
means.   Few even promised to become peaceable for so unconscionable a period as five days a week; or if they did, they made ample
amends on the two days left open to them.   The truce was afterwards
shortened from the Saturday evening to the Monday morning; but
little or no diminution of violence and bloodshed was the consequence.
At the Council of Clermont, Urban II. again solemnly proclaimed the
truce.   So strong was the religious feeling, that every one hastened
to obey.   All minor passions disappeared before the grand passion of
crusading.   The feudal chief ceased to oppress, the robber to plunder,
the people to complain; but one idea was in all hearts, and there
seemed to be no room for any other.

The encampments of these heterogeneous multitudes offered a singular aspect.   Those vassals who ranged themselves under the banners
of their lord erected tents around his castle; while those who undertook the war on their own account constructed booths and huts in
the neighbourhood of the towns or villages, preparatory to their join-
ing some popular leader of the expedition.   The meadows of France
were covered with tents.   As the belligerents were to have remission
of all their sins on their arrival in Palestine, hundreds of them gave
themselves up to the most unbounded licentiousness.   The courtesan,
with the red cross upon her shoulders, plied her shameless trade with
sensual pilgrims without scruple on either side; the lover of good cheer
gave loose reign to his appetite, and drunkenness and debauchery
flourished.   Their zeal in the service of the Lord was to wipe out all
faults and follies, and they had the same surety of salvation as the
rigid anchorite.   This reasoning had charms for the ignorant, and
the sounds of lewd revelry and the voice of prayer rose at the same
instant from the camp.

It is now time to speak of the leaders of the expedition.   Great
multitudes ranged themselves under the command of Peter the Hermit, whom, as the originator, they considered the most appropriate

leader of the war. Others joined the banner of a bold adventurer, whom history has dignified with no other name than that of Gautier sans Avoir, or Walter the Pennyless, but who is represented as having been of noble family, and well skilled in the art of war. A third multitude from Germany flocked around the standard of a monk named Gottschalk, of whom nothing is known except that he was a fanatic of the deepest dye. All these bands, which together are said to have amounted to three hundred thousand men, women, and children, were composed of the vilest rascality of Europe. Without discipline, principle, or true courage, they rushed through the nations like a pestilence, spreading terror and death wherever they went. The first multitude that set forth was led by Walter the Pennyless early in the spring of 1096, within a very few months after the Council of Clermont. Each man of that irregular host aspired to be his own master. Like their nominal leader, each was poor to penury, and trusted for subsistence on his journey to the chances of the road. Rolling through Germany like a tide, they entered Hungary, where, at first, they were received with some degree of kindness by the people. The latter had not yet caught sufficient of the fire of enthusiasm to join the Crusade themselves, but were willing enough to forward the cause by aiding those embarked in it. Unfortunately this good understanding did not last long. The swarm were not contented with food for their necessities, but craved for luxuries also. They attacked and plundered the dwellings of the country people, and thought nothing of murder where resistance was offered. On their arrival before Semlin, the outraged Hungarians collected in large numbers, and, attacking the rear of the crusading host, slew a great many of the stragglers, and, taking away their arms and crosses, affixed them as trophies to the walls of the city. Walter appears to have been in no mood or condition to make reprisals; for his army, destructive as a plague of locusts when plunder urged them on, were useless against any regular attack from a determined enemy. Their rear continued to be thus harassed by the wrathful Hungarians until they were fairly out of their territory. On his entrance into Bulgaria, Walter met with no better fate. The cities and towns refused to let him pass; the villages denied him provisions; and the citizens and country people uniting, slaughtered his followers by hundreds. The progress of the army was more like a retreat than an advance; but as it was impossible to stand still, Walter continued his course till he arrived at Constantinople with a force which famine and the sword had diminished to one-third of its original number.

The greater multitude, led by the enthusiastic Hermit, followed close upon his heels, with a bulky train of baggage, and women and children sufficient to form a host of themselves. If it were possible to find a rabble more vile than the army of Walter the Pennyless, it was that led by Peter the Hermit. Being better provided with means, they were not reduced to the necessity of pillage in their progress through Hungary; and had they taken any other route than that which led through Semlin, might perhaps have traversed the country without molestation. On their arrival before that city, their fury was raised at seeing the arms and red crosses of their predecessors hanging as trophies over the gates. Their pent-up ferocity exploded at the sight. The city was tumultuously attacked, and the besiegers entering, not by dint of bravery, but of superior numbers, it was given up to all the horrors which follow when victory, brutality, and licentiousness are linked together. Every evil passion was allowed to revel with impunity, and revenge, lust, and avarice,—each had its hundreds of victims in unhappy Semlin. Any maniac can kindle a conflagration, but it may require many wise men to put it out. Peter the Hermit had blown the popular fury into a flame, but to cool it again was beyond his power. His followers rioted unrestrained, until the fear of retaliation warned them to desist. When the king of Hungary was informed of the disasters of Semlin, he marched with a sufficient force to chastise the Hermit, who, at the news, broke up his camp and retreated towards the Morava, a broad and rapid stream that joins the Danube a few miles to the eastward of Belgrade. Here a party of indignant Bulgarians awaited him, and so harassed him, as to make the passage of the river a task both of difficulty and danger. Great numbers of his infatuated followers perished in the waters, and many fell under the swords of the Bulgarians. The ancient chronicles do not mention the amount of the Hermit's loss at this passage, but represent it in general terms as very great.

At Nissa, the Duke of Bulgaria fortified himself, in fear of an assault; but Peter, having learned a little wisdom from experience, thought it best to avoid hostilities. He passed three nights in quietness under the walls, and the duke, not wishing to exasperate unnecessarily so fierce and rapacious a host, allowed the townspeople to supply them with provisions. Peter took his departure peaceably on the following morning; but some German vagabonds, falling behind the main body of the army, set fire to the mills and house of a Bulgarian, with whom, it appears, they had had some dispute on the previous evening. The citizens of Nissa, who had throughout mistrusted the Crusaders, and were prepared for the worst, sallied out immediately, and took signal vengeance. The spoilers were cut to pieces, and the townspeople pursuing the Hermit, captured all the women and children who had lagged in the rear, and a great quantity

of baggage. Peter hereupon turned round and marched back to
Nissa, to demand explanation of the Duke of Bulgaria. The latter
fairly stated the provocation given, and the Hermit could urge nothing in palliation of so gross an outrage. A negotiation was entered
into, which promised to be successful, and the Bulgarians were about
to deliver up the women and children, when a party of undisciplined
Crusaders, acting solely upon their own suggestion, endeavoured to
scale the walls and seize upon the town. Peter in vain exerted his
authority; the confusion became general, and after a short but desperate battle, the Crusaders threw down their arms, and fled in all
directions. Their vast host was completely routed, the slaughter
being so great among them, as to be counted, not by hundreds, but
by thousands.

It is said that the Hermit fled from this fatal field to a forest a
few miles from Nissa, abandoned by every human creature. It would
be curious to know whether, after so dire a reverse,

"His enpierced breast
Sharp sorrow did in thousand pieces rive,"

or whether his fiery zeal still rose superior to calamity, and pictured
the eventual triumph of his cause. He, so lately the leader of a hundred thousand men, was now a solitary skulker in the forests, liable
at every instant to be discovered by some pursuing Bulgarian, and
cut off in mid career. Chance at last brought him within sight of
an eminence, where two or three of his bravest knights had collected
five hundred of the stragglers. These gladly received the Hermit,
and a consultation having taken place, it was resolved to gather together the scattered remnants of the army. Fires were lighted on the
hill, and scouts sent out in all directions for the fugitives. Horns
were sounded at intervals, to make known that friends were near;
and before nightfall the Hermit saw himself at the head of seven
thousand men. During the succeeding day, he was joined by twenty
thousand more, and with this miserable remnant of his force, he pursued his route towards Constantinople. The bones of the rest moul-
dered in the forests of Bulgaria.

On his arrival at Constantinople, where he found Walter the
Pennyless awaiting him, he was hospitably received by the Emperor
Alexius. It might have been expected that the sad reverses they
had undergone would have taught his followers common prudence;
but, unhappily for them, their turbulence and love of plunder was
not to be restrained. Although they were surrounded by friends, by
whom all their wants were liberally supplied, they could not refrain
from rapine. In vain the Hermit exhorted them to tranquillity; he
possessed no more power over them, in subduing their passions, than

the obscurest soldier of the host.   They set fire to several public
buildings in Constantinople out of pure mischief, and stripped the
lead from the roofs of the churches, which they afterwards sold for
old metal in the purlieus of the city.   From this time may be dated
the aversion which the Emperor Alexius entertained for the Crusaders,
and which was afterwards manifested in all his actions, even when he
had to deal with the chivalrous and more honourable armies which
arrived after the Hermit.   He seems to have imagined that the Turks
themselves were enemies less formidable to his power than these out-
pourings of the refuse of Europe : he soon found a pretext to hurry
them into Asia Minor.   Peter crossed the Bosphorus with Walter ;
but the excesses of his followers were such, that, despairing of accom-
plishing any good end by remaining at their head, he left them to
themselves, and returned to Constantinople, on the pretext of making
arrangements with the government of Alexius for a proper supply of
provisions.   The Crusaders, forgetting that they were in the enemy's
country, and that union, above all things, was desirable, gave themselves up to dissensions.   Violent disputes arose between the Lom-
bards and Normans commanded by Walter the Pennyless, and the
Franks and Germans led out by Peter.   The latter separated themselves from the former, and choosing for their leader one Reinaldo,
or Reinhold, marched forward, and took possession of the fortress of
Exorogorgon.   The Sultan Solimaun was on the alert, with a superior
force.   A party of Crusaders, which had been detached from the fort,
and stationed at a little distance as an ambuscade, were surprised
and cut to pieces, and Exorogorgon invested on all sides.   The siege
was protracted for eight days, during which the Christians suffered
the most acute agony from the want of water.   It is hard to say how
long the hope of succour or the energy of despair would have enabled
them to hold out : their treacherous leader cut the matter short by
renouncing the Christian faith, and delivering up the fort into the
hands of the sultan.   He was followed by two or three of his officers ;
all the rest, refusing to become Mahometans, were ruthlessly put to
the sword.   Thus perished the last wretched remnant of the vast
multitude which had traversed Europe with Peter the Hermit.

Walter the Pennyless and his multitude met as miserable a fate.
On the news of the disasters of Exorogorgon, they demanded to be
led instantly against the Turks.   Walter, who only wanted good soldiers to have made a good general, was cooler of head, and saw all
the dangers of such a step.   His force was wholly insufficient to make
any decisive movement in a country where the enemy was so much
superior, and where, in case of defeat, he had no secure position to
fall back upon ; and he therefore expressed his opinion against ad-

vancing until the arrival of reinforcements. This prudent counsel found no favour: the army loudly expressed their dissatisfaction at their chief, and prepared to march forward without him. Upon this, the brave Walter put himself at their head, and rushed to destruction. Proceeding towards Nice, the modern Isnik, he was inter-

ISNIK.

cepted by the army of the sultan: a fierce battle ensued, in which the Turks made fearful havoc; out of twenty-five thousand Christians, twenty-two thousand were slain, and among them Gautier himself, who fell pierced by seven mortal wounds. The remaining three thousand retreated upon Civitot, where they entrenched themselves.

Disgusted as was Peter the Hermit at the excesses of the multitude, who, at his call, had forsaken Europe, his heart was moved with grief and pity at their misfortunes. All his former zeal revived: casting himself at the feet of the Emperor Alexius, he implored him, with tears in his eyes, to send relief to the few survivors at Civitot. The emperor consented, and a force was sent, which arrived just in time to save them from destruction. The Turks had beleaguered the place, and the Crusaders were reduced to the last extremity. Negotiations were entered into, and the last three thousand were conducted in safety to Constantinople. Alexius had suffered too much by their former excesses to be very desirous of retaining them in his capital; he therefore caused them all to be disarmed, and, furnishing each with a sum of money, he sent them back to their own country.

While these events were taking place, fresh hordes were issuing from the woods and wilds of Germany, all bent for the Holy Land. They were commanded by a fanatical priest, named Gottschalk, who, like Gautier and Peter the Hermit, took his way through Hungary. History is extremely meagre in her details of the conduct and fate of this host, which amounted to at least one hundred thousand men. Robbery and murder seem to have journeyed with them, and the poor Hungarians were rendered almost desperate by their numbers and rapacity. Karloman, the king of the country, made a bold effort to get rid of them; for the resentment of his people had arrived at such a height, that nothing short of the total extermination of the Crusaders would satisfy them. Gottschalk had to pay the penalty, not only for the ravages of his own bands, but for those of the swarms that had come before him. He and his army were induced, by some means or other, to lay down their arms: the savage Hungarians, seeing them thus defenceless, set upon them, and slaughtered them in great numbers. How many escaped their arrows we are not informed; but not one of them reached Palestine.

Other swarms, under nameless leaders, issued from Germany and France, more brutal and more frantic than any that had preceded them. Their fanaticism surpassed by far the wildest freaks of the followers of the Hermit. In bands, varying in numbers from one to five thousand, they traversed the country in all directions, bent upon plunder and massacre. They wore the symbol of the Crusade upon their shoulders, but inveighed against the folly of proceeding to the Holy Land to destroy the Turks, while they left behind them so many Jews, the still more inveterate enemies of Christ. They swore fierce vengeance against this unhappy race, and murdered all the Hebrews they could lay their hands on, first subjecting them to the most horrible mutilation. According to the testimony of Albert Aquensis, they lived among each other in the most shameless profligacy, and their vice was only exceeded by their superstition. Whenever they were in search of Jews, they were preceded by a goose and goat, which they believed to be holy, and animated with divine power to discover the retreats of the unbelievers. In Germany alone they slaughtered more than a thousand Jews, notwithstanding all the efforts of the clergy to save them. So dreadful was the cruelty of their tormentors, that great numbers of Jews committed self-destruction to avoid falling into their hands.

Again it fell to the lot of the Hungarians to deliver Europe from these pests. When there were no more Jews to murder, the bands collected in one body, and took the old route to the Holy Land, a route stained with the blood of three hundred thousand who had gone before, and destined also to receive theirs. The number of these swarms has never been stated ; but so many of them perished in Hungary, that contemporary writers, despairing of giving any adequate idea of their multitudes, state that the fields were actually heaped with their corpses, and that for miles in its course the waters of the Danube were dyed with their blood. It was at Mersburg, on the Danube, that the greatest slaughter took place,—a slaughter so great as to amount almost to extermination. The Hungarians for a while disputed the passage of the river, but the Crusaders forced their way across, and attacking the city with the blind courage of madness, succeeded in making a breach in the walls. At this moment of victory an unaccountable fear came over them. Throwing down their arms, they fled panic-stricken, no one knew why, and no one knew whither. The Hungarians followed, sword in hand, and cut them down without remorse, and in such numbers, that the stream of the Danube is said to have been choked up by their unburied bodies.

This was the worst paroxysm of the madness of Europe ; and this passed, her chivalry stepped upon the scene. Men of cool heads, mature plans, and invincible courage stood forward to lead and direct the grand movement of Europe upon Asia. It is upon these men that romance has lavished her most admiring epithets, leaving to the condemnation of history the vileness and brutality of those who went before. Of these leaders the most distinguished were Godfrey of Bouillon duke of Lorraine, and Raymond count of Toulouse. Four other chiefs of the royal blood of Europe also assumed the cross, and led each his army to the Holy Land; Hugh count of Vermandois, brother of the king of France ; Robert duke of Normandy, the elder brother of William Rufus ; Robert count of Flanders, and Bohemund prince of Tarentum, eldest son of the celebrated Robert Guiscard. These men were all tinged with the fanaticism of the age, but none of them acted entirely from religious motives. They were neither utterly reckless like Gautier sans Avoir, crazy like Peter the Hermit, nor brutal like Gottschalk the Monk, but possessed each of these qualities in a milder form ; their valour being tempered by caution, their religious zeal by worldly views, and their ferocity by the spirit of chivalry. They saw whither led the torrent of the public will ; and it being nei-

ther their wish nor their interest to stem it, they allowed themselves to
be carried with it, in the hope that it would lead them at last to a haven
of aggrandisement.   Around them congregated many minor chiefs,
the flower of the nobility of France and Italy, with some few from
Germany, England, and Spain. It was wisely conjectured that armies
so numerous would find a difficulty in procuring provisions if they
all journeyed by the same road.   They therefore resolved to separate; Godfrey de Bouillon proceeding through Hungary and Bulgaria,

GODFREY DE BOUILLON.

the Count of Toulouse through Lombardy and Dalmatia, and the
other leaders through Apulia to Constantinople, where the several
divisions were to reunite. The forces under these leaders have been
variously estimated. The Princess Anna Comnena talks of them as
having been as numerous as the sands on the sea-shore, or the stars in
the firmament. Fulcher of Chartres is more satisfactory, and exag-
gerates less magnificently, when he states, that all the divisions,

when they had sat down before Nice in Bithynia, amounted to one hundred thousand horsemen, and six hundred thousand men on foot, exclusive of the priests, women, and children. Gibbon is of opinion that this amount is exaggerated; but thinks the actual numbers did not fall very far short of the calculation. The Princess Anna afterwards gives the number of those under Godfrey of Bouillon as eighty thousand foot and horse; and supposing that each of the other chiefs led an army as numerous, the total would be near half a million. This must be over rather than under the mark, as the army of Godfrey of Bouillon was confessedly the largest when it set out, and suffered less by the way than any other.

The Count of Vermandois was the first who set foot on the Grecian territory. On his arrival at Durazzo he was received with every mark of respect and courtesy by the agents of the emperor, and his followers were abundantly supplied with provisions. Suddenly, however, and without cause assigned, the count was arrested by order of the Emperor Alexius, and conveyed a close prisoner to Constantinople. Various motives have been ass'gned by different authors as having induced the emperor to this treacherous and imprudent proceeding. By every writer he has been condemned for so flagrant a breach of hospitality and justice. The most probable reason for his conduct appears to be that suggested by Guibert of Nogent, who states that Alexius, fearful of the designs of the Crusaders upon his throne, resorted to this extremity in order afterwards to force the count to take the oath of allegiance to him, as the price of his liberation. The example of a prince so eminent as the brother of the king of France, would, he thought, be readily followed by the other chiefs of the Crusade. In the result he was wofully disappointed, as every man deserves to be who commits positive evil that doubtful good may ensue. But this line of policy accorded well enough with the narrowmindedness of the emperor, who, in the enervating atmosphere of his highly civilised and luxurious court, dreaded the influx of the hardy and ambitious warriors of the West, and strove to nibble away by unworthy means the power which he had not energy enough to confront. If danger to himself had existed from the residence of the chiefs in his dominions, he might easily have averted it, by the simple means of placing himself at the head of the European movement, and directing its energies to their avowed object, the conquest of the Holy Land. But the emperor, instead of being, as he might have been, the lord and leader of the Crusades, which he had himself aided in no inconsiderable degree to suscitate by his embassies to the Pope, became the slave of men who hated and despised him. No doubt the barbarous excesses of the followers of Gautier and Peter the Hermit made him look upon the whole body of them with disgust, but it was the disgust of a little mind, which is glad of any excuse to palliate or justify its own irresolution and love of ease.

Godfrey of Bouillon traversed Hungary in the most quiet and orderly manner. On his arrival at Mersburg he found the country strewed with the mangled corpses of the Jew-killers, and demanded of the king of Hungary for what reason his people had set upon them. The latter detailed the atrocities they had committed, and made it so evident to Godfrey that the Hungarians had only acted in self-defence, that the high-minded leader declared himself satisfied, and passed on without giving or receiving molestation. On his arrival at Philippopoli he was informed for the first time of the imprisonment of the count of Vermandois. He immediately sent messengers to the emperor, demanding the count's release, and threatening, in case of refusal, to lay waste the country with fire and sword. After waiting a day at Philippopoli, he marched on to Adrianople, where he was met by his messengers returning with the emperor's refusal. Godfrey, the bravest and most determined of the leaders of the Crusade, was not a man to swerve from his word, and the country was given up to pillage. Alexius here committed another blunder. No sooner did he learn from dire experience that the Crusader was not an utterer of idle threats, than he consented to the release of the prisoner. As he had been unjust in the first instance, he became cowardly in the second, and taught his enemies (for so the Crusaders were forced to consider themselves) a lesson which they took care to remember to his cost, that they could hope nothing from his sense of justice, but every thing from his fears. Godfrey remained encamped for several weeks in the neighbourhood of Constantinople, to the great annoyance of Alexius, who sought by every means to extort from him the homage he had extorted from Vermandois. Sometimes he acted as if at open and declared war with the Crusaders, and sent his troops against them. Sometimes he refused to supply them with food, and ordered the markets to be shut against them, while at other times he was all for peace and good-will, and sent costly presents to Godfrey. The honest, straightforward Crusader was at last so wearied by his false kindness, and so pestered by his attacks, that, allowing his indignation to get the better of his judgment, he gave up the country around Constantinople to be plundered by his soldiers. For six days the flames of the farm-houses around struck terror into the heart of Alexius ; but, as Godfrey anticipated, they convinced him of his error. Fearing that Constantinople itself would be the next object of attack, he sent messengers to demand an interview with Godfrey, offering at the same time to leave his son as a hostage for his good faith. God-

frey agreed to meet him ; and, whether to put an end to these useless dissensions, or for some other unexplained reason, he rendered
homage to Alexius as his liege lord. He was thereupon loaded with
honours, and, according to a singular custom of that age, underwent
the ceremony of the "adoption of honour" as son to the emperor.
Godfrey and his brother Baudouin de Bouillon conducted themselves
with proper courtesy on this occasion, but were not able to restrain
the insolence of their followers, who did not conceive themselves
bound to keep any terms with a man so insincere as he had shewn
himself. One barbarous chieftain, Count Robert of Paris, carried his
insolence so far as to seat himself upon the throne ; an insult which
Alexius merely resented with a sneer, but which did not induce him
to look with less mistrust upon the hordes that were still advancing.

It is impossible, notwithstanding his treachery, to avoid feeling
some compassion for the emperor, whose life at this time was rendered one long scene of misery by the presumption of the Crusaders,
and his not altogether groundless fears of the evil they might inflict
upon him, should any untoward circumstance force the current of
their ambition to the conquest of his empire. His daughter Anna
Comnena feelingly deplores his state of life at this time, and a learned
German,* in a recent work, describes it, on the authority of the princess, in the following manner :

"To avoid all occasion of offence to the Crusaders, Alexius com-
plied with all their whims and their (on many occasions) unreasonable
demands, even at the expense of great bodily exertion, at a time when
he was suffering severely under the gout, which eventually brought
him to his grave. No Crusader who desired an interview with him
was refused access ; he listened with the utmost patience to the long-
winded harangues which their loquacity or zeal continually wearied
him with ; he endured, without expressing any impatience, the un-
becoming and haughty language which they permitted themselves to
employ towards him, and severely reprimanded his officers when they
undertook to defend the dignity of the imperial station from these
rude assaults, for he trembled with apprehension at the slightest disputes, lest they might become the occasion of greater evil. Though
the counts often appeared before him with trains altogether unsuit-
able to their dignity and to his—sometimes with an entire troop,
which completely filled the royal apartment—the emperor held his
peace. He listened to them at all hours ; he often seated himself on
his throne at day-break to attend to their wishes and requests, and
the evening twilight saw him still in the same place. Very frequently
he could not snatch time to refresh himself with meat and drink.

* M. Wilken's *Geschichte der Kreuzzüge.*

During many nights he could not obtain any repose, and was obliged to indulge in an unrefreshing sleep upon his throne, with his head resting on his hands.   Even this slumber was continually disturbed by the appearance and harangues of some newly-arrived rude knights. When all the courtiers, wearied out by the efforts of the day and by night-watching, could no longer keep themselves on their feet, and sank down exhausted—some upon benches and others on the floor— Alexius still rallied his strength to listen with seeming attention to the wearisome chatter of the Latins, that they might have no occasion or pretext for discontent.   In such a state of fear and anxiety, how could Alexius comport himself with dignity and like an emperor ?''

Alexius, however, had himself to blame, in a great measure, for the indignities he suffered : owing to his insincerity, the Crusaders mistrusted him so much, that it became at last a common saying, that the Turks and Saracens were not such inveterate foes to the Western or Latin Christians as the Emperor Alexius and the Greeks.* It would be needless in this sketch, which does not profess to be so much a history of the Crusades, as of the madness of Europe, from which they sprang, to detail the various acts of bribery and intimidation, cajolery and hostility, by which Alexius contrived to make each of the leaders in succession, as they arrived, take the oath of allegiance to him as their suzerain.   One way or another he exacted from each the barren homage on which he had set his heart, and they were then allowed to proceed into Asia Minor.   One only, Raymond de St. Gilles count of Toulouse, obstinately refused the homage.

Their residence in Constantinople was productive of no good to the armies of the cross.   Bickerings and contentions on the one hand, and the influence of a depraved and luxurious court on the other, destroyed the elasticity of their spirits, and cooled the first ardour of their enthusiasm.   At one time the army of the Count of Toulouse was on the point of disbanding itself ; and, had not their leader energetically removed them across the Bosphorus, this would have been the result.   Once in Asia, their spirits in some degree revived, and the presence of danger and difficulty nerved them to the work they had undertaken.   The first operation of the war was the siege of Nice, to gain possession of which all their efforts were directed.

Godfrey of Bouillon and the Count of Vermandois were joined under its walls by each host in succession as it left Constantinople. Among the celebrated Crusaders who fought at this siege we find, besides the leaders already mentioned, the brave and generous Tancred, whose name and fame have been immortalised in the

* Wilken.

Gerusalemme Liberata, the valorous Bishop of Puy, Baldwin, after-wards king of Jerusalem, and Peter the Hermit, now an almost soli-tary soldier, shorn of all the power and influence he had formerly possessed. Kilij Aslaun the sultan of Roum and chief of the Sel-jukian Turks, whose deeds, surrounded by the false halo of romance, are familiar to the readers of Tasso, under the name of Soliman, marched to defend this city, but was defeated after several obstinate engagements, in which the Christians shewed a degree of heroism that quite astonished him. The Turkish chief had expected to find a wild undisciplined multitude, like that under Peter the Hermit, without leaders capable of enforcing obedience ; instead of which, he found the most experienced leaders of the age at the head of armies that had just fanaticism enough to be ferocious, but not enough to render them ungovernable. In these engagements, many hundreds fell on both sides ; and on both sides the most revolting barbarity was practised : the Crusaders cut off the heads of the fallen Mussulmans, and sent them in panniers to Constantinople, as trophies of their victory. After the temporary defeat of Kilij Aslaun, the siege of Nice was carried on with redoubled vigour. The Turks defended themselves with the greatest obstinacy, and discharged showers of poisoned arrows upon the Crusaders. When any unfortunate wretch was killed under the walls, they let down iron hooks from above, and drew the body up, which, after strip-ping and mutilating, they threw back again at the besiegers. The latter were well supplied with provisions, and for six-and-thirty days the siege continued without any relaxation of the efforts on either side. Many tales are told of the almost superhuman heroism of the Christian leaders—how one man put a thousand to flight ; and how the arrows of the faithful never missed their mark. One anec-dote of Godfrey of Bouillon, related by Albert of Aix, is worth re-cording, not only as shewing the high opinion entertained of his valour, but as shewing the contagious credulity of the armies—a cre-dulity which has often led them to the very verge of defeat, as it in-cited them to victory. One Turk, of gigantic stature, took his station day by day on the battlements of Nice, and, bearing an enormous bow, committed great havoc among the Christian host. Not a shaft he sped but bore death upon its point ; and although the Crusaders aimed repeatedly at his breast, and he stood in the most exposed position, their arrows fell harmless at his feet. He seemed to be invulnerable to attack ; and a report was soon spread abroad, that he was no other than the Arch Fiend himself, and that mortal hand could not prevail against him. Godfrey of Bouillon, who had no faith in the supernatural character of the Mussulman, determined, if possible, to put an end to the dismay which was rapidly paralysing the exertions of his best soldiers. Taking a huge cross-bow, he stood forward in front of the army, to try the steadiness of his hand against the much-dreaded archer : the shaft was aimed directly at his heart, and took fatal effect. The Moslem fell amid the groans of the besieged and the shouts of *Deus adjuva! Deus adjuva!* the war-cry of the besiegers.

At last the Crusaders imagined that they had overcome all obstacles, and were preparing to take possession of the city, when, to their great astonishment, they saw the flag of the Emperor Alexius flying from the battlements. An emissary of the emperor, named Faticius or Tatin, had contrived to gain admission, with a body of Greek troops, at a point which the Crusaders had left unprotected, and had persuaded the Turks to surrender to him rather than to the crusading forces. The greatest indignation prevailed in the army when this stratagem was discovered, and the soldiers were, with the utmost difficulty, prevented from renewing the attack and besieging the Greek emissary.

The army, however, continued its march, and, by some means or other, was broken into two divisions; some historians say accidentally,* while others affirm by mutual consent, and for the convenience of obtaining provisions on the way.† The one division was composed of the forces under Bohemund, Tancred, and the Duke of Normandy ; while the other, which took a route at some distance on the right, was commanded by Godfrey of Bouillon and the other chiefs. The Sultan of Roum, who, after his losses at Nice, had been silently making great efforts to crush the Crusaders at one blow, collected in a very short time all the multitudinous tribes that owed him allegiance, and with an army which, according to a moderate calculation, amounted to two hundred thousand men, chiefly cavalry, he fell upon the first division of the Christian host in the valley of Dorylæum. It was early in the morning of the 1st of July 1097, when the Crusaders saw the first companies of the Turkish horsemen pouring down upon them from the hills. Bohemund had hardly time to set himself in order, and transport his sick and helpless to the rear, when the overwhelming force of the Orientals was upon him. The Christian army, composed principally of men on foot, gave way on all sides, and the hoofs of the Turkish steeds, and the poisoned arrows of their bowmen, mowed them down by hundreds. After having lost the flower of their chivalry, the Christians retreated upon their baggage, when a dreadful slaughter took place. Neither

* Fulcher of Chartres; Guibert de Nogent; Vital.
† William of Tyre; Mills; Wilken, &c.

women nor children, nor the sick, were spared. Just as they were reduced to the last extremity, Godfrey of Bouillon and the Count of Toulouse made their appearance on the field, and turned the tide of battle. After an obstinate engagement the Turks fled, and their rich camp fell into the hands of the enemy. The loss of the Crusaders amounted to about four thousand men, with several chiefs of renown, among whom were Count Robert of Paris and William the brother of Tancred. The loss of the Turks, which did not exceed this number, taught them to pursue a different mode of warfare. The sultan was far from being defeated. With his still gigantic army, he laid waste all the country on either side of the Crusaders. The latter, who were unaware of the tactics of the enemy, found plenty of provisions in the Turkish camp; but so far from economising these resources, they gave themselves up for several days to the most unbounded extravagance. They soon paid dearly for their heedlessness. In the ravaged country of Phrygia, through which they advanced towards Antiochetta, they suffered dreadfully for want of food for themselves and pasture for their cattle. Above them was a scorching sun, almost sufficient of itself to dry up the freshness of the land, a task which the firebrands of the sultan had but too surely effected, and water was not to be had after the first day of their march. The pilgrims died at the rate of five hundred a day. The horses of the knights perished on the road, and the baggage which they had aided to transport was either placed upon dogs, sheep, and swine, or abandoned altogether. In some of the calamities that afterwards befel them, the Christians gave themselves up to the most reckless profligacy; but upon this occasion, the dissensions which prosperity had engendered were all forgotten. Religion, often disregarded, arose in the stern presence of misfortune, and cheered them as they died by the promises of eternal felicity.

At length they reached Antiochetta, where they found water in abundance, and pastures for their expiring cattle. Plenty once more surrounded them, and here they pitched their tents. Untaught by the bitter experience of famine, they again gave themselves up to luxury and waste.

On the 18th of October they sat down before the strong city of Antioch, the siege of which, and the events to which it gave rise, are among the most extraordinary incidents of the Crusade. The city, which is situated on an eminence, and washed by the river Orontes, is naturally a very strong position, and the Turkish garrison were well supplied with provisions to endure a long siege. In this respect the Christians were also fortunate, but unluckily for themselves, unwise. Their force amounted to three hundred thousand fighting men; and we are informed by Raymond d'Argilles, that they had so much provision, that they threw away the greater part of every animal they killed, being so dainty, that they would only eat particular parts of the beast. So insane was their extravagance, that in less than ten days famine began to stare them in the face. After making a fruitless attempt to gain possession of the city by a *coup de main*, they, starving themselves, sat down to starve out the enemy. But with want came a cooling of enthusiasm. The chiefs began to grow weary of the expedition. Baldwin had previously detached himself from the main body of the army, and, proceeding to Edessa, had intrigued himself into the supreme power in that little principality. The other leaders were animated with less zeal than heretofore. Stephen of Chartres and Hugh of Vermandois began to waver, unable to endure the privations which their own folly and profusion had brought upon them. Even Peter the Hermit became sick at heart ere all was over. When the famine had become so urgent that they were reduced to eat human flesh in the extremity of their hunger, Bohemund and Robert of Flanders set forth on an expedition to procure a supply. They were in a slight degree successful; but the relief they brought was not economised, and in two days they were as destitute as before. Faticius, the Greek commander and representative of Alexius, deserted with his division under pretence of seeking for food, and his example was followed by various bodies of Crusaders.

Misery was rife among those who remained, and they strove to alleviate it by a diligent attention to signs and omens. These, with extraordinary visions seen by the enthusiastic, alternately cheered and depressed them according as they foretold the triumph or pictured the reverses of the cross. At one time a violent hurricane arose, levelling great trees with the ground, and blowing down the tents of the Christian leaders. At another time an earthquake shook the camp, and was thought to prognosticate some great impending evil to the cause of Christendom. But a comet which appeared shortly afterwards raised them from the despondency into which they had fallen; their lively imaginations making it assume the form of a flaming cross leading them on to victory. Famine was not the least of the evils they endured. Unwholesome food, and the impure air from the neighbouring marshes, engendered pestilential diseases, which carried them off more rapidly than the arrows of the enemy. A thousand of them died in a day, and it became at last a matter of extreme difficulty to afford them burial. To add to their misery, each man grew suspicious of his neighbour; for the camp was infested by Turkish spies, who conveyed daily to the besieged intelligence of the movements and distresses of the enemy. With a ferocity, engendered by despair, Bohemund caused two spies, whom he had detected, to be roasted alive in presence of the army, and within sight of the battlements of Antioch. But even this example failed to reduce their numbers, and the Turks continued to be as well informed as the Christians themselves of all that was passing in the camp.

The news of the arrival of a reinforcement of soldiers from Europe, with an abundant stock of provisions, came to cheer them when reduced to the last extremity. The welcome succour landed at St. Simeon, the port of Antioch, and about six miles from that city. Thitherwards the famishing Crusaders proceeded in tumultuous bands, followed by Bohemund and the Count of Toulouse, with strong detachments of their retainers and vassals, to escort the supplies in safety to the camp. The garrison of Antioch, forewarned of this arrival, was on the alert, and a corps of Turkish archers was despatched to lie in ambuscade among the mountains and intercept their return. Bohemund, laden with provisions, was encountered in the rocky passes by the Turkish host. Great numbers of his followers were slain, and he himself had just time to escape to the camp with the news of his defeat. Godfrey of Bouillon, the Duke of Normandy, and the other leaders had heard the rumour of this battle, and were at that instant preparing for the rescue. The army was immediately in motion, animated both by zeal and by hunger, and marched so rapidly as to intercept the victorious Turks before they had time to reach Antioch with their spoil. A fierce battle ensued, which lasted from noon till the going down of the sun. The Christians gained and maintained the advantage, each man fighting as if upon himself alone had depended the fortune of the day. Hundreds of Turks perished in the Orontes, and more than two thousand were left dead upon the field of battle. All the provision was recaptured and brought in safety to the camp, whither the Crusaders returned singing *Alleluia!* or shouting *Deus adjuva! Deus adjuva!*

This relief lasted for some days, and, had it been duly economised, would have lasted much longer; but the chiefs had no authority, and were unable to exercise any control over its distribution. Famine again approached with rapid strides, and Stephen count of Blois, not liking the prospect, withdrew from the camp with four thousand of his retainers, and established himself at Alexandretta. The moral influence of this desertion was highly prejudicial upon those who remained; and Bohemund, the most impatient and ambitious of the chiefs, foresaw that, unless speedily checked, it would lead to the utter failure of the expedition. It was necessary to act decisively; the army murmured at the length of the siege, and the sultan was collecting his forces to crush them. Against the efforts of the Crusaders

Antioch might have held out for months; but treason within effected that which courage without might have striven for in vain.

Baghasihan, the Turkish prince or emir of Antioch, had under his command an Armenian of the name of Phirouz, whom he had entrusted with the defence of a tower on that part of the city wall which overlooked the passes of the mountains. Bohemund, by means of a spy who had embraced the Christian religion, and to whom he had given his own name at baptism, kept up a daily communication with this captain, and made him the most magnificent promises of reward, if he would deliver up his post to the Crusaders. Whether the proposal was first made by Bohemund or by the Armenian is uncertain, but that a good understanding soon existed between them is undoubted ; and a night was fixed for the execution of the project. Bohemund communicated the scheme to Godfrey and the Count of Toulouse, with the stipulation that, if the city were won, he, as the soul of the enterprise, should enjoy the dignity of Prince of Antioch. The other leaders hesitated : ambition and jealousy prompted them to refuse their aid in furthering the views of the intriguer. More mature consideration decided them to acquiesce, and seven hundred of the bravest knights were chosen for the expedition, the real object of which, for fear of spies, was kept a profound secret from the rest of the army. When all was ready, a report was promulgated that the seven hundred were intended to form an ambuscade for a division of the sultan's army, which was stated to be approaching.

Every thing favoured the treacherous project of the Armenian captain, who, on his solitary watch-tower, received due intimation of the approach of the Crusaders. The night was dark and stormy; not a star was visible above, and the wind howled so furiously as to overpower all other sounds : the rain fell ih torrents, and the watchers on the towers adjoining to that of Phirouz could not hear the tramp of the armed knights for the wind, nor see them for the obscurity of the night and the dismalness of the weather. When within shot of the walls, Bohemund sent forward an interpreter to confer with the Armenian. The latter urged them to make haste, and seize the favourable interval, as armed men, with lighted torches, patrolled the battlements every half hour, and at that instant they had just passed. The chiefs were instantly at the foot of the wall : Phirouz let down a rope ; Bohemund attached it to the end of a ladder of hides, which was then raised by the Armenian, and held while the knights mounted. A momentary fear came over the spirits of the adventurers, and every one hesitated. At last Bohemund,* encouraged by

* Vide William of Tyre.

Phirouz from above, ascended a few steps on the ladder, and was followed by Godfrey, Count Robert of Flanders, and a number of other knights. As they advanced, others pressed forward, until their

SIEGE OF ANTIOCH.

weight became too great for the ladder, which, breaking, precipitated about a dozen of them to the ground, where they fell one upon the other, making a great clatter with their heavy coats of mail. For a moment they thought that all was lost; but the wind made so loud a howling as it swept in fierce gusts through the mountain gorges, and the Orontes, swollen by the rain, rushed so noisily along, that the guards heard nothing. The ladder was easily repaired, and the knights ascended two at a time, and reached the platform in safety. When sixty of them had thus ascended, the torch of the coming patrol was seen to gleam at the angle of the wall. Hiding themselves behind a buttress, they awaited his coming in breathless silence. As soon as he arrived at arm's length, he was suddenly seized, and, before he could open his lips to raise an alarm, the silence of death closed them up for ever. They next descended rapidly the spiral staircase of the tower, and opening the portal, admitted the whole of their companions. Raymond of Toulouse, who, cognisant of the whole plan, had been left behind with the main body of the army, heard at this instant the signal horn, which announced that an entry had been effected, and, leading on his legions, the town was attacked from within and without.

Imagination cannot conceive a scene more dreadful than that presented by the devoted city of Antioch on that night of horror. The Crusaders fought with a blind fury, which fanaticism and suffering alike incited. Men, women, and children were indiscriminately slaughtered, till the streets ran with blood. Darkness increased the destruction, for when morning dawned the Crusaders found themselves with their swords at the breasts of their fellow-soldiers, whom they had mistaken for foes. The Turkish commander fled, first to the citadel, and that becoming insecure, to the mountains, whither he was pursued and slain, and his grey head brought back to Antioch as a trophy. At daylight the massacre ceased, and the Crusaders gave themselves up to plunder. They found gold, and jewels, and silks, and velvets in abundance, but of provisions, which were of more importance to them, they found but little of any kind. Corn was excessively scarce, and they discovered to their sorrow that in this respect the besieged had been but little better off than the besiegers.

Before they had time to instal themselves in their new position, and take the necessary measures for procuring a supply, the city was invested by the Turks. The sultan of Persia had raised an immense army, which he entrusted to the command of Kerbogha, the emir of Mosul, with instructions to sweep the Christian locusts from the face of the land. The emir effected a junction with Kilij Aslaun, and the two armies surrounded the city. Discouragement took complete possession of the Christian host, and numbers of them contrived to elude the vigilance of the besiegers, and escape to Count Stephen of Blois at Alexandretta, to whom they related the most exaggerated tales of

the misery they had endured, and the utter hopelessness of continuing the war. Stephen forthwith broke up his camp and retreated
towards Constantinople. On his way he was met by the Emperor
Alexius, at the head of a considerable force, hastening to take possession of the conquests made by the Christians in Asia. As soon as he
heard of their woful plight, he turned back, and proceeded with the
Count of Blois to Constantinople, leaving the remnant of the Crusaders to shift for themselves.

The news of this defection increased the discouragement at Antioch. All the useless horses of the army had been slain and eaten,
and dogs, cats, and rats were sold at enormous prices. Even vermin
were becoming scarce. With increasing famine came a pestilence, so
that in a short time but sixty thousand remained of the three hundred thousand that had originally invested Antioch. But this bitter
extremity, while it annihilated the energy of the host, only served to
knit the leaders more firmly together ; and Bohemund, Godfrey, and
Tancred swore never to desert the cause as long as life lasted. The
former strove in vain to reanimate the courage of his followers. They
were weary and sick at heart, and his menaces and promises were
alike thrown away. Some of them had shut themselves up in the
houses, and refused to come forth. Bohemund, to drive them to
their duty, set fire to the whole quarter, and many of them perished
in the flames, while the rest of the army looked on with the utmost
indifference. Bohemund, animated himself by a worldly spirit, did
not know the true character of the Crusaders, nor understand the religious madness which had brought them in such shoals from Europe.
A priest, more clear-sighted, devised a scheme which restored all their
confidence, and inspired them with a courage so wonderful as to make
the poor sixty thousand emaciated, sick, and starving zealots put to
flight the well-fed and six times as numerous legions of the Sultan of
Persia.

This priest, a native of Provence, was named Peter Barthelemy,
and whether he were a knave or an enthusiast, or both ; a principal,
or a tool in the hands of others, will ever remain a matter of doubt.
Certain it is, however, that he was the means of raising the siege of
Antioch, and causing the eventual triumph of the armies of the cross.
When the strength of the Crusaders was completely broken by their
sufferings, and hope had fled from every bosom, Peter came to Count
Raymond of Toulouse, and demanded an interview on matters of
serious moment. He was immediately admitted. He said that, some
weeks previously, at the time the Christians were besieging Antioch,
he was reposing alone in his tent, when he was startled by the shock
of the earthquake which had so alarmed the whole host. Through

violent terror of the shock he could only ejaculate, God help me!
when turning round he saw two men standing before him, whom he
at once recognised by the halo of glory around them as beings of
another world.   One of them appeared to be an aged man, with red-
dish hair sprinkled with grey, black eyes, and a long flowing grey
beard.   The other was younger, larger, and handsomer, and had something more divine in his aspect.   The elderly man alone spoke, and
informed him that he was the holy apostle St. Andrew, and desired
him to seek out the Count Raymond, the Bishop of Puy, and Raymond of Altapulto, and ask them why the bishop did not exhort the
people, and sign them with the cross which he bore.   The apostle
then took him, naked in his shirt as he was, and transported him
through the air into the heart of the city of Antioch, where he led
him into the church of St. Peter, at that time a Saracen mosque.
The apostle made him stop by the pillar close to the steps by which
they ascend on the south side to the altar, where hung two lamps,
which gave out a light brighter than that of the noonday sun ; the
younger man, whom he did not at that time know, standing afar off,
near the steps of the altar.   The apostle then descended into the
ground and brought up a lance, which he gave into his hand, telling
him that it was the very lance that had opened the side whence had
flowed the salvation of the world.   With tears of joy he held the holy
lance, and implored the apostle to allow him to take it away and
deliver it into the hands of Count Raymond.   The apostle refused,
and buried the lance again in the ground, commanding him, when
the city was won from the infidels, to go with twelve chosen men,
and dig it up again in the same place.   The apostle then transported
him back to his tent, and the two vanished from his sight.   He had
neglected, he said, to deliver this message, afraid that his wonderful
tale would not obtain credence from men of such high rank.   After
some days he again saw the holy vision, as he was going out of the
camp to look for food.   This time the divine eyes of the younger
looked reproachfully upon him.   He implored the apostle to choose
some one else more fitted for the mission, but the apostle refused,
and smote him with a disorder of the eyes, as a punishment for his
disobedience.   With an obstinacy unaccountable even to himself, he
had still delayed.   A third time the apostle and his companion had
appeared to him, as he was in a tent with his master William at St.
Simeon.   On that occasion St. Andrew told him to bear his command
to the Count of Toulouse not to bathe in the waters of the Jordan
when he came to it, but to cross over in a boat, clad in a shirt and
breeches of linen, which he should sprinkle with the sacred waters of
the river.   These clothes he was afterwards to preserve along with

the holy lance. His master William, although he could not see the saint, distinctly heard the voice giving orders to that effect. Again he neglected to execute the commission, and again the saints appeared to him, when he was at the port of Mamistra, about to sail for Cyprus, and St. Andrew threatened him with eternal perdition if he refused longer. Upon this he made up his mind to divulge all that had been revealed to him.

The Count of Toulouse, who, in all probability, concocted this tale with the priest, appeared struck with the recital, and sent immediately for the Bishop of Puy and Raymond of Altapulto. The bishop at once expressed his disbelief of the whole story, and refused to have any thing to do in the matter. The Count of Toulouse, on the contrary, saw abundant motives, if not for believing, for pretending to believe; and, in the end, he so impressed upon the mind of the bishop the advantage that might be derived from it, in working up the popular mind to its former excitement, that the latter reluctantly agreed to make search in due form for the holy weapon. The day after the morrow was fixed upon for the ceremony; and, in the mean time, Peter was consigned to the care of Raymond, the count's chaplain, in order that no profane curiosity might have an opportunity of cross-examining him, and putting him to a nonplus.

Twelve devout men were forthwith chosen for the undertaking, among whom were the Count of Toulouse and his chaplain. They began digging at sunrise, and continued unwearied till near sunset, without finding the lance; they might have dug till this day with no better success, had not Peter himself sprung into the pit, praying to God to bring the lance to light, for the strengthening and victory of his people. Those who hide know where to find; and so it was with Peter, for both he and the lance found their way into the hole at the same time. On a sudden he and Raymond the chaplain beheld its point in the earth, and Raymond, drawing it forth, kissed it with tears of joy, in sight of the multitude which had assembled in the church. It was immediately enveloped in a rich purple cloth, already prepared to receive it, and exhibited in this state to the faithful, who made the building resound with their shouts of gladness.

THE HOLY LANCE

Peter had another vision the same night, and became from that day forth " dreamer of dreams" in general to the army. He stated on the following day, that the Apostle Andrew and "the youth with the divine aspect" appeared to him again, and directed that the Count of Toulouse, as a reward for his persevering piety, should carry the Holy Lance at the head of the army, and that the day on which it was found should be observed as a solemn festival throughout Christendom. St. Andrew shewed him at the same time the holes in the feet and hands of his benign companion ; and he became convinced that he stood in the awful presence of THE REDEEMER.

Peter gained so much credit by his visions that dreaming became contagious. Other monks beside himself were visited by the saints, who promised victory to the host if it would valiantly hold out to the last, and crowns of eternal glory to those who fell in the fight. Two deserters, wearied of the fatigues and privations of the war, who had stealthily left the camp, suddenly returned, and seeking Bohemund, told him that they had been met by two apparitions, who, with great anger, had commanded them to return. The one of them said, that he recognised his brother, who had been killed in battle some months before, and that he had a halo of glory around his head. The other, still more hardy, asserted that the apparition which had spoken to him was the Saviour himself, who had promised eternal happiness as his reward if he returned to his duty, but the pains of eternal fire if he rejected the cross. No one thought of disbelieving these men. The courage of the army immediately revived ; despondency gave way to hope ; every arm grew strong again, and the pangs of hunger were for a time disregarded. The enthusiasm which had led them from Europe burned forth once more as brightly as ever, and they demanded, with loud cries, to be led against the enemy. The leaders were not unwilling. In a battle lay their only chance of salvation ; and although Godfrey, Bohemund, and Tancred received the story of the lance with much suspicion, they were too wise to throw discredit upon an imposture which bade fair to open the gates of victory.

Peter the Hermit was previously sent to the camp of Kerbogha to propose that the quarrel between the two religions should be decided by a chosen number of the bravest soldiers of each army. Kerbogha turned from him with a look of contempt, and said he could agree to no proposals from a set of such miserable beggars and robbers. With this uncourteous answer Peter returned to Antioch. Preparations were immediately commenced for an attack upon the enemy : the latter continued to be perfectly well informed of all the proceedings of the Christian camp. The citadel of Antioch, which remained in their possession, overlooked the town, and the commander of the fortress could distinctly see all that was passing within. On the morning of the 28th of June, 1098, a black flag, hoisted from its highest tower, announced to the besieging army that the Christians were about to sally forth.

The Moslem leaders knew the sad inroads that famine and disease had made upon the numbers of the foe ; they knew that not above two hundred of the knights had horses to ride upon, and that the foot soldiers were sick and emaciated ; but they did not know the almost incredible valour which superstition had infused into their hearts. The story of the lance they treated with the most supreme contempt, and, secure of an easy victory, they gave themselves no trouble in preparing for the onslaught. It is related that Kerbogha was playing a game at chess, when the black flag on the citadel gave warning of the enemy's approach, and that, with true oriental coolness, he insisted upon finishing the game ere he bestowed any of his attention upon a foe so unworthy. The defeat of his advanced post of two thousand men aroused him from his apathy.

The Crusaders, after this first victory, advanced joyfully towards the mountains, hoping to draw the Turks to a place where their cavalry would be unable to manœuvre. Their spirits were light and their courage high, as, led on by the Duke of Normandy, Count Robert of Flanders, and Hugh of Vermandois, they came within sight of the splendid camp of the enemy. Godfrey of Bouillon and Adhemar Bishop of Puy followed immediately after these leaders, the latter clad in complete armour, and bearing the Holy Lance within sight of the whole army : Bohemund and Tancred brought up the rear.

Kerbogha, aware at last that his enemy was not so despicable, took vigorous measures to remedy his mistake, and, preparing himself to meet the Christians in front, he despatched the Sultan Soliman of Roum to attack them in the rear. To conceal this movement, he set fire to the dried weeds and grass with which the ground was covered, and Soliman, taking a wide circuit with his cavalry, succeeded, under cover of the smoke, in making good his position in the rear. The battle raged furiously in front ; the arrows of the Turks fell thick as hail, and their well-trained squadrons trod the Crusaders under their hoofs like stubble. Still the affray was doubtful ; for the Christians had the advantage of the ground, and were rapidly gaining upon the enemy, when the overwhelming forces of Soliman arrived in the rear. Godfrey and Tancred flew to the rescue of Bohemund, spreading dismay in the Turkish ranks by their fierce impetuosity. The Bishop of Puy was left almost alone with the Provençals to oppose the legions commanded by Kerbogha in person ; but the presence of the Holy Lance made a hero of the meanest soldier in his train. Still, however, the numbers of the enemy seemed interminable. The Christians, attacked on every side, began at last to give way, and the Turks made sure of victory.

At this moment a cry was raised in the Christian host that the saints were fighting on their side. The battle-field was clear of the smoke from the burning weeds, which had curled away, and hung in white clouds of fantastic shape on the brow of the distant mountains. Some imaginative zealot, seeing this dimly through the dust of the battle, called out to his fellows, to look at the army of saints, clothed in white, and riding upon white horses, that were pouring over the hills to the rescue. All eyes were immediately turned to the distant smoke; faith was in every heart; and the old battle-cry, *God wills it! God wills it!* resounded through the field, as every soldier, believing that God was visibly sending his armies to his aid, fought with an energy unfelt before. A panic seized the Persian and Turkish hosts, and they gave way in all directions. In vain Kerbogha tried to rally them. Fear is more contagious than enthusiasm, and they fled over the mountains like deer pursued by the hounds. The two leaders, seeing the uselessness of further efforts, fled with the rest; and that immense army was scattered over Palestine, leaving nearly seventy thousand of its dead upon the field of battle.

Their magnificent camp fell into the hands of the enemy, with its rich stores of corn, and its droves of sheep and oxen. Jewels, gold, and rich velvets in abundance, were distributed among the army. Tancred followed the fugitives over the hills, and reaped as much plunder as those who had remained in the camp. The way, as they fled, was covered with valuables, and horses of the finest breed of Arabia became so plentiful that every knight of the Christians was provided with a steed. The Crusaders, in this battle, acknowledge to have lost nearly ten thousand men.

Their return to Antioch was one of joy indeed: the citadel was surrendered at once, and many of the Turkish garrison embraced the Christian faith, and the rest were suffered to depart. A solemn thanksgiving was offered up by the Bishop of Puy, in which the whole army joined, and the Holy Lance was visited by every soldier.

The enthusiasm lasted for some days, and the army loudly demanded to be led forward to Jerusalem, the grand goal of all their wishes: but none of their leaders was anxious to move;—the more prudent among them, such as Godfrey and Tancred, for reasons of expediency; and the more ambitious, such as the Count of Toulouse and Bohemund, for reasons of self-interest. Violent dissensions sprang up again between all the chiefs. Raymond of Toulouse, who was left at Antioch to guard the town, had summoned the citadel to surrender, as soon as he saw that there was no fear of any attack upon the part of the Persians; and the other chiefs found, upon their return, his banner waving on its walls. This had given great offence to Bohemund, who had stipulated the principality of Antioch as his reward for winning the town in the first instance. Godfrey and Tancred supported his claim, and, after a great deal of bickering, the flag of Raymond was lowered from the tower, and that of Bohemund hoisted in its stead, who assumed from that time the title of Prince of Antioch. Raymond, however, persisted in retaining possession of one of the city gates and its adjacent towers, which he held for several months, to the great annoyance of Bohemund and the scandal of the army. The count became in consequence extremely unpopular, although his ambition was not a whit more unreasonable than that of Bohemund himself, nor of Baldwin, who had taken up his quarters at Edessa, where he exercised the functions of a petty sovereign.

The fate of Peter Barthelemy deserves to be recorded. Honours and consideration had come thick upon him after the affair of the lance, and he consequently felt bound in conscience to continue the dreams which had made him a personage of so much importance. The mischief of it was, that, like many other liars, he had a very bad memory, and he contrived to make his dreams contradict each other in the most palpable manner. St. John one night appeared to him, and told one tale; while, a week after, St. Paul told a totally different story, and held out hopes quite incompatible with those of his apostolic brother. The credulity of that age had a wide maw, and Peter's visions must have been absurd and outrageous indeed, when the very men who had believed in the lance refused to swallow any more of his wonders. Bohemund at last, for the purpose of annoying the Count of Toulouse, challenged poor Peter to prove the truth of his story of the lance by the fiery ordeal. Peter could not refuse a trial so common in that age, and being besides encouraged by the count and his chaplain Raymond, an early day was appointed for the ceremony. The previous night was spent in prayer and fasting, according to custom, and Peter came forth in the morning bearing the lance in his hand, and walked boldly up to the fire. The whole army gathered round, impatient for the result; many thousands still believing that the lance was genuine, and Peter a holy man. Prayers having been said by Raymond d'Agilles, Peter walked into the flames, and had got nearly through, when pain caused him to lose his presence of mind: the heat, too, affected his eyes, and, in his anguish, he turned round unwittingly, and passed through the fire again, instead of stepping out of it, as he should have done. The result was, that he was burned so severely that he never recovered, and, after lingering for some days, he expired in great agony.

Most of the soldiers were suffering either from wounds, disease, or weariness ; and it was resolved by Godfrey,—the tacitly acknowledged chief of the enterprise,—that the army should have time to refresh itself ere they advanced upon Jerusalem. It was now July, and he proposed that they should pass the hot months of August and September within the walls of Antioch, and march forward in October with renewed vigour, and numbers increased by fresh arrivals from Europe. This advice was finally adopted, although the enthusiasts of the army continued to murmur at the delay. In the mean time the Count of Vermandois was sent upon an embassy to the Emperor Alexius at Constantinople, to reproach him for his base desertion of the cause, and urge him to send the reinforcements he had promised. The count faithfully executed his mission (of which, by the way, Alexius took no notice whatever), and remained for some time at Constantinople, till his zeal, never very violent, totally evaporated. He then returned to France, sick of the Crusade, and determined to intermeddle with it no more.

The chiefs, though they had determined to stay at Antioch for two months, could not remain quiet for so long a time. They would, in all probability, have fallen upon each other, had there been no Turks in Palestine upon whom they might vent their impetuosity. Godfrey proceeded to Edessa, to aid his brother Baldwin in expelling the Saracens from his principality, and the other leaders carried on separate hostilities against them as caprice or ambition dictated. At length the impatience of the army to be led against Jerusalem became so great that the chiefs could no longer delay, and Raymond, Tancred, and Robert of Normandy marched forward with their divisions, and laid siege to the small but strong town of Marah. With their usual improvidence, they had not food enough to last a beleaguering army for a week. They suffered great privations in consequence, till Bohemund came to their aid and took the town by storm. In connexion with this siege, the chronicler, Raymond d'Agilles (the same Raymond the chaplain who figured in the affair of the holy lance), relates a legend, in the truth of which he devoutly believed, and upon which Tasso has founded one of the most beautiful passages of his poem. It is worth preserving, as shewing the spirit of the age and the source of the extraordinary courage manifested by the Crusaders on occasions of extreme difficulty. "One day," says Raymond, "Anselme de Ribeaumont beheld young Engelram, the son of the Count de St. Paul, who had been killed at Marah, enter his tent. ' How is it,' said Anselme to him, ' that you, whom I saw lying dead on the field of battle, are full of life?'—'You must know,' replied Engelram, ' that those who fight for Jesus Christ never die.' ' But whence,' re-

sumed Anselme, 'comes that strange brightness that surrounds you ?'
Upon this Engelram pointed to the sky, where Anselme saw a palace
of diamond and crystal. ' It is thence,' said he, ' that I derive the
beauty which surprises you. My dwelling is there; a still finer one is
prepared for you, and you shall soon come to inhabit it. Farewell !
we shall meet again to-morrow.' With these words Engelram returned
to heaven. Anselme, struck by the vision, sent the next morning
for the priests, received the sacrament, and although full of health,
took a last farewell of all his friends, telling them that he was about
to leave this world. A few hours afterwards, the enemy having made
a sortie, Anselme went out against them sword in hand, and was
struck on the forehead by a stone from a Turkish sling, which sent
him to heaven, to the beautiful palace that was prepared for him."

New disputes arose between the Prince of Antioch and the Count
of Toulouse with regard to the capture of this town, which were with
the utmost difficulty appeased by the other chiefs. Delays also took

SHRINE OF THE NATIVITY.

place in the progress of the army, especially before Archas, and the
soldiery were so exasperated that they were on the point of choosing
new leaders to conduct them to Jerusalem. Godfrey, upon this, set

fire to his camp at Archas, and marched forward. He was immediately joined by hundreds of the Provençals of the Count of Toulouse.
The latter, seeing the turn affairs were taking, hastened after them,
and the whole host proceeded towards the holy city, so long desired
amid sorrow, and suffering, and danger. At Emmaus they were met
by a deputation from the Christians of Bethlehem, praying for immediate aid against the oppression of the infidels. The very name of
Bethlehem, the birthplace of their Saviour, was music to their ears,
and many of them wept with joy to think they were approaching
a spot so hallowed. Albert of Aix informs us that their hearts were
so touched that sleep was banished from the camp, and that, instead
of waiting till the morning's dawn to recommence their march, they
set out shortly after midnight, full of hope and enthusiasm. For upwards of four hours the mail-clad legions tramped stedfastly forward
in the dark, and when the sun arose in unclouded splendour, the
towers and pinnacles of Jerusalem gleamed upon their sight. All the

THE PILGRIMS AT THE FIRST SIGHT OF JERUSALEM.

tender feelings of their nature were touched ; no longer brutal fanatics, but meek and humble pilgrims, they knelt down upon the sod,
and with tears in their eyes, exclaimed to one another, "*Jerusalem !
Jerusalem !*" Some of them kissed the holy ground, others stretched

themselves at full length upon it, in order that their bodies might come in contact with the greatest possible extent of it, and others prayed aloud. The women and children who had followed the camp from Europe, and shared in all its dangers, fatigues, and privations, were more boisterous in their joy; the former from long-nourished enthusiasm, and the latter from mere imitation,* and prayed, and wept, and laughed till they almost put the more sober to the blush.

The first ebullition of their gladness having subsided, the army marched forward and invested the city on all sides. The assault was almost immediately begun; but after the Christians had lost some of their bravest knights, that mode of attack was abandoned, and the army commenced its preparations for a regular siege. Mangonels, movable towers, and battering-rams, together with a machine called a sow, made of wood, and covered with raw hides, inside of which miners worked to undermine the walls, were forthwith constructed; and to restore the courage and discipline of the army, which had suffered from the unworthy dissensions of the chiefs, the latter held out the hand of friendship to each other, and Tancred and the Count of Toulouse embraced in sight of the whole camp. The clergy aided the cause with their powerful voice, and preached union and goodwill to the highest and the lowest. A solemn procession was also ordered round the city, in which the entire army joined, prayers being offered up at every spot which gospel records had taught them to consider as peculiarly sacred.

The Saracens upon the ramparts beheld all these manifestations without alarm. To incense the Christians, whom they despised, they constructed rude crosses, and fixed them upon the walls, and spat upon and pelted them with dirt and stones. This insult to the symbol of their faith raised the wrath of the Crusaders to that height that bravery became ferocity, and enthusiasm madness. When all the engines of war were completed, the attack was recommenced, and every soldier of the Christian army fought with a vigour which the sense of private wrong invariably inspires. Every man had been personally outraged, and the knights worked at the battering-rams with as much readiness as the meanest soldiers. The Saracen arrows and balls of fire fell thick and fast among them, but the tremendous

* Guibert de Nogent relates a curious instance of the imitativeness of these juvenile Crusaders. He says that, during the siege of Antioch, the Christian and Saracen boys used to issue forth every evening from the town and camp in great numbers, under the command of captains chosen from among themselves. Armed with sticks instead of swords, and stones instead of arrows, they ranged themselves in battle order, and, shouting each the war-cry of their country, fought with the utmost desperation. Some of them lost their eyes, and many became cripples for life from the injuries they received on these occasions.

rams still heaved against the walls, while the best marksmen of the host were busily employed in the several floors of the movable towers in dealing death among the Turks upon the battlements. Godfrey, Raymond, Tancred, and Robert of Normandy, each upon his tower, fought for hours with unwearied energy, often repulsed, but ever ready to renew the struggle. The Turks, no longer despising the enemy, defended themselves with the utmost skill and bravery till darkness brought a cessation of hostilities. Short was the sleep that night in the Christian camp. The priests offered up solemn prayers in the midst of the attentive soldiery for the triumph of the cross in this last great struggle; and as soon as morning dawned, every one was in readiness for the affray. The women and children lent their aid, the latter running unconcerned to and fro while the arrows fell fast around them, bearing water to the thirsty combatants. The saints were believed to be aiding their efforts, and the army, impressed with this idea, surmounted difficulties under which a force thrice as numerous, but without their faith, would have quailed and been defeated. Raymond of Toulouse at last forced his way into the city by escalade, while at the very same moment Tancred and Robert of Normandy succeeded in bursting open one of the gates. The Turks flew to repair the mischief, and Godfrey of Bouillon, seeing the battlements comparatively deserted, let down the drawbridge of his movable tower, and sprang forward, followed by all the knights of his train. In an instant after, the banner of the cross floated upon the walls of Jerusalem. The Crusaders, raising once more their redoubtable war-cry, rushed on from every side, and the city was taken. The battle raged in the streets for several hours, and the Christians, remembering their insulted faith, gave no quarter to young or old, male or female, sick or strong. Not one of the leaders thought himself at liberty to issue orders for staying the carnage, and if he had, he would not have been obeyed. The Saracens fled in great numbers to the mosque of Soliman, but they had not time to fortify themselves within it ere the Christians were upon them. Ten thousand persons are said to have perished in that building alone.

Peter the Hermit, who had remained so long under the veil of neglect, was repaid that day for all his zeal and all his sufferings. As soon as the battle was over, the Christians of Jerusalem issued forth from their hiding-places to welcome their deliverers. They instantly recognised the Hermit as the pilgrim who, years before, had spoken to them so eloquently of the wrongs and insults they had endured, and promised to stir up the princes and people of Europe in their behalf. They clung to the skirts of his garments in the fervour of their gratitude, and vowed to remember him for ever in their prayers. Many of them shed tears about his neck, and attributed the deliverance of Jerusalem solely to his courage and perseverance. Peter afterwards held some ecclesiastical office in the holy city, but

SIEGE OF JERUSALEM.

what it was, or what was his ultimate fate, history has forgotten to inform us. Some say that he returned to France and founded a monastery, but the story does not rest upon sufficient authority.

The grand object for which the popular swarms of Europe had forsaken their homes was now accomplished. The Moslem mosques of Jerusalem were converted into churches for a purer faith, and the Mount of Calvary and the sepulchre of Christ were profaned no longer by the presence or the power of the infidel. Popular frenzy had fulfilled its mission, and, as a natural consequence, it began to subside from that time forth. The news of the capture of Jerusalem brought numbers of pilgrims from Europe, and, among others, Stephen count of Chartres and Hugh of Vermandois, to atone for their desertion; but nothing like the former enthusiasm existed among the nations.

Thus, then, ends the history of the first Crusade. For the better understanding of the second, it will be necessary to describe the interval between them, and to enter into a slight sketch of the history of Jerusalem under its Latin kings, the long and fruitless wars they continued to wage with the unvanquished Saracens, and the poor and miserable results which sprang from so vast an expenditure of zeal and so deplorable a waste of human life.

The necessity of having some recognised chief was soon felt by the Crusaders, and Godfrey de Bouillon, less ambitious than Bohemund or Raymond of Toulouse, gave his cold consent to wield a sceptre which the latter chiefs would have clutched with eagerness. He was hardly invested with the royal mantle before the Saracens menaced his capital. With much vigour and judgment he exerted himself to follow up the advantages he had gained, and marching out to meet the enemy before they had time to besiege him in Jerusalem, he gave them battle at Ascalon, and defeated them with great loss. He did not, however, live long to enjoy his new dignity, being seized with a fatal illness when he had only reigned nine months. To him succeeded his brother, Baldwin of Edessa. The latter monarch did much to improve the condition of Jerusalem and to extend its territory, but was not able to make a firm footing for his successors. For fifty years, in which the history of Jerusalem is full of interest to the historical student, the Crusaders were exposed to fierce and constant hostilities, often gaining battles and territory, and as often losing them, but becoming every day weaker and more divided, while the Saracens became stronger and more united to harass and root them out. The battles of this period were of the most chivalrous character, and deeds of heroism were done by the handful of brave knights that remained in Syria which have hardly their parallel in the annals of war. In the course of time, however, the Christians could not avoid feeling some respect for the courage, and admiration for the polished manners and advanced civilisation of the Saracens, so much superior to the rudeness and semi-barbarism of Europe at that day. Difference of faith

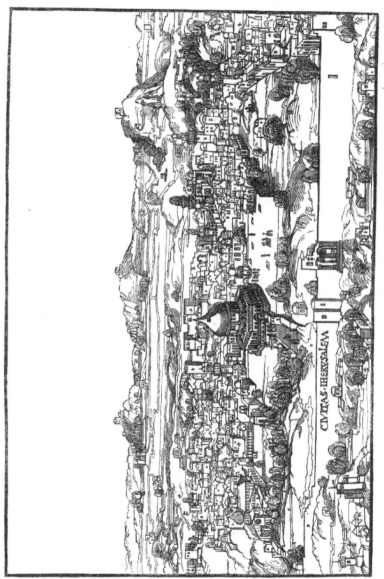

JERUSALEM.

did not prevent them from forming alliances with the dark-eyed maidens of the East.   One of the first to set the example of taking a Paynim spouse was King Baldwin himself, and these connexions in time became not only frequent, but almost universal, among such of the knights as had resolved to spend their lives in Palestine. These Eastern ladies were obliged, however, to submit to the ceremony of baptism before they could be received to the arms of a Christian lord. These, and their offspring, naturally looked upon the Saracens with less hatred than did the zealots who conquered Jerusalem, and who thought it a sin deserving the wrath of God to spare an unbeliever. We find, in consequence, that the most obstinate battles waged during the reigns of the later kings of Jerusalem were fought by the new and

BIBLE OF BALDWIN'S QUEEN.

raw levies who from time to time arrived from Europe, lured by the hope of glory or spurred by fanaticism. The latter broke without scruple the truces established between the original settlers and the Saracens, and drew down severe retaliation upon many thousands of their brethren in the faith, whose prudence was stronger than their zeal, and whose chief desire was to live in peace.

Things remained in this unsatisfactory state till the close of the year 1145, when Edessa, the strong frontier town of the Christian kingdom, fell into the hands of the Saracens. The latter were commanded by Zenghi, a powerful and enterprising monarch, and, after his death, by his son Nourheddin, as powerful and enterprising as his father. An unsuccessful attempt was made by the Count of Edessa to regain the fortress, but Nourheddin with a large army came to the rescue, and after defeating the count with great slaughter, marched into Edessa and caused its fortifications to be razed to the ground, that the town might never more be a bulwark of defence for the king-dom of Jerusalem. The road to the capital was now open, and con-sternation seized the hearts of the Christians. Nourheddin, it was known, was only waiting for a favourable opportunity to advance upon Jerusalem, and the armies of the cross, weakened and divided, were not in a condition to make any available resistance. The clergy were filled with grief and alarm, and wrote repeated letters to the Pope and the sovereigns of Europe, urging the expediency of a new Crusade for the relief of Jerusalem. By far the greater number of the priests of Palestine were natives of France, and these naturally looked first to their own country. The solicitations they sent to Louis VII. were urgent and oft repeated, and the chivalry of France began to talk once more of arming in defence of the birthplace of Jesus. The kings of Europe, whose interest it had not been to take any part in the first Crusade, began to bestir themselves in this; and a man appeared, eloquent as Peter the Hermit, to arouse the people as that preacher had done.

We find, however, that the enthusiasm of the second did not equal that of the first Crusade; in fact, the mania had reached its climax in the time of Peter the Hermit, and decreased regularly from that period. The third Crusade was less general than the second, and the fourth than the third, and so on, until the public enthusiasm was quite extinct, and Jerusalem returned at last to the dominion of its old masters without a convulsion in Christendom. Various reasons have been assigned for this; and one very generally put forward is, that Europe was wearied with continued struggles, and had become sick of "precipitating itself upon Asia." M. Guizot, in his admirable lectures upon European civilisation, successfully combats this opinion, and offers one of his own, which is far more satisfactory. He says, in his eighth lecture, " It has been often repeated that Europe was tired of continually invading Asia. This expression appears to me exceedingly incorrect. It is not possible that human beings can be wearied with what they have not done—that the labours of their forefathers can fatigue them. Weariness is a personal, not an in-herited feeling. The men of the thirteenth century were not fatigued by the Crusades of the twelfth. They were influenced by another cause. A great change had taken place in ideas, sentiments, and social conditions. The same desires and the same wants were no longer felt. The same things were no longer believed. The people refused to believe what their ancestors were persuaded of."

This is, in fact, the secret of the change; and its truth becomes more apparent as we advance in the history of the Crusades, and com-pare the state of the public mind at the different periods when God-

frey of Bouillon, Louis VII., and Richard I., were chiefs and leaders
of the movement.   The Crusades themselves were the means of operating a great change in national ideas, and advancing the civilisation
of Europe.   In the time of Godfrey, the nobles were all-powerful and
all-oppressive, and equally obnoxious to kings and people.   During
their absence along with that portion of the community the deepest
sunk in ignorance and superstition, both kings and people fortified
themselves against the renewal of aristocratic tyranny, and in proportion as they became free became civilised.   It was during this period
that in France, the grand centre of the crusading madness, the *communes* began to acquire strength, and the monarch to possess a practical
and not a merely theoretic authority.   Order and comfort began to
take root, and, when the second Crusade was preached, men were in
consequence much less willing to abandon their homes than they had
been during the first.   Such pilgrims as had returned from the Holy
Land came back with minds more liberal and expanded than when
they set out.   They had come in contact with a people more civilised
than themselves ; they had seen something more of the world, and had
lost some portion, however small, of the prejudice and bigotry of
ignorance.   The institution of chivalry had also exercised its human-
ising influence, and coming bright and fresh through the ordeal of
the Crusades, had softened the character and improved the hearts of
the aristocratic order.   The *trouvères* and *troubadours*, singing of love
and war in strains pleasing to every class of society, helped to root
out the gloomy superstitions which, at the first Crusade, filled the
minds of all those who were able to think.   Men became in consequence less exclusively under the mental thraldom of the priesthood,
and lost much of the credulity which formerly distinguished them.

The Crusades appear never to have excited so much attention in
England as on the continent of Europe ; not because the people were
less fanatical than their neighbours, but because they were occupied
in matters of graver interest.   The English were suffering too severely
from the recent successful invasion of their soil, to have much sympathy to bestow upon the distresses of people so far away as the
Christians of Palestine ; and we find that they took no part in the
first Crusade, and very little in the second.   Even then those who
engaged in it were chiefly Norman knights and their vassals, and not
the Saxon franklins and population, who no doubt thought, in their
sorrow, as many wise men have thought since, that charity should
begin at home.

Germany was productive of more zeal in the cause, and her raw
uncivilised hordes continued to issue forth under the banners of the
cross in numbers apparently undiminished, when the enthusiasm had

long been on the wane in other countries. They were sunk at that time in a deeper slough of barbarism than the livelier nations around them, and took, in consequence, a longer period to free themselves from their prejudices. In fact, the second Crusade drew its chief supplies of men from that quarter, where alone the expedition can be said to have retained any portion of popularity.

Such was the state of mind of Europe when Pope Eugenius, moved by the reiterated entreaties of the Christians of Syria, commissioned St. Bernard to preach a new Crusade. St. Bernard was a man eminently qualified for the mission. He was endowed with an eloquence of the highest order, could move an auditory to tears, or laughter, or fury, as it pleased him, and had led a life of such rigid and self-denying virtue, that not even calumny could lift her finger and point it at him. He had renounced high prospects in the Church, and contented himself with the simple abbacy of Clairvaux, in order that he might have the leisure he desired, to raise his powerful voice against abuses wherever he found them. Vice met in him an austere and uncompromising reprover ; no man was too high for his reproach, and none too low for his sympathy. He was just as well suited for his age as Peter the Hermit had been for the age preceding. He appealed more to the reason, his predecessor to the passions ; Peter the Hermit collected a mob, while St. Bernard collected an army. Both were endowed with equal zeal and perseverance, springing in the one from impulse, and in the other from conviction, and a desire to increase the influence of the Church, that great body of which he was a pillar and an ornament.

One of the first converts he made was in himself a host. Louis VII. was both superstitious and tyrannical, and, in a fit of remorse for the infamous slaughter he had authorised at the sacking of Vitry, he made a vow to undertake the journey to the Holy Land.* He was in this disposition when St. Bernard began to preach, and wanted but little persuasion to embark in the cause. His example had great influence upon the nobility, who, impoverished as many of them were

* The sacking of Vitry reflects indelible disgrace upon Louis VII. His predecessors had been long engaged in resistance to the outrageous powers assumed by the Popes, and Louis continued the same policy. The ecclesiastical chapter of Bourges, having elected an archbishop without his consent, he proclaimed the election to be invalid, and took severe and prompt measures against the refractory clergy. Thibault count de Champagne took up arms in defence of the Papal authority, and entrenched himself in the town of Vitry. Louis immediately took the field to chastise the rebel, and he besieged the town with so much vigour that the count was forced to surrender. Upwards of thirteen hundred of the inhabitants, fully one-half of whom were women and children, took refuge in the church; and when the gates of the city were opened, and all resistance had ceased, Louis inhumanly gave orders to set fire to the sacred edifice, and a thousand persons perished in the flames.

by the sacrifices made by their fathers in the holy wars, were anxious to repair their ruined fortunes by conquests on a foreign shore.
These took the field with such vassals as they could command, and
in a very short time an army was raised amounting to two hundred

CATHEDRAL OF VEZELAI.

thousand men. At Vezelai the monarch received the cross from the
hands of St. Bernard, on a platform elevated in sight of all the people. Several nobles, three bishops, and his queen Eleanor of Aquitaine were present at this ceremony, and enrolled themselves under

the banner of the cross, St. Bernard cutting up his red sacerdotal vestments and making crosses of them, to be sewn on the shoulders of the people. An exhortation from the Pope was read to the multitude, granting remission of their sins to all who should join the Crusade, and directing that no man on that holy pilgrimage should encumber himself with heavy baggage and vain superfluities; and that the nobles should not travel with dogs or falcons, to lead them from the direct road, as had happened to so many during the first Crusade.

The command of the army was offered to St. Bernard; but he wisely refused to accept a station for which his habits had unqualified him. After consecrating Louis with great solemnity, at St. Denis, as chief of the expedition, he continued his course through the country, stirring up the people wherever he went. So high an opinion was entertained of his sanctity, that he was thought to be animated by the spirit of prophecy, and to be gifted with the power of working miracles. Many women, excited by his eloquence, and encouraged by his predictions, forsook their husbands and children, and, clothing themselves in male attire, hastened to the war. St. Bernard himself wrote a letter to the Pope detailing his success, and stating, that in several towns there did not remain a single male inhabitant capable of bearing arms, and that every where castles and towns were to be seen filled with women weeping for their absent husbands. But in spite of this apparent enthusiasm, the numbers who really took up arms were inconsiderable, and not to be compared to the swarms of the first Crusade. A levy of no more than two hundred thousand men, which was the utmost the number amounted to, could hardly have depopulated a country like France, to the extent mentioned by St. Bernard. His description of the state of the country appears, therefore, to have been much more poetical than true.

Suger, the able minister of Louis, endeavoured to dissuade him from undertaking so long a journey at a time when his own dominions so much needed his presence. But the king was pricked in his conscience by the cruelties of Vitry, and was anxious to make the only reparation which the religion of that day considered sufficient. He was desirous, moreover, of testifying to the world, that though he could brave the temporal power of the Church when it encroached upon his prerogatives, he could render all due obedience to its spiritual decrees whenever it suited his interest or tallied with his prejudices to do so. Suger, therefore, implored in vain, and Louis received the pilgrim's staff at St. Denis, and made all preparations for his pilgrimage.

In the mean time St. Bernard passed into Germany, where similar success attended his preaching. The renown of his sanctity had gone before him, and he found every where an admiring audience. Thousands of people, who could not understand a word he said, flocked around him to catch a glimpse of so holy a man; and the knights enrolled themselves in great numbers in the service of the cross, each receiving from his hands the symbol of the cause. But the people were not led away as in the days of Gottschalk. We do not find that they rose in such tremendous masses of two and three hundred thousand men, swarming over the country like a plague of locusts. Still the enthusiasm was very great. The extraordinary tales that were told and believed of the miracles worked by the preacher brought the country people from far and near. Devils were said to vanish at his sight, and diseases of the most malignant nature to be cured by his touch.* The Emperor Conrad caught at last the contagion from his subjects, and declared his intention to follow the cross.

The preparations were carried on so vigorously under the orders of Conrad, that in less than three months he found himself at the head of an army containing at least one hundred and fifty thousand effective men, besides a great number of women who followed their husbands and lovers to the war. One troop of them rode in the attitude and armour of men : their chief wore gilt spurs and buskins, and thence acquired the epithet of the golden-footed lady. Conrad was ready to set out long before the French monarch, and in the month of June 1147 he arrived before Constantinople, having passed through Hungary and Bulgaria without offence to the inhabitants.

PILGRIM'S
STAFF.

Manuel Comnenus, the Greek emperor, successor not only to the throne but to the policy of Alexius, looked with alarm upon the new levies who had come to eat up his capital and imperil its tranquillity. Too weak to refuse them a passage through his dominions, too distrustful of them to make them welcome when they came, and too little assured of the advantages likely to result to himself from the war, to feign a friendship which he did not feel, the Greek emperor gave offence at the very outset. His subjects, in the pride of superior civilisation, called the Germans barbarians; while the latter, who, if

---

* Philip, Archdeacon of the cathedral of Liege, wrote a detailed account of all the miracles performed by St. Bernard during thirty-four days of his mission. They averaged about ten per day. The disciples of St. Bernard complained bitterly that the people flocked around their master in such numbers, that they could not see half the miracles he performed. But they willingly trusted the eyes of others, as far as faith in the miracles went, and seemed to vie with each other whose credulity should be greatest.

semi-barbarous, were at least honest and straightforward, retorted upon the Greeks by calling them double-faced knaves and traitors. Disputes continually arose between them, and Conrad, who had preserved so much good order among his followers during their passage, was unable to restrain their indignation when they arrived at Constantinople. For some offence or other which the Greeks had given them, but which is rather hinted at than stated by the scanty historians of the day, the Germans broke into the magnificent pleasure-garden of the emperor, where he had a valuable collection of tame animals, for which the grounds had been laid out in woods, caverns, groves, and streams, that each might follow in captivity his natural habits. The enraged Germans, meriting the name of barbarians that had been bestowed upon them, laid waste this pleasant retreat, and killed or let loose the valuable animals it contained. Manuel, who is said to have beheld the devastation from his palace-windows without power or courage to prevent it, was completely disgusted with his guests, and resolved, like his predecessor Alexius, to get rid of them on the first opportunity. He sent a message to Conrad respectfully desiring an interview, but the German refused to trust himself within the walls of Constantinople. The Greek emperor, on his part, thought it compatible neither with his dignity nor his safety to seek the German, and several days were spent in insincere negotiations. Manuel at length agreed to furnish the crusading army with guides to conduct it through Asia Minor ; and Conrad passed over the Hellespont with his forces, the advanced guard being commanded by himself, and the rear by the warlike Bishop of Freysinghen.

Historians are almost unanimous in their belief that the wily Greek gave instructions to his guides to lead the army of the German emperor into dangers and difficulties. It is certain that, instead of guiding them through such districts of Asia Minor as afforded water and provisions, they led them into the wilds of Cappadocia, where neither was to be procured, and where they were suddenly attacked by the sultan of the Seljukian Turks, at the head of an immense force. The guides, whose treachery is apparent from this fact alone, fled at the first sight of the Turkish army, and the Christians were left to wage unequal warfare with their enemy, entangled and bewildered in desert wilds. Toiling in their heavy mail, the Germans could make but little effective resistance to the attacks of the Turkish light horse, who were down upon them one instant, and out of sight the next. Now in the front and now in the rear, the agile foe showered his arrows upon them, enticing them into swamps and hollows, from which they could only extricate themselves after long struggles and great losses. The Germans, confounded by this mode of warfare, lost all conception of the direction they were pursuing, and went back instead of forward. Suffering at the same time for want of provisions, they fell an easy prey to their pursuers. Count Bernhard, one of the bravest leaders of the German expedition, was surrounded, with his whole division, not one of whom escaped the Turkish arrows. The emperor himself had nearly fallen a victim, and was twice severely wounded. So persevering was the enemy, and so little able were the Germans to make even a show of resistance, that when Conrad at last reached the city of Nice, he found that, instead of being at the head of an imposing force of one hundred thousand foot and seventy thousand horse, he had but fifty or sixty thousand men, and these in the most worn and wearied condition.

Totally ignorant of the treachery of the Greek emperor, although he had been warned to beware of it, Louis VII. proceeded at the head of his army, through Worms and Ratisbon, towards Constantinople. At Ratisbon, he was met by a deputation from Manuel, bearing letters so full of hyperbole and flattery, that Louis is reported to have blushed when they were read to him by the Bishop of Langres. The object of the deputation was to obtain from the French king a promise to pass through the Grecian territories in a peaceable and friendly manner, and to yield to the Greek emperor any conquest he might make in Asia Minor. The first part of the proposition was immediately acceded to, but no notice was taken of the second and more unreasonable. Louis marched on, and, passing through Hungary, pitched his tents in the outskirts of Constantinople.

On his arrival, Manuel sent him a friendly invitation to enter the city at the head of a small train. Louis at once accepted it, and was met by the emperor at the porch of his palace. The fairest promises were made; every art that flattery could suggest was resorted to, and every argument employed, to induce him to yield his future conquests to the Greek. Louis obstinately refused to pledge himself, and returned to his army convinced that the emperor was a man not to be trusted. Negotiations were, however, continued for several days, to the great dissatisfaction of the French army. The news that arrived of a treaty entered into between Manuel and the Turkish sultan changed their dissatisfaction into fury, and the leaders demanded to be led against Constantinople, swearing that they would raze the treacherous city to the ground. Louis did not feel inclined to accede to this proposal, and, breaking up his camp, he crossed over into Asia.

Here he heard, for the first time, of the mishaps of the German emperor, whom he found in a woful plight under the walls of Nice. The two monarchs united their forces, and marched together along the sea-coast to Ephesus; but Conrad, jealous, it would appear, of the superior numbers of the French, and not liking to sink into a vassal, for the time being, of his rival, withdrew abruptly with the remnant of his legions, and returned to Constantinople. Manuel was all smiles and courtesy. He condoled with the German so feelingly upon his losses, and cursed the stupidity or treachery of the guides with such apparent heartiness, that Conrad was half inclined to believe in his sincerity.

Louis, marching onward in the direction of Jerusalem, came up with the enemy on the banks of the Meander. The Turks contested the passage of the river, but the French bribed a peasant to point out a ford lower down: crossing the river without difficulty, they attacked the Turks with much vigour, and put them to flight. Whether the Turks were really defeated, or merely pretended to be so, is doubtful; but the latter supposition seems to be the true one. It is probable that it was part of a concerted plan to draw the invaders onwards to more unfavourable ground, where their destruction might be more certain. If such were the scheme, it succeeded to the heart's wish of its projectors. The Crusaders, on the third day after their victory, arrived at a steep mountain-pass, on the summit of which the Turkish host lay concealed so artfully, that not the slightest vestige of their presence could be perceived. "With labouring steps and slow," they toiled up the steep ascent, when suddenly a tremendous fragment of rock came bounding down the precipices with an awful crash, bearing dismay and death before it. At the same instant the Turkish archers started from their hiding-places, and discharged a shower of arrows upon the foot-soldiers, who fell by hundreds at a time. The arrows rebounded harmlessly against the iron mail of the knights, which the Turks observing, took aim at their steeds, and horse and rider fell down the steep into the rapid torrent which rushed below. Louis, who commanded the rear-guard, received the first intimation of the onslaught from the sight of the wounded and flying soldiers, and, not knowing the numbers of the enemy, he pushed vigorously forward to stay, by his presence, the panic which had taken possession of his army. All his efforts were in vain. Immense stones continued to be hurled upon them as they advanced, bearing men and horse before them; and those who succeeded in forcing their way to the top were met hand-to-hand by the Turks, and cast down headlong upon their companions. Louis himself fought with the energy of desperation, but had great difficulty to avoid falling into the enemy's hands. He escaped at last under cover of the night, with the remnant of his forces, and took up his position before Attalia. Here he restored the discipline and the courage of his disorganised and disheartened followers, and debated with his

captains the plan that was to be pursued. After suffering severely
both from disease and famine, it was resolved that they should
march to Antioch, which still remained an independent principality
under the successors of Bohemund of Tarentum. At this time the
sovereignty was vested in the person of Raymond, the uncle of Eleanor
of Aquitaine. This prince, presuming upon his relationship to the
French queen, endeavoured to withdraw Louis from the grand object
of the Crusade—the defence of the kingdom of Jerusalem, and secure
his co-operation in extending the limits and the power of his principality of Antioch. The Prince of Tripoli formed a similar design ;
but Louis rejected the offers of both, and marched, after a short
delay, to Jerusalem. The Emperor Conrad was there before him,
having left Constantinople with promises of assistance from Manuel
Comnenus—assistance which never arrived, and was never intended.

A great council of the Christian princes of Palestine, and the
leaders of the Crusade, was then summoned, to discuss the future
operations of the war. It was ultimately determined that it would
further the cause of the cross in a greater degree if the united armies,
instead of proceeding to Edessa, laid siege to the city of Damascus,

DAMASCUS.

and drove the Saracens from that strong position. This was a bold
scheme, and, had it been boldly followed out, would have insured,
in all probability, the success of the war. But the Christian leaders

never learned from experience the necessity of union, that very soul of great enterprises. Though they all agreed upon the policy of the plan, yet every one had his own notions as to the means of executing it. The princes of Antioch and Tripoli were jealous of each other, and of the king of Jerusalem. The Emperor Conrad was jealous of the king of France, and the king of France was disgusted with them all. But he had come out to Palestine in accordance with a solemn vow; his religion, though it may be called bigotry, was sincere; and he determined to remain to the very last moment that a chance was left of effecting any good for the cause he had set his heart on.

The siege of Damascus was accordingly commenced, and with so much ability and vigour that the Christians gained a considerable advantage at the very outset. For weeks the siege was pressed, till the shattered fortifications and diminishing resistance of the besieged gave evidence that the city could not hold out much longer. At that moment the insane jealousy of the leaders led to dissensions that soon caused the utter failure, not only of the siege but of the Crusade. A modern cookery-book, in giving a recipe for cooking a hare, says, "first catch your hare, and then kill it"—a maxim of indisputable wisdom. The Christian chiefs, on this occasion, had not so much sagacity, for they began a violent dispute among themselves for the possession of a city which was still unconquered. There being already a prince of Antioch and a prince of Tripoli, twenty claimants started for the principality of Damascus; and a grand council of the leaders was held to determine the individual on whom the honour should devolve. Many valuable days were wasted in this discussion, the enemy in the meanwhile gaining strength from their inactivity. It was at length, after a stormy deliberation, agreed that Count Robert of Flanders, who had twice visited the Holy Land, should be invested with the dignity. The other claimants refused to recognise him or to co-operate in the siege until a more equitable arrangement had been made. Suspicion filled the camp; the most sinister rumours of intrigues and treachery were set afloat; and the discontented candidates withdrew at last to the other side of the city, and commenced operations on their own account without a probability of success. They were soon joined by the rest of the army. The consequence was that the weakest side of the city, and that on which they had already made considerable progress in the work of demolition, was left uncovered. The enemy was prompt to profit by the mistake, and received an abundant supply of provisions, and refortified the walls, before the Crusaders came to their senses again. When this desirable event happened, it was too late. Saph Eddin, the powerful emir of Mousoul, was in the neighbourhood, at the head of a large army, advancing by forced marches to the relief of the city. The siege was abruptly abandoned, and the foolish Crusaders returned to Jerusalem, having done nothing to weaken the enemy, but every thing to weaken themselves.

The freshness of enthusiasm had now completely subsided; even the meanest soldiers were sick at heart. Conrad, from whose fierce zeal at the outset so much might have been expected, was wearied with reverses, and returned to Europe with the poor remnant of his host. Louis lingered a short time longer, for very shame, but the pressing solicitations of his minister Suger induced him to return to France. Thus ended the second Crusade. Its history is but a chronicle of defeats. It left the kingdom of Jerusalem in a worse state than when it quitted Europe, and gained nothing but disgrace for its leaders, and discouragement for all concerned.

St. Bernard, who had prophesied a result so different, fell after this into some disrepute, and experienced, like many other prophets, the fate of being without honour in his own country. What made the matter worse, he could not obtain it in any other. Still, however, there were not wanting zealous advocates to stand forward in his behalf, and stem the tide of incredulity, which, unopposed, would have carried away his reputation. The Bishop of Freysinghen declared that prophets were not always able to prophesy, and that the vices of the Crusaders drew down the wrath of heaven upon them. But the most ingenious excuse ever made for St. Bernard is to be found in his life by Geoffroi de Clairvaux, where he pertinaciously insists that the Crusade was not unfortunate. St. Bernard, he says, had prophesied a happy result, and that result could not be considered other than happy which had peopled heaven with so glorious an army of martyrs. Geoffroi was a cunning pleader, and, no doubt, convinced a few of the zealous; but plain people, who were not wanting even in those days, retained their own opinion, or, what amounts to the same thing, " were convinced against their will."

We now come to the consideration of the third Crusade, and of the causes which rendered it necessary. The epidemic frenzy, which had been cooling ever since the issue of the first expedition, was now extinct, or very nearly so, and the nations of Europe looked with cold indifference upon the armaments of their princes. But chivalry had flourished in its natural element of war, and was now in all its glory. It continued to supply armies for the Holy Land when the popular ranks refused to deliver up their able-bodied swarms. Poetry, which, more than religion, inspired the third Crusade, was then but " caviare to the million," who had other matters, of sterner import, to claim all their attention. But the knights and their retainers listened with delight to the martial and amatory strains of the minstrels, minnesängers, trouvères, and troubadours, and burned to win favour in ladies' eyes by shewing prowess in the Holy Land. The third was truly the romantic era of the Crusades. Men fought then, not so much for the sepulchre of Jesus and the maintenance of a Christian kingdom in the East, as to gain glory for themselves in the best and almost only field where glory could be obtained. They fought, not as zealots, but as soldiers; not for religion, but for honour; not for the crown of martyrdom, but for the favour of the lovely.

It is not necessary to enter into a detail of the events by which Saladin attained the sovereignty of the East, or how, after a succession of engagements, he planted the Moslem banner once more upon the battlements of Jerusalem. The Christian knights and population, including the grand orders of St. John, the Hospitallers, and the Templars, were sunk in an abyss of vice, and, torn by unworthy jealousies and dissensions, were unable to resist the well-trained armies which the wise and mighty Saladin brought forward to crush them. But the news of their fall created a painful sensation among the chivalry of Europe, whose noblest members were linked to the dwellers in Palestine by many ties, both of blood and friendship. The news of the great battle of Tiberias, in which Saladin defeated the Christian host with terrible slaughter, arrived first in Europe, and was followed in quick succession by that of the capture of Jerusalem, Antioch, Tripoli, and other cities. Dismay seized upon the clergy. The Pope (Urban III.) was so affected by the news that he pined away for grief, and was scarcely seen to smile again, until he sank into the sleep of death.* His successor, Gregory VIII., felt the loss as acutely, but had better strength to bear it, and instructed all the clergy of the Christian world to stir up the people to arms for the recovery of the Holy Sepulchre. William Archbishop of Tyre, a humble follower in the path of Peter the Hermit, left Palestine to preach to the kings of Europe the miseries he had wit-

SEAL OF BARBAROSSA.

nessed, and to incite them to the rescue. The renowned Frederick Barbarossa, the emperor of Germany, speedily collected an army, and

* James of Vitry; William de Nangis.

passing over into Syria with less delay than had ever before awaited a crusading force, defeated the Saracens, and took possession of the city of Iconium. He was unfortunately cut off in the middle of his successful career, by imprudently bathing in the Cydnus* while he was overheated, and the Duke of Suabia took the command of the expedition. The latter did not prove so able a general, and met with nothing but reverses, although he was enabled to maintain a footing at Antioch until assistance arrived from Europe.

HENRY II. OF ENGLAND.

Henry II. of England and Philip Augustus of France, at the head of their chivalry, supported the Crusade with all their influence, until wars and dissensions nearer home estranged them from it for a time. The two kings met at Gisors in Normandy in the month of January,

* The desire of comparing two great men has tempted many writers to drown Frederick in the river Cydnus, in which Alexander so imprudently bathed (Q. Curt. lib. iii. c. 4, 5); but, from the march of the emperor I rather judge that his Saleph is the Cacadnus, a stream of less fame, but of a longer course— *Gibbon.*

1188, accompanied by a brilliant train of knights and warriors. William of Tyre was present, and expounded the cause of the cross with considerable eloquence, and the whole assembly bound themselves by oath to proceed to Jerusalem. It was agreed at the same time that

CHATEAU OF GISORS.

a tax, called Saladin's tithe, and consisting of the tenth part of all possessions, whether landed or personal, should be enforced over Christendom, upon every one who was either unable or unwilling to assume the cross. The lord of every feof, whether lay or ecclesiastical, was charged to raise the tithe within his own jurisdiction; and any one who refused to pay his quota became by that act the bondsman and absolute property of his lord. At the same time the greatest indulgence was shewn to those who assumed the cross; no man was at liberty to stay them by process of any kind, whether for debt, or robbery, or murder. The king of France, at the breaking up of the conference, summoned a parliament at Paris, where these resolutions were solemnly confirmed, while Henry II. did the same for his Norman possessions at Rouen, and for England at Geddington, in Northamptonshire. To use the words of an ancient chronicler,* "he

* Stowe.

held a parliament about the voyage into the Holy Land, and troubled
the whole land with the paying of tithes towards it."

PHILIP AUGUSTUS.

But it was not England alone
that was "*troubled*" by the tax.
The people of France also looked upon it with no pleasant feelings, and
appear from that time forth to have
changed their indifference for the
Crusade into aversion. Even the
clergy, who were exceedingly willing
that other people should contribute
half, or even all their goods in furtherance of their favourite scheme,
were not at all anxious to contribute
a single sous themselves. Millot* relates that several of them cried out
against the impost. Among the rest,
the clergy of Rheims were called upon to pay their quota, but sent a
deputation to the king, begging him
to be contented with the aid of their
prayers, as they were too poor to contribute in any other shape. Philip
Augustus knew better, and by way
of giving them a lesson, employed
three nobles of the vicinity to lay
waste the Church lands. The clergy,
informed of the outrage, applied to the king for redress. "I will
aid you with my prayers," said the monarch condescendingly, "and
will entreat those gentlemen to let the Church alone." He did
as he had promised, but in such a manner that the nobles, who
appreciated the joke, continued their devastations as before. Again
the clergy applied to the king. "What would you have of me?"
he replied, in answer to their remonstrances : "you gave me your
prayers in my necessity, and I have given you mine in yours." The
clergy understood the argument, and thought it the wiser course to
pay their quota of Saladin's tithe without further parley.

This anecdote shews the unpopularity of the Crusade. If the
clergy disliked to contribute, it is no wonder that the people felt still
greater antipathy. But the chivalry of Europe was eager for the
affray : the tithe was rigorously collected, and armies from England,
France, Burgundy, Italy, Flanders, and Germany were soon in the

* *Elémens de l'Histoire de France.*

field. The two kings who were to have led it were, however, drawn
into broils by an aggression of Richard duke of Guienne, better known
as Richard Cœur de Lion, upon the territory of the Count of Toulouse,
and the 'proposed journey to Palestine was delayed. War continued
to rage between France and England, and with so little probability
of a speedy termination, that many of the nobles, bound to the Crusade, left the two monarchs to settle the differences at their leisure,
and proceeded to Palestine without them.

Death at last stepped in and removed Henry II. from the hostility
of his foes, and the treachery and ingratitude of his children. His
son Richard immediately concluded an alliance with Philip Augustus; and the two young, valiant, and impetuous monarchs united
all their energies to forward the Crusade. They met with a numerous and brilliant retinue at Nonancourt in Normandy, where, in
sight of their assembled chivalry, they embraced as brothers, and
swore to live as friends and true allies, until a period of forty days
after their return from the Holy Land. With a view of purging
their camp from the follies and vices which had proved so ruinous
to preceding expeditions, they drew up a code of laws for the government of the army. Gambling had been carried to a great extent,
and proved the fruitful source of quarrels and bloodshed; and one of
their laws prohibited any person in the army, beneath the degree of
a knight, from playing at any game for money.* Knights and clergymen might play for money, but no one was permitted to lose or gain
more than twenty shillings in a day, under a penalty of one hundred
shillings. The personal attendants of the monarchs were also allowed to play to the same extent. The penalty in their case for in-
fraction was that they should be whipped naked through the army
for the space of three days. Any Crusader who struck another and
drew blood was ordered to have his hand cut off; and whoever slew
a brother Crusader was condemned to be tied alive to the corpse of
his victim, and buried with him. No young women were allowed to
follow the army, to the great sorrow of many vicious and of many virtuous dames, who had not courage to elude the decree by dressing in
male attire. But many high-minded and affectionate maidens and
matrons, bearing the sword or the spear, followed their husbands
and lovers to the war in spite of King Richard, and in defiance of
danger. The only women allowed to accompany the army in their
own habiliments were washerwomen of fifty years complete, and any
others of the fair sex who had reached the same age.

These rules having been promulgated, the two monarchs marched
together to Lyons, where they separated, agreeing to meet again at

* Strutt's *Sports and Pastimes.*

Messina. Philip proceeded across the Alps to Genoa, where he took ship, and was conveyed in safety to the place of rendezvous. Richard turned in the direction of Marseilles, where he also took ship for Messina. His impetuous disposition hurried him into many squabbles by the way, and his knights and followers, for the most part as brave and as foolish as himself, imitated him very zealously in this particular. At Messina the Sicilians charged the most exorbitant prices for every necessary of life. Richard's army in vain remonstrated. From words they came to blows, and, as a last resource, plundered the Sicilians, since they could not trade with them. Continual

THE ISLAND OF RHODES.

battles were the consequence, in one of which Lebrun, the favourite attendant of Richard, lost his life. The peasantry from far and near came flocking to the aid of the townspeople, and the battle soon became general. Richard, irritated at the loss of his favourite, and incited by a report that Tancred, the king of Sicily, was fighting at the head of his own people, joined the *mêlée* with his boldest knights, and, beating back the Sicilians, attacked the city sword in hand, stormed the battlements, tore down the flag of Sicily, and planted his own in its stead. This collision gave great offence to the king of France, who became from that time jealous of Richard, and apprehensive that his design was not so much to re-establish the Christian kingdom of Jerusalem as to make conquests for himself. He, however, exerted his influence to restore peace between the English and Sicilians, and shortly afterwards set sail for Acre, with distrust of his ally germinating in his heart.

Richard remained behind for some weeks in a state of inactivity quite unaccountable in one of his temperament. He appears to have had no more squabbles with the Sicilians, but to have lived an easy, luxurious life, forgetting, in the lap of pleasure, the objects for which he had quitted his own dominions and the dangerous laxity he was introducing into his army. The superstition of his soldiers recalled him at length to a sense of his duty: a comet was seen for several successive nights, which was thought to menace them with the vengeance of Heaven for their delay. Shooting stars gave them similar warning; and a fanatic, of the name of Joachim, with his drawn sword in his hand, and his long hair streaming wildly over his shoulders, went through the camp, howling all night long, and predicting plague, famine, and every other calamity, if they did not set out immediately. Richard did not deem it prudent to neglect the intimations; and, after doing humble penance for his remissness, he set sail for Acre.

A violent storm dispersed his fleet, but he arrived safely at Rhodes with the principal part of the armament. Here he learned that three of his ships had been stranded on the rocky coasts of Cyprus, and that the ruler of the island, Isaac Comnenus, had permitted his people to pillage the unfortunate crews, and had refused shelter to his betrothed bride, the Princess Berengaria, and his sister, who, in one of the vessels, had been driven by stress of weather into the port of Limisso. The fiery monarch swore to be revenged, and, collecting all his vessels, sailed back to Limisso. Isaac Comnenus refused to apologise or explain, and Richard, in no mood to be trifled with, landed on the island, routed with great loss the forces sent to oppose him, and laid the whole country under contribution.

On his arrival at Acre he found the whole of the chivalry of Europe there before him. Guy of Lusignan, the king of Jerusalem, had long before collected the bold Knights of the Temple, the Hospital, and St. John, and had laid siege to Acre, which was resolutely defended by the Sultan Saladin, with an army magnificent both for its numbers and its discipline. For nearly two years the Crusaders had pushed the siege, and made efforts almost superhuman to dis-

RICHARD I. AND BERENGARIA.

lodge the enemy. Various battles had taken place in the open fields with no decisive advantage to either party, and Guy of Lusignan had begun to despair of taking that strong position without aid from

Europe. His joy was extreme on the arrival of Philip with all his chivalry, and he only waited the coming of Cœur de Lion to make one last decisive attack upon the town. When the fleet of England was first seen approaching the shores of Syria, a universal shout arose from the Christian camp; and when Richard landed with his train, one louder still pierced to the very mountains of the south, where Saladin lay with all his army.

It may be remarked as characteristic of this Crusade, that the Christians and the Moslems no longer looked upon each other as barbarians, to whom mercy was a crime. Each host entertained the highest admiration for the bravery and magnanimity of the other, and, in their occasional truces, met upon the most friendly terms. The Moslem warriors were full of courtesy to the Christian knights, and had no other regret than to think that such fine fellows were not Mahomedans. The Christians, with a feeling precisely similar, extolled to the skies the nobleness of the Saracens, and sighed to think that such generosity and valour should be sullied by disbelief in the Gospel of Jesus. But when the strife began, all these feelings disappeared, and the struggle became mortal.

The jealousy excited in the mind of Philip by the events of Messina still rankled, and the two monarchs refused to act in concert. Instead of making a joint attack upon the town, the French monarch assailed it alone, and was repulsed. Richard did the same, and with the same result. Philip tried to seduce the soldiers of Richard from their allegiance by the offer of three gold pieces per month to every knight who would forsake the banners of England for those of France. Richard endeavoured to neutralise the offer by a larger one, and promised four pieces to every French knight who should join the Lion of England. In this unworthy rivalry their time was wasted, to the great detriment of the discipline and efficiency of their followers. Some good was nevertheless effected; for the mere presence of two such armies prevented the besieged city from receiving supplies, and the inhabitants were reduced by famine to the most woful straits. Saladin did not deem it prudent to risk a general engagement by coming to their relief, but preferred to wait till dissension had weakened his enemy, and made him an easy prey. Perhaps if he had been aware of the real extent of the extremity in Acre, he would have changed his plan; but, cut off from the town, he did not know its misery till it was too late. After a short truce the city capitulated upon terms so severe that Saladin afterwards refused to ratify them. The chief conditions were, that the precious wood of the true cross, captured by the Moslems in Jerusalem, should be restored; that a sum of two hundred thousand gold pieces should be paid; and that all the Christian prisoners in Acre should be released, together with two hundred knights and a thousand soldiers detained in captivity by Saladin. The eastern monarch, as may be well conceived, did not set much store on the wood of the cross, but was nevertheless anxious to keep it, as he knew its possession by the Christians would do more than a victory to restore their courage. He refused, therefore, to deliver it up, or to accede to any of the conditions; and Richard, as he had previously threatened, barbarously ordered all the Saracen prisoners in his power to be put to death.

The possession of the city only caused new and unhappy dissensions between the Christian leaders. The Archduke of Austria unjustifiably hoisted his flag on one of the towers of Acre, which Richard no sooner saw than he tore it down with his own hands, and trampled it under his feet. Philip, though he did not sympathise with the archduke, was piqued at the assumption of Richard, and the breach between the two monarchs became wider than ever. A foolish dispute arose at the same time between Guy of Lusignan and Conrad of Montferrat for the crown of Jerusalem. The inferior knights were not slow to imitate the pernicious example, and jealousy, distrust, and ill-will reigned in the Christian camp. In the midst of this confusion the king of France suddenly announced his intention to return to his own country. Richard was filled with indignation, and exclaimed, " Eternal shame light on him, and on all France, if, for any cause, he leave this work unfinished !" But Philip was not to be stayed. His health had suffered by his residence in the East; and, ambitious of playing a first part, he preferred to play none at all than to play second to King Richard. Leaving a small detachment of Burgundians behind, he returned to France with the remainder of his army; and Cœur de Lion, without feeling, in the multitude of his rivals, that he had lost the greatest, became painfully convinced that the right arm of the enterprise was lopped off.

After his departure, Richard refortified Acre, restored the Christian worship in the churches, and leaving a Christian garrison to protect it, marched along the sea-coast towards Ascalon. Saladin was on the alert, and sent his light horse to attack the rear of the Christian army, while he himself, miscalculating their weakness since the defection of Philip, endeavoured to force them to a general engagement. The rival armies met near Azotus. A fierce battle ensued, in which Saladin was defeated and put to flight, and the road to Jerusalem left free for the Crusaders.

Again discord exerted its baleful influence, and prevented Richard from following up his victory. His opinion was constantly opposed by the other leaders, all jealous of his bravery and influence; and the army, instead of marching to Jerusalem, or even to Ascalon, as was first intended, proceeded to Jaffa, and remained in idleness until Saladin was again in a condition to wage war against them.

Many months were spent in fruitless hostilities and as fruitless negotiations. Richard's wish was to recapture Jerusalem; but there were difficulties in the way, which even his bold spirit could not conquer. His own intolerable pride was not the least cause of the evil; for it estranged many a generous spirit, who would have been willing to co-operate with him in all cordiality. At length it was agreed to march to the Holy City; but the progress made was so slow and painful, that the soldiers murmured, and the leaders meditated retreat. The weather was hot and dry, and there was little water to be pro-

BETHLEHEM.

cured. Saladin had choked up the wells and cisterns on the route, and the army had not zeal enough to push forward amid such privation. At Bethlehem a council was held, to debate whether they should retreat or advance. Retreat was decided upon, and immediately commenced. It is said, that Richard was first led to a hill, whence he could obtain a sight of the towers of Jerusalem, and that he was so affected at being so near it, and so unable to relieve it, that he hid his face behind his shield, and sobbed aloud.

The army separated into two divisions, the smaller falling back upon Jaffa, and the larger, commanded by Richard and the Duke of Burgundy, returning to Acre. Before the English monarch had made all his preparations for his return to Europe, a messenger reached Acre with the intelligence that Jaffa was besieged by Saladin, and that unless relieved immediately, the city would be taken. The French, under the Duke of Burgundy, were so wearied with the war, that they refused to aid their brethren in Jaffa. Richard, blushing with shame at their pusillanimity, called his English to the rescue, and arrived just in time to save the city. His very name put the Saracens to flight, so great was their dread of his prowess. Saladin regarded him with the warmest admiration, and when Richard, after his victory, demanded peace, willingly acceded. A truce was concluded for three years and eight months, during which Christian pilgrims were to enjoy the liberty of visiting Jerusalem without hindrance or payment of any tax. The Crusaders were allowed to retain the cities of Tyre and Jaffa, with the country intervening. Saladin, with a princely generosity, invited many of the Christians to visit Jerusalem; and several of the leaders took advantage of his offer to feast their eyes upon a spot which all considered so sacred. Many of them were entertained for days in the sultan's own palace, from which they returned with their tongues laden with the praises of the noble infidel. Richard and Saladin never met, though the impression that they did will remain on many minds, who have been dazzled by the glorious fiction of Sir Walter Scott. But each admired the prowess and nobleness of soul of his rival, and agreed to terms far less onerous than either would have accepted, had this mutual admiration not existed.*

The king of England no longer delayed his departure, for messengers from his own country brought imperative news that his presence was required to defeat the intrigues that were fomenting against his crown. His long imprisonment in the Austrian dominions and final ransom are too well known to be dwelt upon. And thus ended the third Crusade, less destructive of human life than the two first, but quite as useless.

---

* Richard left a high reputation in Palestine. So much terror did his name occasion, that the women of Syria used it to frighten their children for ages afterwards. Every disobedient child became still when told that King Richard was coming. Even men shared the panic that his name created; and a hundred years afterwards, whenever a horse shied at any object in the way, his rider would exclaim, "What! dost thou think King Richard is in the bush?"

The flame of popular enthusiasm now burned pale indeed, and all the efforts of popes and potentates were insufficient to rekindle it. At last, after flickering unsteadily, like a lamp expiring in the socket, it burned up brightly for one final instant, and was extinguished for ever.

The fourth Crusade, as connected with popular feeling, requires little or no notice. At the death of Saladin, which happened a year after the conclusion of his truce with Richard of England, his vast empire fell to pieces. His brother Saif Eddin, or Saphaddin, seized upon Syria, in the possession of which he was troubled by the sons of Saladin. When this intelligence reached Europe, the pope, Celestine III., judged the moment favourable for preaching a new Crusade. But every nation in Europe was unwilling and cold towards it. The people had no ardour, and kings were occupied with more weighty matters at home. The only monarch of Europe who encouraged it was the Emperor Henry of Germany, under whose auspices the Dukes of Saxony and Bavaria took the field at the head of a considerable force. They landed in Palestine, and found any thing but a welcome from the Christian inhabitants. Under the mild sway of Saladin, they had enjoyed repose and toleration, and both were endangered by the arrival of the Germans. They looked upon them in consequence as over-officious intruders, and gave them no encouragement in the warfare against Saphaddin. The result of this Crusade was even more disastrous than the last; for the Germans contrived not only to embitter the Saracens against the Christians of Judea, but to lose the strong city of Jaffa, and cause the destruction of nine-tenths of the army with which they had quitted Europe. And so ended the fourth Crusade.

The fifth was more important, and had a result which its projectors never dreamed of—no less than the sacking of Constantinople, and the placing of a French dynasty upon the imperial throne of the eastern Cæsars. Each succeeding pope, however much he may have differed from his predecessors on other points, zealously agreed in one, that of maintaining by every possible means the papal ascendency. No scheme was so likely to aid in this endeavour as the Crusades. As long as they could persuade the kings and nobles of Europe to fight and die in Syria, their own sway was secured over the minds of men at home. Such being their object, they never inquired whether a Crusade was or was not likely to be successful, whether the time were well or ill chosen, or whether men and money could be procured in sufficient abundance. Pope Innocent III. would have been proud if he could have bent the refractory monarchs of England and France into so much submission. But John and Philip Augustus were both engaged. Both had deeply offended the Church, and had been laid under her ban, and both were occupied in important reforms at home; Philip in bestowing immunities upon his subjects, and John in having them forced from him. The emissaries of the pope therefore plied them in vain; but as in the first and second Crusades, the eloquence of a powerful preacher incited the nobility, and through them a certain portion of the people: Foulque bishop of Neuilly, an ambitious and enterprising prelate, entered fully into the views of the court of Rome, and preached the Crusade wherever he could find an audience. Chance favoured him to a degree he did not himself expect, for he had in general found but few proselytes, and those few but cold in the cause. Theobald count of Champagne had instituted a grand tournament, to which he had invited all the nobles from far and near. Upwards of two thousand knights were present with their retainers, besides a vast concourse of people to witness the sports. In the midst of the festivities Foulque arrived upon the spot, and conceiving the opportunity to be a favourable one, he addressed the multitude in eloquent language, and passionately called upon them to enrol themselves for the new Crusade. The Count de Champagne, young, ardent, and easily excited, received the cross at his hands. The enthusiasm spread rapidly. Charles count of Blois followed the example, and of the two thousand knights present, scarcely one hundred and fifty refused. The popular phrensy seemed on the point of breaking out as in the days of yore. The Count of Flanders, the Count of Bar, the Duke of Burgundy, and the Marquis of Montferrat brought all their vassals to swell the train, and in a very short space of time an effective army was on foot and ready to march to Palestine.

The dangers of an overland journey were too well understood, and the Crusaders endeavoured to make a contract with some of the Italian states to convey them over in their vessels. Dandolo, the aged doge of Venice, offered them the galleys of the Republic; but the Crusaders, on their arrival in that city, found themselves too poor to pay even half the sum demanded. Every means was tried to raise money; the Crusaders melted down their plate, and ladies gave up their trinkets. Contributions were solicited from the faithful, but came in so slowly as to make it evident to all concerned, that the faithful of Europe were outnumbered by the prudent. As a last resource, Dandolo offered to convey them to Palestine at the expense of the Republic, if they would previously aid in the recapture of the city of Zara, which had been seized from the Venetians a short time previously by the king of Hungary. The Crusaders consented, much to the displeasure of the pope, who threatened excommunication upon all who should be turned aside from the voyage to Jerusalem. But notwithstanding the fulminations of the Church, the expedition never reached Palestine. The siege of Zara was speedily undertaken. After a long and brave defence, the city surrendered at discretion, and the Crusaders were free, if they had so chosen it, to use their swords against the Saracens. But the ambition of the chiefs had been directed, by unforeseen circumstances, elsewhere.

After the death of Manuel Comnenus, the Greek empire had fallen a prey to intestine divisions. His son Alexius II. had succeeded him, but was murdered after a short reign by his uncle Andronicus, who seized upon the throne. His reign also was but of short duration. Isaac Angelus, a member of the same family, took up arms against the usurper, and having defeated and captured him in a pitched battle, had him put to death. He also mounted the throne only to be cast down from it. His brother Alexius deposed him, and to incapacitate him from reigning, put out his eyes, and shut him up in a dungeon. Neither was Alexius III. allowed to remain in peaceable possession of the throne; the son of the unhappy Isaac, whose name also was Alexius, fled from Constantinople, and hearing that the Crusaders had undertaken the siege of Zara, made them the most magnificent offers if they would afterwards aid him in deposing his uncle. His offers were, that if by their means he was re-established in his father's dominions, he would place the Greek Church under the authority of the Pope of Rome, lend the whole force of the Greek empire to the conquest of Palestine, and distribute two hundred thousand marks of silver among the crusading army. The offer was accepted, with a proviso on the part of some of the leaders, that they should be free to abandon the design, if it met with the disapproval of the pope. But this was not to be feared. The submission of the schismatic Greeks to the See of Rome was a greater bribe to the pontiff than the utter annihilation of the Saracen power in Palestine would have been.

The Crusaders were soon in movement for the imperial city. Their operations were skilfully and courageously directed, and spread such dismay as to paralyse the efforts of the usurper to retain possession of his throne. After a vain resistance, he abandoned the city to its fate, and fled no one knew whither. The aged and blind Isaac was taken from his dungeon by his subjects, and placed upon the throne ere the Crusaders were apprised of the flight of his rival. His son Alexius IV. was afterwards associated with him in the sovereignty.

But the conditions of the treaty gave offence to the Grecian people, whose prelates refused to place themselves under the dominion of the See of Rome. Alexius at first endeavoured to persuade his subjects to submission, and prayed the Crusaders to remain in Con-

stantinople until they had fortified him in the possession of a throne
which was yet far from secure. He soon became unpopular with his
subjects; and breaking faith with regard to the subsidies, he offended
the Crusaders. War was at length declared upon him by both parties; by his people for his tyranny, and by his former friends for his
treachery. He was seized in his palace by his own guards, and thrown
into prison, while the Crusaders were making ready to besiege his
capital. The Greeks immediately proceeded to the election of a new
monarch; and looking about for a man of courage, energy, and perseverance, they fixed upon Alexius Ducas, who, with almost every
bad quality, was possessed of the virtues they needed. He ascended

CONSTANTINOPLE.

the throne under the name of Murzuphlis. One of his first acts was
to rid himself of his youngest predecessor—a broken heart had already removed the blind old Isaac, no longer a stumbling-block in
his way—and the young Alexius was soon after put to death in his
prison.

War to the knife was now declared between the Greeks and the
Franks; and early in the spring of the year 1204, preparations were
commenced for an assault upon Constantinople. The French and
Venetians entered into a treaty for the division of the spoils among
their soldiery; for so confident were they of success, that failure
never once entered into their calculations. This confidence led them

on to victory; while the Greeks, cowardly as treacherous people always are, were paralysed by a foreboding of evil. It has been a matter of astonishment to all historians, that Murzuphlis, with the reputation for courage which he had acquired, and the immense resources at his disposal, took no better measures to repel the onset of the Crusaders. Their numbers were as a mere handful in comparison with those which he could have brought against them; and if they had the hopes of plunder to lead them on, the Greeks had their homes to fight for, and their very existence as a nation to protect. After an impetuous assault, repulsed for one day, but renewed with double impetuosity on another, the Crusaders lashed their vessels against the walls, slew every man who opposed them, and, with little loss to themselves, entered the city. Murzuphlis fled, and Constantinople was given over to be pillaged by the victors. The wealth they found was enormous. In money alone there was sufficient to distribute twenty marks of silver to each knight, ten to each squire or servant at arms, and five to each archer. Jewels, velvets, silks, and every luxury of attire, with rare wines and fruits, and valuable merchandise of every description, also fell into their hands, and were bought by the trading Venetians, and the proceeds distributed among the army. Two thousand persons were put to the sword; but had there been less plunder to take up the attention of the victors, the slaughter would in all probability have been much greater.

In many of the bloody wars which defile the page of history, we find that soldiers, utterly reckless of the works of God, will destroy his masterpiece, man, with unsparing brutality, but linger with respect round the beautiful works of art. They will slaughter women and children, but spare a picture; will hew down the sick, the helpless, and the hoary-headed, but refrain from injuring a fine piece of sculpture. The Latins, on their entrance into Constantinople, respected neither the works of God nor man, but vented their brutal ferocity upon the one, and satisfied their avarice upon the other. Many beautiful bronze statues, above all price as works of art, were broken into pieces to be sold as old metal. The finely-chiselled marble, which could be put to no such vile uses, was also destroyed with a recklessness, if possible, still more atrocious.*

* The following is a list of some of the works of art thus destroyed, from Nicetas, a contemporary Greek author: 1st. A colossal Juno, from the forum of Constantine, the head of which was so large that four horses could scarcely draw it from the place where it stood to the palace. 2d. The statue of Paris, presenting the apple to Venus. 3d. An immense bronze pyramid, crowned by a female figure, which turned with the wind. 4th. The colossal statue of Bellerophon, in bronze, which was broken down and cast into the furnace. Under the inner nail of the horse's hind foot on the left side, was found a seal wrapped in a woollen cloth. 5th. A figure of Hercules, by Lysimachus, of such vast

The carnage being over, and the spoil distributed, six persons were chosen from among the Franks and six from among the Venetians, who were to meet and elect an emperor, previously binding themselves by oath to select the individual best qualified among the candidates. The choice wavered between Baldwin count of Flanders and Boniface marquis of Montferrat, but fell eventually upon the former. He was straightway robed in the imperial purple, and became the founder of a new dynasty. He did not live long to enjoy his power, or to consolidate it for his successors, who, in their turn, were soon swept away. In less than sixty years the rule of the Franks at Constantinople was brought to as sudden and disastrous a termination as the reign of Murzuphlis: and this was the grand result of the fifth Crusade.

Pope Innocent III., although he had looked with no very unfavourable eye upon these proceedings, regretted that nothing had been done for the relief of the Holy Land; still, upon every convenient occasion, he enforced the necessity of a new Crusade. Until the year 1213, his exhortations had no other effect than to keep the subject in the mind of Europe. Every spring and summer detachments of pilgrims continued to set out for Palestine to the aid of their brethren, but not in sufficient numbers to be of much service. These periodical passages were called the *passagium Martii*, or the passage of March, and the *passagium Johannis*, or the passage of the festival of St. John. These did not consist entirely of soldiers, armed against the Saracen, but of pilgrims led by devotion, and in performance of their vows, bearing nothing with them but their staff and their wallet. Early in the spring of 1213 a more extraordinary body of Crusaders was raised in France and Germany. An immense number of boys and girls, amounting, according to some accounts, to thirty thousand, were incited by the persuasion of two monks to undertake the journey to Palestine. They were no doubt composed of the idle and deserted children who generally swarm in great cities, nurtured in vice and daring, and ready for any thing. The object of the monks seems to have been the atrocious one of inveigling them into slave-ships, on pretence of sending them to Syria, and selling them for slaves on the coast of Africa.* Great numbers of these poor victims were shipped

dimensions that the thumb was equal in circumference to the waist of a man. 6th. The Ass and his Driver, cast by order of Augustus after the battle of Actium, in commemoration of his having discovered the position of Anthony through the means of an ass-driver. 7th. The Wolf suckling the Twins of Rome. 8th. The Gladiator in combat with a Lion. 9th. The Hippopotamus. 10th. The Sphinxes. 11th. An Eagle fighting with a Serpent. 12th. A beautiful statue of Helen. 13th. A group, with a monster somewhat resembling a bull engaged in deadly conflict with a serpent; and many other works of art, too numerous to mention.

* See Jacob de Voragine and Albericus.

at Marseilles; but the vessels, with the exception of two or three, were wrecked on the shores of Italy, and every soul perished. The remainder arrived safely in Africa, and were bought up as slaves, and sent off into the interior of the country. Another detachment arrived at Genoa; but the accomplices in this horrid plot having taken no measures at that port, expecting them all at Marseilles, they were induced to return to their homes by the Genoese.

Fuller, in his quaint history of the *Holy Warre*, says that this Crusade was done by the instinct of the devil; and he adds a reason, which may provoke mirth now, but which was put forth by the worthy historian in all soberness and sincerity. He says, "the devil, being cloyed with the murdering of men, desired a cordial of children's blood to comfort his weak stomach;" as epicures, when tired of mutton, resort to lamb for a change.

It appears from other authors that the preaching of the vile monks had such an effect upon these deluded children that they ran about the country, exclaiming, "O Lord Jesus, restore thy cross to us!" and that neither bolts nor bars, the fear of fathers, nor the love of mothers, was sufficient to restrain them from journeying to Jerusalem.

The details of these strange proceedings are exceedingly meagre and confused, and none of the contemporary writers who mention the subject have thought it worth while to state the names of the monks who originated the scheme, or the fate they met for their wickedness. Two merchants of Marseilles, who were to have shared in the profits, were, it is said, brought to justice for some other crime, and suffered death; but we are not informed whether they divulged any circumstances relating to this matter.

Pope Innocent III. does not seem to have been aware that the causes of this juvenile Crusade were such as have been stated, for, upon being informed that numbers of them had taken the cross, and were marching to the Holy Land, he exclaimed, "These children are awake while we sleep!" He imagined, apparently, that the mind of Europe was still bent on the recovery of Palestine, and that the zeal of these children implied a sort of reproach upon his own lukewarmness. Very soon afterwards, he bestirred himself with more activity, and sent an encyclical letter to the clergy of Christendom, urging them to preach a new Crusade. As usual, a number of adventurous nobles, who had nothing else to do, enrolled themselves with their retainers. At a Council of Lateran, which was held while these bands were collecting, Innocent announced that he himself would take the Cross, and lead the armies of Christ to the defence of his sepulchre. In all probability he would have done so, for he was zealous enough; but death stepped in, and destroyed his project ere it was ripe. His successor encouraged the Crusade, though he refused to accompany it ; and the armament continued in France, England, and Germany. No leaders of any importance joined it from the former countries. Andrew king of Hungary was the only monarch who had leisure or inclination to leave his dominions. The Dukes of Austria and Bavaria joined him with a considerable army of Germans, and marching to Spalatro, took ship for Cyprus, and from thence to Acre.

The whole conduct of the king of Hungary was marked by pusillanimity and irresolution. He found himself in the Holy Land at the head of a very efficient army ; the Saracens were taken by surprise, and were for some weeks unprepared to offer any resistance to his arms. He defeated the first body sent to oppose him, and marched towards Mount Tabor with the intention of seizing upon an important fortress which the Saracens had recently constructed. He arrived without impediment at the mount, and might have easily taken it ; but a sudden fit of cowardice came over him, and he returned to Acre without striking a blow. He very soon afterwards abandoned the enterprise altogether, and returned to his own country.

Tardy reinforcements arrived at intervals from Europe ; and the Duke of Austria, now the chief leader of the expedition, had still sufficient forces at his command to trouble the Saracens very seriously. It was resolved by him, in council with the other chiefs, that the whole energy of the Crusade should be directed upon Egypt, the seat of the Saracen power in its relationship to Palestine, and from whence were drawn the continual levies that were brought against them by the sultan. Damietta, which commanded the river Nile, and was one of the most important cities of Egypt, was chosen as the first point of attack. The siege was forthwith commenced, and carried on with considerable energy, until the Crusaders gained possession of a tower, which projected into the middle of the stream, and was looked upon as the very key of the city.

While congratulating themselves upon this success, and wasting in revelry the time which should have been employed in turning it to further advantage, they received the news of the death of the wise Sultan Saphaddin. His two sons, Camhel and Cohreddin, divided his empire between them. Syria and Palestine fell to the share of Cohreddin, while Egypt was consigned to the other brother, who had for some time exercised the functions of lieutenant of that country. Being unpopular among the Egyptians, they revolted against him, giving the Crusaders a finer opportunity for making a conquest than they had ever enjoyed before. But, quarrelsome and licentious as they had been from time immemorial, they did not see that the favourable moment had come ; or seeing, could not profit by it. While they were revelling or fighting among themselves under the walls of Damietta, the revolt was suppressed, and Camhel firmly established on the throne of Egypt. In conjunction with his brother Cohreddin, his next care was to drive the Christians from Damietta, and for upwards of three months they bent all their efforts to throw in supplies to the besieged, or draw on the besiegers to a general engagement. In neither were they successful ; and the famine in Damietta became so dreadful that vermin of every description were thought luxuries, and sold for exorbitant prices. A dead dog became more valuable than a live ox in time of prosperity. Unwholesome food brought on disease, and the city could hold out no longer for absolute want of men to defend the walls.

Cohreddin and Camhel were alike interested in the preservation of so important a position, and, convinced of the certain fate of the city, they opened a conference with the crusading chiefs, offering to yield the whole of Palestine to the Christians upon the sole condition of the evacuation of Egypt. With a blindness and wrong-headedness almost incredible, these advantageous terms were refused, chiefly through the persuasion of Cardinal Pelagius, an ignorant and obstinate fanatic, who urged upon the Duke of Austria and the French and English leaders, that infidels never kept their word ; that their offers were deceptive, and merely intended to betray. The conferences were brought to an abrupt termination by the Crusaders, and a last attack made upon the walls of Damietta. The besieged made but slight resistance, for they had no hope, and the Christians entered the city, and found, out of seventy thousand people, but three thousand remaining : so fearful had been the ravages of the twin fiends plague and famine.

Several months were spent in Damietta. The climate either weakened the frames or obscured the understandings of the Christians ; for, after their conquest, they lost all energy, and abandoned themselves more unscrupulously than ever to riot and debauchery. John of Brienne, who by right of his wife was the nominal sovereign of Jerusalem, was so disgusted with the pusillanimity, arrogance, and dissensions of the chiefs, that he withdrew entirely from them and retired to Acre. Large bodies also returned to Europe, and Cardinal Pelagius was left at liberty to blast the whole enterprise whenever it pleased him. He managed to conciliate John of Brienne, and marched forward with these combined forces to attack Cairo. It was only when he had approached within a few hours' march of that city that he discovered the inadequacy of his army. He turned back immediately ; but the Nile had risen since his departure ; the sluices were opened, and there was no means of reaching Damietta. In this strait, he sued for the peace he had formerly spurned, and, happily for himself, found the generous brothers Camhel and Cohreddin still willing to grant it. Damietta was soon afterwards given up, and the cardinal returned to Europe. John of Brienne retired to Acre, to mourn the loss of his kingdom, embittered against the folly of his pretended friends, who had ruined where they should have aided him. And thus ended the sixth Crusade.

The seventh was more successful. Frederic II., emperor of Germany, had often vowed to lead his armies to the defence of Palestine, but was as often deterred from the journey by matters of more pressing importance. Cohreddin was a mild and enlightened monarch, and the Christians of Syria enjoyed repose and toleration under his rule : but John of Brienne was not willing to lose his kingdom without an effort ; and the popes in Europe were ever willing to embroil the nations for the sake of extending their own power. No monarch of that age was capable of rendering more effective assistance than Frederic of Germany. To inspire him with more zeal, it was proposed that he should wed the young Princess Violante, daughter of John of Brienne, and heiress of the kingdom of Jerusalem. Frederic consented with joy and eagerness. The princess was brought from Acre to Rome without delay, and her marriage celebrated on a scale of great magnificence. Her father, John of Brienne, abdicated all his rights in favour of his son-in-law, and Jerusalem had once more a king, who had not only the will, but the power, to enforce his claims. Preparations for the new Crusade were immediately commenced, and in the course of six months the emperor was at the head of a well-disciplined army of sixty thousand men. Matthew Paris informs us, that an army of the same amount was gathered in England ; and most of the writers upon the Crusades adopt his statement. When John of Brienne was in England, before his daughter's marriage with the emperor was thought of, praying for the aid of Henry III. and his nobles to recover his lost kingdom, he did not meet with much encouragement. Grafton, in his *Chronicle*, says, " he departed again without any great comfort." But when a man of more influence in European politics appeared upon the scene, the English nobles were as ready to sacrifice themselves in the cause as they had been in the time of Cœur de Lion.

The army of Frederic encamped at Brundusium ; but a pestilential disease having made its appearance among them, their departure was delayed for several months. In the mean time the Empress Violante died in childbed. John of Brienne, who had already repented of his abdication, and was besides incensed against Frederic for many acts of neglect and insult, no sooner saw the only tie which bound them severed by the death of his daughter, than he began to bestir himself, and make interest with the pope to undo what he had done, and regain the honorary crown he had renounced. Pope Gregory IX., a man of a proud, unconciliating, and revengeful character, owed the emperor a grudge for many an act of disobedience to his authority, and encouraged the overtures of John of Brienne more than he should have done. Frederic, however, despised them both, and, as soon as his army was convalescent, set sail for Acre. He had not been many days at sea when he was himself attacked with the malady, and obliged to return to Otranto, the nearest port. Gregory, who had by this time decided in the interest of John of Brienne, excommunicated the emperor for returning from so holy an expedition on any pretext whatever. Frederic at first treated the excommunication with supreme contempt; but when he got well, he gave his holiness to understand that he was not to be outraged with impunity, and sent some of his troops to ravage the papal territories. This, however, only made the matter worse, and Gregory despatched messengers to Palestine forbidding the faithful, under severe pains and penalties, to hold any intercourse with the excommunicated emperor. Thus, between them both, the scheme which they had so much at heart bade fair to be as effectually ruined as even the Saracens could have wished. Frederic still continued his zeal in the Crusade, for he was now king of Jerusalem, and fought for himself, and not for Christendom, or its representative, Pope Gregory. Hearing that John of Brienne was preparing to leave Europe, he lost no time in taking his own departure, and arrived safely at Acre. It was here that he first experienced the evil effects of excommunication. The Christians of Palestine refused to aid him in any way, and looked with distrust, if not with abhorrence, upon him. The Templars, Hospitallers, and other knights, shared at first the general feeling; but they were not men to yield a blind obedience to a distant potentate, especially when it compromised their own interests. When, therefore, Frederic prepared to march upon Jerusalem without them, they joined his banners to a man.

It is said that, previous to quitting Europe, the German emperor had commenced a negotiation with the Sultan Camhel for the restoration of the Holy Land, and that Camhel, who was jealous of the ambition of his brother Cohreddin, was willing to stipulate to that effect, on condition of being secured by Frederic in the possession of the more important territory of Egypt. But before the Crusaders reached Palestine, Camhel was relieved from all fears by the death of his brother. He nevertheless did not think it worth while to contest with the Crusaders the barren corner of the earth which had already been dyed with so much Christian and Saracen blood, and proposed a truce of three years, only stipulating, in addition, that the Moslems should be allowed to worship freely in the temple of Jerusalem. This happy termination did not satisfy the bigoted Christians of Palestine. The tolerance they sought for themselves, they were not willing to extend to others, and they complained bitterly of the privilege of free worship allowed to their opponents. Unmerited good fortune had made them insolent, and they contested the right of the emperor to become a party to any treaty, as long as he remained under the ecclesiastical ban. Frederic was disgusted with his new subjects; but, as the Templars and Hospitallers remained true to him, he marched to Jeru-

TEMPLAR AND HOSPITALLER.

salem to be crowned. All the churches were shut against him, and he could not even find a priest to officiate at his coronation. He had despised the papal authority too long to quail at it now, when it was so unjustifiably exerted, and, as there was nobody to crown him, he very wisely crowned himself. He took the royal diadem from the altar with his own hands, and boldly and proudly placed it on his brow. No shouts of an applauding populace made the welkin ring;

no hymns of praise and triumph resounded from the ministers of religion ; but a thousand swords started from their scabbards to testify that their owners would defend the new monarch to the death.

It was hardly to be expected that he would renounce for any long period the dominion of his native land for the uneasy crown and barren soil of Palestine. He had seen quite enough of his new subjects before he was six months among' them, and more important interests called him home. John of Brienne, openly leagued with Pope Gregory against him, was actually employed in ravaging his territories at the head of a papal army. This intelligence decided his return. As a preliminary step, he made those who had contemned his authority feel, to their sorrow, that he was their master. He then set sail, loaded with the curses of Palestine. And thus ended the seventh Crusade, which, in spite of every obstacle and disadvantage, had been productive of more real service to the Holy Land than any that had gone before ; a result solely attributable to the bravery of Frederic and the generosity of the Sultan Camhel.

Soon after the emperor's departure a new claimant started for the throne of Jerusalem, in the person of Alice queen of Cyprus, and half-sister of the Mary who, by her marriage, had transferred her right to John of Brienne. The grand military orders, however, clung to Frederic, and Alice was obliged to withdraw.

So peaceful a termination to the Crusade did not give unmixed pleasure in Europe. The chivalry of France and England were unable to rest, and long before the conclusion of the truce, were collecting their armies for an eighth expedition. In Palestine also the contentment was far from universal. Many petty Mahomedan states in the immediate vicinity were not parties to the truce, and harassed the frontier towns incessantly. The Templars, ever turbulent, waged bitter war with the sultan of Aleppo, and in the end were almost exterminated. So great was the slaughter among them that Europe resounded with the sad story of their fate, and many a noble knight took arms to prevent the total destruction of an order associated with so many high and inspiring remembrances. Camhel, seeing the preparations that were making, thought that his generosity had been sufficiently shewn, and the very day the truce was at an end assumed the offensive, and marching forward to Jerusalem, took possession of it, after routing the scanty forces of the Christians. Before this intelligence reached Europe a large body of Crusaders was on the march, headed by the King of Navarre, the Duke of Burgundy, the Count de Bretagne, and other leaders. On their arrival, they learned that Jerusalem had been taken, but that the sultan was dead, and his kingdom torn by rival claimants to the supreme power. The dissensions of their foes ought to have made them united; but, as in all previous Crusades, each feudal chief was master of his own host, and acted upon his own responsibility, and without reference to any general plan. The consequence was that nothing could be done. A temporary advantage was gained by one leader, who had no means of improving it; while another was defeated, without means of retrieving himself. Thus the war lingered till the battle of Gaza, when the king of Navarre was defeated with great loss, and compelled to save himself from total destruction by entering into a hard and oppressive treaty with the emir of Karac.

At this crisis aid arrived from England, commanded by Richard earl of Cornwall, the namesake of Cœur de Lion, and inheritor of his valour. His army was strong and full of hope. They had confidence in themselves and in their leader, and looked like men accustomed to victory. Their coming changed the aspect of affairs. The new sultan of Egypt was at war with the sultan of Damascus, and had not forces to oppose two enemies so powerful. He therefore sent messengers to meet the English earl, offering an exchange of prisoners and the complete cession of the Holy Land. Richard, who had not come to fight for the mere sake of fighting, agreed at once to terms so advantageous, and became the deliverer of Palestine without striking a blow. The sultan of Egypt then turned his whole force against his Moslem enemies, and the Earl of Cornwall returned to Europe. Thus ended the eighth Crusade, the most beneficial of all. Christendom had no further pretence for sending her fierce levies to the East. To all appearance the holy wars were at an end: the Christians had entire possession of Jerusalem, Tripoli, Antioch, Edessa, Acre, Jaffa, and, in fact, of nearly all Judea; and, could they have been at peace among themselves, they might have overcome, without great difficulty, the jealousy and hostility of their neighbours. A circumstance, as unforeseen as it was disastrous, blasted this fair prospect, and reillumed, for the last time, the fervour and fury of the Crusades.

Gengis Khan and his successors had swept over Asia like a tropical storm, overturning in their progress the landmarks of ages. Kingdom after kingdom was cast down as they issued, innumerable, from the far recesses of the North and East, and, among others, the empire of Korasmin was overrun by these all-conquering hordes. The Korasmins, a fierce, uncivilised race, thus driven from their homes, spread themselves, in their turn, over the south of Asia with fire and sword, in search of a resting-place. In their impetuous course they directed themselves towards Egypt, whose sultan, unable to withstand the swarm that had cast their longing eyes on the fertile valleys of the Nile, endeavoured to turn them from their course. For this purpose, he sent emissaries to Barbaquan, their leader, inviting them to settle in Palestine; and the offer being accepted by the wild horde, they entered the country before the Christians received the slightest intimation of their coming. It was as sudden as it was overwhelming. Onwards, like the simoom, they came, burning and slaying, and were at the walls of Jerusalem before the inhabitants had time to look round them. They spared neither life nor property; they slew women and children, and priests at the altar, and profaned even the graves of those who had slept for ages. They tore down every vestige of the Christian faith, and committed horrors unparalleled in the history of warfare. About seven thousand of the inhabitants of Jerusalem sought safety in retreat; but before they were out of sight, the banner of the cross was hoisted upon the walls by the savage foe to decoy them back. The artifice

JAFFA.

was but too successful. The poor fugitives imagined that help had arrived from another direction, and turned back to regain their homes. Nearly the whole of them were massacred, and the streets of Jerusalem ran with blood.

The Templars, Hospitallers, and Teutonic knights forgot their long and bitter animosities, and joined hand in hand to rout out this desolating foe. They entrenched themselves in Jaffa, with all the chivalry of Palestine that yet remained, and endeavoured to engage the sultans of Emissa and Damascus to assist them against the common enemy. The aid obtained from the Moslems amounted at first to only four thousand men, but with these reinforcements Walter of Brienne, the lord of Jaffa, resolved to give battle to the Korasmins. The conflict was as deadly as despair on the one side, and unmitigated ferocity on the other, could make it. It lasted with varying fortune for two days, when the sultan of Emissa fled to his fortifications, and Walter of Brienne fell into the enemy's hands. The brave knight was suspended by the arms to a cross in sight of the walls of Jaffa, and the Korasminian leader declared that he should remain in that position until the city surrendered. Walter raised his feeble voice, not to advise surrender, but to command his soldiers to hold out to the last. But his gallantry was unavailing. So great had been the slaughter, that out of the grand array of knights, there now remained but sixteen Hospitallers, thirty-three Templars, and three Teutonic cavaliers. These, with the sad remnant of the army, fled to Acre, and the Korasmins were masters of Palestine.

The sultans of Syria preferred the Christians to this fierce horde for their neighbours. Even the sultan of Egypt began to regret the aid he had given to such barbarous foes, and united with those of Emissa and Damascus to root them from the land. The Korasmins amounted to but twenty thousand men, and were unable to resist the determined hostility which encompassed them on every side. The sultans defeated them in several engagements, and the peasantry rose up in masses to take vengeance upon them. Gradually their numbers were diminished. No mercy was shewn them in defeat. Barbaquan their leader was slain; and after five years of desperate struggles, they were finally extirpated, and Palestine became once more the territory of the Mussulmans.

A short time previous to this devastating eruption, Louis IX. fell sick in Paris, and dreamed in the delirium of his fever that he saw the Christian and Moslem host fighting before Jerusalem, and the Christians defeated with great slaughter. The dream made a great impression on his superstitious mind, and he made a solemn vow, that if ever he recovered his health, he would take a pilgrimage to the Holy Land. When the news of the misfortunes of Palestine, and the awful massacres at Jerusalem and Jaffa, arrived in Europe, St. Louis remembered him of his dream. More persuaded than ever that it was an intimation direct from heaven, he prepared to take the cross at the head of his armies, and march to the deliverance of the Holy Sepulchre. From that moment he doffed the royal mantle of purple and ermine, and dressed in the sober serge becoming a pilgrim. All his thoughts were directed to the fulfilment of his design, and although his kingdom could but ill spare him, he made every preparation to leave it. Pope Innocent IV. applauded his zeal and afforded him every assistance. He wrote to Henry III. of England to forward the cause in his dominions, and called upon the clergy and laity all over Europe to contribute towards it. William Longsword,

WILLIAM LONGSWORD.

the celebrated Earl of Salisbury, took the cross at the head of a great number of valiant knights and soldiers. But the fanaticism of the people was not to be awakened either in France or England. Great armies were raised, but the masses no longer sympathised. Taxation had been the great cooler of zeal. It was no longer a disgrace even

to a knight if he refused to take the cross.   Rutebeuf, a French
minstrel, who flourished about this time (1250), composed a dialogue between a Crusader and a non-Crusader, which the reader will
find translated in Way's *Fabliaux*.   The Crusader uses every argument to persuade the non-Crusader to take up arms, and forsake
every thing in the holy cause; but it is evident from the greater
force of the arguments used by the non-Crusader, that he was the
favourite of the minstrel.   To a most urgent solicitation of his friend
the Crusader, he replies:

> "I read thee right, thou holdest good
>   To this same land I straight should hie,
> And win it back with mickle blood,
>   Nor gaine one foot of soil thereby;
> While here dejected and forlorn
> My wife and babes are left to mourn;
> My goodly mansion rudely marred,
> All trusted to my dogs to guard.
> But I, fair comrade, well I wot
>   An ancient saw of pregnant wit
> Doth bid us keep what we have got;
>   And troth I mean to follow it."

This being the general feeling, it is not to be wondered at that Louis IX.
was occupied fully three years in organising his forces, and in making
the necessary preparations for his departure.   When all was ready he
set sail for Cyprus, accompanied by his queen, his two brothers, the
Counts d'Anjou and d'Artois, and a long train of the noblest chivalry
of France.   His third brother, the Count de Poitiers, remained behind to collect another corps of Crusaders, and followed him in a few
months afterwards.   The army united at Cyprus, and amounted to
fifty thousand men, exclusive of the English Crusaders under William
Longsword.   Again, a pestilential disease made its appearance, to
which many hundreds fell victims.   It was in consequence found
necessary to remain in Cyprus until the spring.   Louis then embarked
for Egypt with his whole host; but a violent tempest separated his
fleet, and he arrived before Damietta with only a few thousand men.
They were, however, impetuous and full of hope; and although the
Sultan Melick Shah was drawn up on the shore with a force infi-
nitely superior, it was resolved to attempt a landing without waiting
the arrival of the rest of the army.   Louis himself, in wild impatience,
sprang from his boat, and waded on shore; while his army, inspired
by his enthusiastic bravery, followed, shouting the old war-cry of
the first Crusaders, *Dieu le veut! Dieu le veut!*   A panic seized the
Turks.   A body of their cavalry attempted to bear down upon the
Crusaders, but the knights fixed their large shields deep in the sands

of the shore, and rested their lances upon them, so that they projected above, and formed a barrier so imposing, that the Turks, afraid to breast it, turned round and fairly took to flight. At the moment of this panic, a false report was spread in the Saracen host, that the sultan had been slain. The confusion immediately became general—the *deroute* was complete: Damietta itself was abandoned, and the same night the victorious Crusaders fixed their head-quarters in that city. The soldiers who had been separated from their chief by the tempest arrived shortly afterwards; and Louis was in a position to justify the hope, not only of the conquest of Palestine, but of Egypt itself.

But too much confidence proved the bane of his army. They thought, as they had accomplished so much, that nothing more remained to be done, and gave themselves up to ease and luxury. When, by the command of Louis, they marched towards Cairo, they were no longer the same men; success, instead of inspiring, had unnerved them; debauchery had brought on disease, and disease was aggravated by the heat of a climate to which none of them were accustomed. Their progress towards Massoura, on the road to Cairo, was checked by the Thanisian canal, on the banks of which the Saracens were drawn up to dispute the passage. Louis gave orders that a bridge should be thrown across: and the operations commenced under cover of two cat-castles, or high movable towers. The Saracens soon destroyed them by throwing quantities of Greek fire, the artillery of that day, upon them, and Louis was forced to think of some other means of effecting his design. A peasant agreed, for a considerable bribe, to point out a ford where the army might wade across, and the Count d'Artois was despatched with fourteen hundred men to attempt it, while Louis remained to face the Saracens with the main body of the army. The Count d'Artois got safely over, and defeated the detachment that had been sent to oppose his landing. Flushed with the victory, the brave count forgot the inferiority of his numbers, and pursued the panic-stricken enemy into Massoura. He was now completely cut off from the aid of his brother Crusaders, which the Moslems perceiving, took courage and returned upon him, with a force swollen by the garrison of Massoura, and by reinforcements from the surrounding districts. The battle now became hand to hand. The Christians fought with the energy of desperate men, but the continually increasing numbers of the foe surrounded them completely, and cut off all hope, either of victory or escape. The Count d'Artois was among the foremost of the slain; and when Louis arrived to the rescue, the brave advanced-guard was nearly cut to pieces. Of the fourteen hundred, but three hundred remained. The fury of the battle was now increased threefold. The French king and his troops performed prodigies of valour, and the Saracens, under the command of the Emir Ceccidun, fought as if they were determined to exterminate, in one last decisive effort, the new European swarm that had settled upon their coast. At the fall of the evening dews the Christians were masters of the field of Massoura, and flattered themselves that they were the victors. Self-love would not suffer them to confess that the Saracens had withdrawn, and not retreated ; but their leaders were too wofully convinced that that fatal field had completed the disorganisation of the Christian army, and that all hopes of future conquest were at an end.

Impressed with this truth, the Crusaders sued for peace. The sultan insisted upon the immediate evacuation of Damietta, and that Louis himself should be delivered as hostage for the fulfilment of the condition. His army at once refused, and the negotiations were broken off. It was now resolved to attempt a retreat ; but the agile Saracens, now in the front and now in the rear, rendered it a matter of extreme difficulty, and cut off the stragglers in great numbers. Hundreds of them were drowned in the Nile ; and sickness and famine worked sad ravages upon those who escaped all other casualties. Louis himself was so weakened by disease, fatigue, and discouragement, that he was hardly able to sit upon his horse. In the confusion of the flight he was separated from his attendants, and left a total stranger upon the sands of Egypt, sick, weary, and almost friendless. One knight, Geffry de Sergines, alone attended him, and led him to a miserable hut in a small village, where for several days he lay in the hourly expectation of death. He was at last discovered and taken prisoner by the Saracens, who treated him with all the honour due to his rank and all the pity due to his misfortunes. Under their care his health rapidly improved, and the next consideration was that of his ransom.

The Saracens demanded, besides money, the cession of Acre, Tripoli, and other cities of Palestine. Louis unhesitatingly refused, and conducted himself with so much pride and courage that the sultan declared he was the proudest infidel he had ever beheld. After a good deal of haggling, the sultan agreed to waive these conditions, and a treaty was finally concluded. The city of Damietta was restored, a truce, of ten years agreed upon, and ten thousand golden bezants paid for the release of Louis and the liberation of all the captives. Louis then withdrew to Jaffa, and spent two years in putting that city, and Cesarea, with the other possessions of the Christians in Palestine, into a proper state of defence. He then returned to his own country, with great reputation as a saint, but very little as a soldier,

Matthew Paris informs us that, in the year 1250, while Louis was in Egypt, "thousands of the English were resolved to go to the holy, war, had not the king strictly guarded his ports and kept his people from running out of doors." When the news arrived of the reverses and captivity of the French king, their ardour cooled; and the Crusade was sung of only, but not spoken of.

In France, a very different feeling was the result. The news of the king's capture spread consternation through the country. A fanatic monk of Citeaux suddenly appeared in the villages, preaching to the people, and announcing that the Holy Virgin, accompanied by a whole army of saints and martyrs, had appeared to him, and commanded him to stir up the shepherds and farm-labourers, to the defence of the cross. To them only was his discourse addressed; and his eloquence was such, that thousands flocked around him, ready to follow wherever he should lead. The pastures and the corn-fields were deserted, and the shepherds, or *pastoureaux*, as they were termed, became at last so numerous as to amount to upwards of fifty thousand,—Millot says one hundred thousand men.* The Queen Blanche, who governed as regent during the absence of the king, encouraged at first the armies of the *pastoureaux;* but they soon gave way to such vile excesses that the peaceably disposed were driven to resistance. Robbery, murder, and violation marked their path; and all good men, assisted by the government, united in putting them down. They were finally dispersed, but not before three thousand of them had been massacred. Many authors say that the slaughter was still greater.

The ten years' truce concluded in 1264, and St. Louis was urged by two powerful motives to undertake a second expedition for the relief of Palestine. These were, fanaticism on the one hand, and a desire of retrieving his military fame on the other, which had suffered more than his parasites liked to remind him of. The pope, of course, encouraged his design, and once more the chivalry of Europe began to bestir themselves. In 1268, Edward, the heir of the English monarchy, announced his determination to join the Crusade; and the pope (Clement IV.) wrote to the prelates and clergy to aid the cause by their persuasions and their revenues. In England, they agreed to contribute a tenth of their possessions; and by a parliamentary order, a twentieth was taken from the corn and movables of all the laity at Michaelmas.

In spite of the remonstrances of the few clear-headed statesmen who surrounded him, urging the ruin that might in consequence fall upon his then prosperous kingdom, Louis made every preparation for

* *Elémens de l'Histoire de France.*

his departure. The warlike nobility were nothing loath; and in the spring of 1270, the king set sail with an army of sixty thousand men. He was driven by stress of weather into Sardinia, and while there, a change in his plans took place. Instead of proceeding to Acre, as he originally intended, he shaped his course for Tunis, on the African coast. The king of Tunis had some time previously expressed himself favourably disposed towards the Christians and their religion, and Louis, it appears, had hopes of converting him, and securing his aid against the sultan of Egypt. "What honour would be mine," he used to say, "if I could become godfather to this Mussulman king!" Filled with this idea he landed in Africa, near the site of the city of Carthage, but found that he had reckoned without his host. The king of Tunis had no thoughts of renouncing his religion, nor intention of aiding the Crusaders in any way. On the contrary, he opposed their landing with all the forces that could be collected on so sudden an emergency. The French, however, made good their first position, and defeated the Moslems with considerable loss. They also gained some advantage over the reinforcements that were sent to oppose them; but an infectious flux appeared in the army, and put a stop to all future victories. The soldiers died at the rate of a hundred in a day. The enemy, at the same time, made as great havoc as the plague. St. Louis himself was one of the first attacked by the disease. His constitution had been weakened by fatigues, and even before he left France he was unable to bear the full weight of his armour. It was soon evident to his sorrowing soldiers that their beloved monarch could not long survive. He lingered for some days, and died in Carthage in the fifty-sixth year of his age, deeply regretted by his army and his subjects, and leaving behind him one of the most singular reputations in history. He is the model king of ecclesiastical writers, in whose eyes his very defects became virtues, because they were manifested in furtherance of their cause. More unprejudiced historians, while they condemn his fanaticism, admit that he was endowed with many high and rare qualities; that he was in no one point behind his age, and in many in advance of it.

His brother, Charles of Anjou, in consequence of a revolution in Sicily, had become king of that country. Before he heard of the death of Louis, he had sailed from Messina with large reinforcements. On his landing near Carthage, he advanced at the head of his army, amid the martial music of drums and trumpets. He was soon informed how inopportune was his rejoicing, and shed tears before his whole army, such as no warrior would have been ashamed to shed. A peace was speedily agreed upon with the king of Tunis, and the armies of France and Sicily returned to their homes.

So little favour had the Crusade found in England, that even the exertions of the heir to the throne had only collected a small force of fifteen hundred men. With these few Prince Edward sailed from Dover to Bourdeaux, in the expectation that he would find the French king in that city. St. Louis, however, had left a few weeks previously; upon which Edward followed him to Sardinia, and afterwards to Tunis. Before his arrival in Africa, St. Louis was no more, and peace had been concluded between France and Tunis. He determined, however, not to relinquish the Crusade. Returning to Sicily, he passed the winter in that country, and endeavoured to augment his little army. In the spring he set sail for Palestine, and arrived in safety at Acre. The Christians were torn, as usual, by mutual jealousies and animosities. The two great military orders were as virulent and as intractable as ever; opposed to each other, and to all the world. The arrival of Edward had the effect of causing them to lay aside their unworthy contention, and of uniting heart

SEAL OF EDWARD I.

to heart in one last effort for the deliverance of their adopted country. A force of six thousand effective warriors was soon formed to join those of the English prince, and preparations were made for the renewal of hostilities. The Sultan Bibars or Bendocdar,* a fierce Mamluke, who had been placed on the throne by a bloody revolution, was

* Mills, in his history, gives the name of this chief as " Al Malek al Dhaker Rok neddin Abulfeth Bibars al Ali al Bundokdari al Salehi."

at war with all his neighbours, and unable, for that reason, to con-
centrate his whole strength against them.   Edward took advantage
of this, and marching boldly forward to Nazareth, defeated the Turks
and gained possession of that city.   This was the whole amount of
his successes.   The hot weather engendered disease among his troops,
and he himself, the life and soul of the expedition, fell sick among
the first.   He had been ill for some time, and was slowly recovering,
when a messenger desired to speak with him on important matters,
and to deliver some despatches into his own hand.   While the prince
was occupied in examining them, the traitorous messenger drew a
dagger from his belt and stabbed him in the breast.   The wound fortunately was not deep, and Edward had regained a portion of his
strength.   He struggled with the assassin, and put him to death with
his own dagger, at the same time calling loudly for assistance.*   His
attendants came at his call, and found him bleeding profusely, and
ascertained on inspection that the dagger was poisoned.   Means were
instantly taken to purify the wound, and an antidote was sent by the
Grand Master of the Templars which removed all danger from the
effects of the poison.   Camden, in his history, has adopted the more
popular, and certainly more beautiful version of this story, which
says that the Princess Eleonora, in her love for her gallant husband,
sucked the poison from his wound at the risk of her own life : to use
the words of old Fuller, " it is a pity so pretty a story should not be
true ; and that so sovereign a remedy as a woman's tongue, anointed
with the virtue of loving affection," should not have performed the
good deed.

   Edward suspected, and doubtless not without reason, that the
assassin was employed by the sultan of Egypt.   But it amounted to
suspicion only ; and by the sudden death of the assassin the principal
clue to the discovery of the truth was lost for ever.   Edward, on his
recovery, prepared to resume the offensive ; but the sultan, embar-
rassed by the defence of interests which, for the time being, he considered of more importance, made offers of peace to the Crusaders.
This proof of weakness on the part of the enemy was calculated to
render a man of Edward's temperament more anxious to prosecute
the war ; but he had also other interests to defend.   News arrived in
Palestine of the death of his father, King Henry III. ; and his presence being necessary in England, he agreed to the terms of the sultan.   These were, that the Christians should be allowed to retain
their possessions in the Holy Land, and that a truce of ten years

---

   * The reader will recognise the incident which Sir Walter Scott has introduced into
his beautiful romance, *The Talisman*, and which, with the license claimed by poets and
romancers, he represents as having befallen King Richard I.

should be proclaimed. Edward then set sail for England; and thus ended the last Crusade.

The after-fate of the Holy Land may be told in a few words. The Christians, unmindful of their past sufferings and of the jealous neighbours they had to deal with, first broke the truce by plundering some

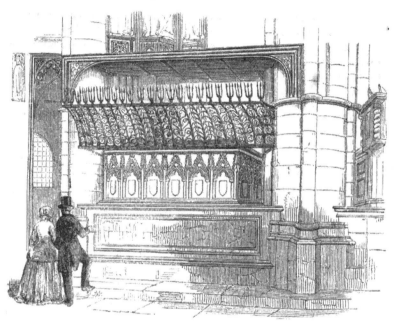

TOMB OF QUEEN ELEANOR.

Egyptian traders near Margat. The sultan immediately revenged the outrage by taking possession of Margat, and war once more raged between the nations. Margat made a gallant defence, but no reinforcements arrived from Europe to prevent its fall. Tripoli was the next, and other cities in succession, until at last Acre was the only city of Palestine that remained in possession of the Christians.

The Grand Master of the Templars collected together his small and devoted band, and with the trifling aid afforded by the king of Cyprus, prepared to defend to the death the last possession of his order. Europe was deaf to his cry for aid, the numbers of the foe were overwhelming, and devoted bravery was of no avail. In that

disastrous siege the Christians were all but exterminated.   The king
of Cyprus fled when he saw that resistance was vain, and the Grand
Master fell at the head of his knights, pierced with a hundred wounds.
Seven Templars, and as many Hospitallers, alone escaped from the
dreadful carnage.   The victorious Moslems then set fire to the city,
and the rule of the Christians in Palestine was brought to a close for
ever.

This intelligence spread alarm and sorrow among the clergy of
Europe, who endeavoured to rouse once more the energy and enthusiasm of the nations in the cause of the Holy Land.   But the popular
mania had run its career; the spark of zeal had burned its appointed
time, and was never again to be re-illumined.   Here and there a solitary knight announced his determination to take up arms, and now
and then a king gave cold encouragement to the scheme; but it
dropped almost as soon as spoken of, to be renewed again, still more
feebly, at some longer interval.

Now what was the grand result of all these struggles?   Europe
expended millions of her treasures, and the blood of two millions of
her children; and a handful of quarrelsome knights retained possession of Palestine for about one hundred years!   Even had Christendom retained it to this day, the advantage, if confined to that, would
have been too dearly purchased.   But notwithstanding the fanaticism
that originated, and the folly that conducted them, the Crusades were
not productive of unmitigated evil.   The feudal chiefs became better
members of society by coming in contact, in Asia, with a civilisation
superior to their own; the people secured some small instalments of
their rights; kings, no longer at war with their nobility, had time to
pass some good laws; the human mind learned some little wisdom
from hard experience, and, casting off the slough of superstition in
which the Roman clergy had so long enveloped it, became prepared
to receive the seeds of the approaching Reformation.   Thus did the
all-wise Disposer of events bring good out of evil, and advance the
civilisation and ultimate happiness of the nations of the West by means
of the very fanaticism that had led them against the East.   But the
whole subject is one of absorbing interest, and if carried fully out in
all its bearings, would consume more space than the plan of this work
will allow.   The philosophic student will draw his own conclusions;
and he can have no better field for the exercise of his powers than
this European madness—its advantages and disadvantages, its causes
and results.

ARRAS.

THE WITCH MANIA.

What wrath of gods, or wicked influence
Of tears, conspiring wretched men t' afflict,
Hath pour'd on earth this noyous pestilence
That mortal minds doth inwardly infect
With love of blindness and of ignorance?

Spencer's Tears of the Muses.

Countrymen. Hang her! beat her! kill her!

Justice. How now? Forbear this violence!

Mother Sawyer. A crew of villains—a knot of bloody hangmen! set to torment me! I know not why.

Justice. Alas, neighbour Banks! are you a ringleader in mischief? Fie! to abuse an aged woman!

Banks. Woman! a she hell-cat, a witch! To prove her one, we no sooner set fire on the thatch of her house, but in she came running, as if the devil had sent her in a barrel of gunpowder.

Ford's Witch of Edmonton.

THE belief that disembodied spirits may be permitted to revisit this world has its foundation upon that sublime hope of immortality which is at once the chief solace and greatest triumph of our reason.   Even if revelation did not teach us, we feel that we have that within us which shall never die; and all our experience of this life but makes us cling the more fondly to that one repaying hope. But in the early days of "little knowledge" this grand belief became the source of a whole train of superstitions, which, in their turn, became the fount .from whence flowed a deluge of blood and horror. Europe, for a period of two centuries and a half, brooded upon the idea, not only that parted spirits walked the earth to meddle in the affairs of men, but that men had power to summon evil spirits to their aid to work woe upon their fellows. An epidemic terror seized upon the nations; no man thought himself secure, either in his person or possessions, from the machinations of the devil and his agents. Every calamity that befell him he attributed to a witch. If a storm arose and blew down his barn, it was witchcraft; if his cattle died of a murrain—if disease fastened upon his limbs, or death entered suddenly and snatched a beloved face from his hearth—they were not visitations of Providence, but the works of some neighbouring hag, whose wretchedness or insanity caused the ignorant to raise their finger and point at her as a witch. The word was upon every body's tongue. France, Italy, Germany, England, Scotland, and the far north successively ran mad upon this subject, and for a long series of years furnished their tribunals with so many trials for witchcraft, that other crimes were seldom or never spoken of. Thousands upon thousands of unhappy persons fell victims to this cruel and absurd delusion. In many cities of Germany, as will be shewn more fully in its due place hereafter, the average number of executions for this pretended crime was six hundred annually, or two every day, if we leave out the Sundays, when it is to be supposed that even this madness refrained from its work.

A misunderstanding of the famous text of the Mosaic law, "Thou shalt not suffer a witch to live," no doubt led many conscientious men astray, whose superstition, warm enough before, wanted but a little corroboration to blaze out with desolating fury. In all ages of the world men have tried to hold converse with superior beings, and to pierce by their means the secrets of futurity. In the time of Moses, it is evident that there were impostors who trafficked upon the credulity of mankind, and insulted the supreme majesty of the true God by pretending to the power of divination. Hence the law which Moses, by divine command, promulgated against these criminals; but it did not follow, as the superstitious monomaniacs of the middle ages imagined, that the Bible established the existence of the power of divination by its edicts against those who pretended to it. From the best authorities, it appears that the Hebrew word, which has been rendered *venefica* and *witch*, means a poisoner and divineress, a dabbler in spells, or fortune-teller. The modern witch was a very different character, and joined to her pretended power of foretelling future events that of working evil upon the life, limbs, and possessions of mankind. This power was only to be acquired by an express compact, signed in blood, with the devil himself, by which the wizard or witch renounced baptism, and sold his or her immortal soul to the evil one, without any saving clause of redemption.

There are so many wondrous appearances in nature for which science and philosophy cannot even now account, that it is not surprising that, when natural laws were still less understood, men should have attributed to supernatural agency every appearance which they could not otherwise explain. The merest tyro now understands various phenomena which the wisest of old could not fathom. The schoolboy knows why, upon high mountains, there should on certain occasions appear three or four suns in the firmament at once, and why the figure of a traveller upon one eminence should be reproduced, inverted and of a gigantic stature, upon another. We all know the strange pranks which imagination can play in certain diseases; that the hypochondriac can see visions and spectres; and that there have been cases in which men were perfectly persuaded that they were teapots. Science has lifted up the veil, and rolled away all the fantastic horrors in which our forefathers shrouded these and similar cases. The man who now imagines himself a wolf is sent to the hospital instead of to the stake, as in the days of the witch mania; and earth, air, and sea are unpeopled of the grotesque spirits that were once believed to haunt them.

Before entering further into the history of Witchcraft, it may be as well if we consider the absurd impersonation of the evil principle formed by the monks in their legends. We must make acquaintance with the *primum mobile*, and understand what sort of a personage it was who gave the witches, in exchange for their souls, the power to torment their fellow-creatures. The popular notion of the devil was, that he was a large, ill-formed, hairy sprite, with horns, a long tail, cloven feet, and dragon's wings. In this shape he was constantly brought on the stage by the monks in their early "miracles" and "mysteries." In these representations he was an important personage, and answered the purpose of the clown in the modern pantomime. The great fun for the people was to see him well belaboured by the saints with clubs or cudgels, and to hear him howl with pain as he limped off, maimed by the blow of some vigorous anchorite. St. Dunstan generally served him the glorious trick for which he is renowned, catching hold of his nose with a pair of red-hot pincers, till

"Rocks and distant dells resounded with his cries."

Some of the saints spat in his face, to his very great annoyance; and others chopped pieces off of his tail, which, however, always grew on again. This was paying him in his own coin, and amused the populace mightily, for they all remembered the scurvy tricks he had played them and their forefathers. It was believed that he endeavoured to trip people up by laying his long invisible tail in their way, and giving it a sudden whisk when their legs were over it :— that he used to get drunk, and swear like a trooper, and be so mischievous in his cups as to raise tempests and earthquakes, to destroy the fruits of the earth, and the barns and homesteads of true believers ;—that he used to run invisible spits into people by way of amusing himself in the long winter evenings, and to proceed to taverns and regale himself with the best, offering in payment pieces of gold which, on the dawn of the following morning, invariably turned into slates. Sometimes, disguised as a large drake, he used to lurk among the bulrushes, and frighten the weary traveller out of his wits by his awful quack. The reader will remember the lines of Burns in his address to the " De'il," which so well express the popular notion on this point :

> " Ae dreary, windy, winter night,
> The stars shot down wi' sklentin light,
> Wi' you mysel' I got a fright
>   Ayont the lough;
> Ye, like a rash-bush, stood in sight
>   Wi' waving sough.
>
> The cudgel in my nieve did shake,
> Each bristled hair stood like a stake,
> When wi' an eldritch stour, 'quaick! quaick!'
>   Among the springs
> Awa' ye squattered, like a drake,
>   On whistling wings."

In all the stories circulated and believed about him, he was represented as an ugly, petty, mischievous spirit, who rejoiced in playing off all manner of fantastic tricks upon poor humanity. Milton seems to have been the first who succeeded in giving any but a ludicrous description of him. The sublime pride, which is the quintessence of evil, was unconceived before his time. All other limners made him merely grotesque, but Milton made him awful. In this the monks shewed themselves but miserable romancers; for their object undoubtedly was to represent the fiend as terrible as possible. But there was nothing grand about their Satan; on the contrary, he was a low, mean devil, whom it was easy to circumvent, and fine fun to play tricks with. But, as is well and eloquently remarked by a modern writer,*

* See article on "Demonology" in the sixth volume of the *Foreign Quarterly Review*.

the subject has also its serious side. An Indian deity, with its wild distorted shape and grotesque attitude, appears merely ridiculous when separated from its accessories and viewed by daylight in a museum; but restore it to the darkness of its own hideous temple, bring back to our recollection the victims that have bled upon its altar or been crushed beneath its car, and our sense of the ridiculous subsides into aversion and horror. So, while the superstitious dreams of former times are regarded as mere speculative insanities, we may be for a moment amused with the wild incoherencies of the patients; but when we reflect that out of these hideous misconceptions of the principle of evil arose the belief in witchcraft—that this was no dead faith, but one operating on the whole being of society, urging on the wisest and the mildest to deeds of murder, or cruelties scarcely less than murder—that the learned and the beautiful, young and old, male and female, were devoted by its influence to the stake and the scaffold—every feeling disappears, except that of astonishment that such things could be, and humiliation at the thought that the delusion was as lasting as it was universal.

Besides this chief personage, there was an infinite number of inferior demons, who played conspicuous parts in the creed of witchcraft. The pages of Bekker, Leloyer, Bodin, Delrio, and De Lancre, abound with descriptions of the qualities of these imps, and the functions which were assigned them. From these authors,—three of whom were commissioners for the trial of witches, and who wrote from the confessions made by the supposed criminals and the evidence delivered against them,—and from the more recent work of M. Jules Garinet, the following summary of the creed has been, with great pains, extracted. The student who is desirous of knowing more is referred to the works in question; he will find enough in every leaf to make his blood curdle with shame and horror: but the purity of these pages shall not be soiled by any thing so ineffably humiliating and disgusting as a complete exposition of them; what is here culled will be a sufficient sample of the popular belief, and the reader would but lose time who should seek in the writings of the demonologists for more ample details. He will gain nothing by lifting the veil which covers their unutterable obscenities, unless, like Sterne, he wishes to gather fresh evidence of "what a beast man is." In that case, he will find plenty there to convince him that the beast would be libelled by the comparison.

It was thought that the earth swarmed with millions of demons of both sexes, many of whom, like the human race, traced their lineage up to Adam, who after the fall was led astray by devils, assuming the forms of beautiful women to deceive him. These de-

mons "increased and multiplied" among themselves with the most
extraordinary rapidity. Their bodies were of the thin air, and they
could pass through the hardest substances with the greatest ease.
They had no fixed residence or abiding-place, but were tossed to
and fro in the immensity of space. When thrown together in great
multitudes, they excited whirlwinds in the air and tempests in the
waters, and took delight in destroying the beauty of nature and the
monuments of the industry of man. Although they increased among
themselves like ordinary creatures, their numbers were daily aug-
mented by the souls of wicked men, of children still-born, of women who died in childbed, and of persons killed in duels. The
whole air was supposed to be full of them, and many unfortunate
men and women drew them by thousands into their mouths and nostrils at every inspiration; and the demons, lodging in their bowels
or other parts of their bodies, tormented them with pains and diseases of every kind, and sent them frightful dreams. St. Gregory of
Nice relates a story of a nun who forgot to say her *benedicite* and
make the sign of the cross before she sat down to supper, and
who in consequence swallowed a demon concealed among the leaves
of a lettuce. Most persons said the number of these demons was so
great that they could not be counted, but Wierus asserted that they
amounted to no more than seven millions four hundred and five
thousand nine hundred and twenty-six; and that they were divided
into seventy-two companies or battalions, to each of which there was
a prince or captain. They could assume any shape they pleased.
When they were male, they were called incubi; and when female,
succubi. They sometimes made themselves hideous; and at other
times they assumed shapes of such transcendent loveliness, that
mortal eyes never saw beauty to compete with theirs.

Although the devil and his legions could appear to mankind at any
time, it was generally understood that he preferred the night between
Friday and Saturday. If Satan himself appeared in human shape, he
was never perfectly and in all respects like a man. He was either
too black or too white, too large or too small, or some of his limbs
were out of proportion to the rest of his body. Most commonly his
feet were deformed, and he was obliged to curl up and conceal his
tail in some part of his habiliments; for, take what shape he would,
he could not get rid of that encumbrance. He sometimes changed
himself into a tree or a river; and upon one occasion he transformed
himself into a barrister, as we learn from Wierus, book iv. chapter 9.
In the reign of Philippe le Bel, he appeared to a monk in the shape
of a dark man riding a tall black horse, then as a friar, afterwards
as an ass, and finally as a coach-wheel. Instances are not rare in

which both he and his inferior demons have taken the form of handsome young men, and, successfully concealing their tails, have married beautiful young women, who have had children by them. Such
children were easily recognisable by their continual shrieking, by
their requiring five nurses to suckle them, and by their never growing fat.

All these demons were at the command of any individual who
would give up his immortal soul to the prince of evil for the privilege
of enjoying their services for a stated period. The wizard or witch
could send them to execute the most difficult missions : whatever the
witch commanded was performed, except it was a good action, in
which case the order was disobeyed, and evil worked upon herself
instead.

At intervals, according to the pleasure of Satan, there was a general meeting of the demons and all the witches. This meeting was
called the Sabbath, from its taking place on the Saturday, or immediately after midnight on Fridays. These sabbaths were sometimes
held for one district, sometimes for another, and once at least every
year it was held on the Brocken, or among other high mountains, as
a general sabbath of the fiends for the whole of Christendom.

The devil generally chose a place where four roads met as the
scene of this assembly, or if that was not convenient, the neighbourhood of a lake. Upon this spot nothing would ever afterwards grow,
as the hot feet of the demons and witches burnt the principle of fecun-
dity from the earth, and rendered it barren for ever. When orders
had been once issued for the meeting of the sabbath, all the wizards
and witches who failed to attend it were lashed by demons with a rod
made of serpents or scorpions, as a punishment for their inattention
or want of punctuality.

In France and England the witches were supposed to ride uni-
formly upon broomsticks; but in Italy and Spain, the devil himself, in
the shape of a goat, used to transport them on his back, which length-
ened or shortened according to the number of witches he was desirous
of accommodating. No witch, when proceeding to the sabbath, could
get out by a door or window, were she to try ever so much. Their
general mode of ingress was by the keyhole, and of egress by the
chimney, up which they flew, broom and all, with the greatest ease.
To prevent the absence of the witches from being noticed by their
neighbours, some inferior demon was commanded to assume their
shapes and lie in their beds, feigning illness, until the sabbath was
over.

When all the wizards and witches had arrived at the place of
rendezvous, the infernal ceremonies of the sabbath began. Satan,

having assumed his favourite shape of a large he-goat, with a face in front and another in his haunches, took his seat upon a throne ; and all present, in succession, paid their respects to him, and kissed him in his face behind.   This done, he appointed a master of the ceremonies, in company with whom he made a personal examination of all the wizards and witches, to see whether they had the secret mark about them by which they were stamped as the devil's own.   This mark was always insensible to pain.   Those who had not yet been marked, received the mark from the master of the ceremonies, the devil at the same time bestowing nicknames upon them.   This done, they all began to sing and dance in the most furious manner, until some one arrived who was anxious to be admitted into their society.   They were then silent for a while, until the new-comer had denied his salvation, kissed the devil, spat upon the Bible, and sworn obedience to him in all things.   They then began dancing again with all their might, and singing these words,

" Alegremos, Alegremos !
Que gente va tenemos !"

In the course of an hour or two they generally became wearied of this violent exercise, and then they all sat down and recounted the evil deeds they had done since their last meeting.   Those who had not been malicious and mischievous enough towards their fellow-creatures, received personal chastisement from Satan himself, who flogged them with thorns or scorpions till they were covered with blood, and unable to sit or stand.

When this ceremony was concluded, they were all amused by a dance of toads.   Thousands of these creatures sprang out of the earth, and standing on their hind legs, danced, while the devil played the bagpipes or the trumpet.   These toads were all endowed with the faculty of speech, and entreated the witches to reward them with the flesh of unbaptised babes for their exertions to give them pleasure. The witches promised compliance.   The devil bade them remember to keep their word ; and then stamping his foot, caused all the toads to sink into the earth in an instant.   The place being thus cleared, preparation was made for the banquet, where all manner of disgusting things were served up and greedily devoured by the demons and witches ; although the latter were sometimes regaled with choice meats and expensive wines from golden plates and crystal goblets ; but they were never thus favoured unless they had done an extraordinary number of evil deeds since the last period of meeting.

After the feast, they began dancing again ; but such as had no relish for any more exercise in that way, amused themselves by mocking the holy sacrament of baptism. For this purpose, the toads were again called up, and sprinkled with filthy water; the devil making the sign of the cross, and all the witches calling out, "*In nomine Patricâ, Aragueaco Petrica, agora! agora! Valentia, jouando goure gaits goustia!*" which meant, "In the name of Patrick, Petrick of Aragon, now, now, all our ills are over!"

When the devil wished to be particularly amused, he made the witches strip off their clothes and dance before him, each with a cat tied round her neck, and another dangling from her body in form of a tale. When the cock crew, they all disappeared, and the sabbath was ended.

This is a summary of the belief which prevailed for many centuries nearly all over Europe, and which is far from eradicated even at this day. It was varied in some respects in several countries, but the main points were the same in France, Germany, Great Britain, Italy, Spain, and the far North of Europe.

The early annals of France abound with stories of supposed sorcery, but it was not until the time of Charlemagne that the crime acquired any great importance. "This monarch," says M. Jules Garinet,* "had several times given order, that all necromancers, astrologers, and witches should be driven from his states; but as the number of criminals augmented daily, he found it necessary at last to resort to severer measures. In consequence, he published several edicts, which may be found at length in the *Capitulaire de Baluse.* By these, every sort of magic, enchantment, and witchcraft was forbidden; and the punishment of death decreed against those who in any way evoked the devil, compounded love-philters, afflicted either man or woman with barrenness, troubled the atmosphere, excited tempests, destroyed the fruits of the earth, dried up the milk of cows, or tormented their fellow-creatures with sores and diseases. All persons found guilty of exercising these execrable arts were to be executed immediately upon conviction, that the earth might be rid of the burden and curse of their presence; and those even who consulted them might also be punished with death."†

After this time, prosecutions for witchcraft are continually mentioned, especially by the French historians. It was a crime imputed with so much ease, and repelled with so much difficulty, that the

---

* *Histoire de la Magie en France.* Rois de la seconde race, p. 29.

† M. Michaud, in his *History of the Crusades*, M. Guinguené, in his *Literary History of Italy*, and some other critics, have objected to Tasso's poem, that he has attributed to the Crusaders a belief in magic, which did not exist at that time. If these critics had referred to the edicts of Charlemagne, they would have seen that Tasso was right, and that a disposition too eager to spy out imperfections in a great work was leading themselves into error.

powerful, whenever they wanted to ruin the weak, and could fix no other imputation upon them, had only to accuse them of witchcraft to ensure their destruction. Instances in which this crime was made the pretext for the most violent persecution, both of individuals and of communities, whose real offences were purely political or religious, must be familiar to every reader. The extermination of the Stedinger in 1234, of the Templars from 1307 to 1313, the execution of Joan "of Arc in 1429, and the unhappy scenes of Arras in 1459, are the most prominent. The first of these is perhaps the least known, but is not among the least remarkable. The following account, from Dr. Kortüm's interesting history* of the republican confederacies of the middle ages, will shew the horrible convenience of imputations of witchcraft when royal or priestly wolves wanted a pretext for a quarrel with the sheep.

The Frieslanders, inhabiting the district from the Weser to the Zuydersee, had long been celebrated for their attachment to freedom, and their successful struggles in its defence. As early as the eleventh century they had formed a general confederacy against the encroachments of the Normans and the Saxons, which was divided into seven *seelands*, holding annually a diet under a large oak-tree at Aurich, near the Upstalboom. Here they managed their own affairs, without the control of the clergy and ambitious nobles who surrounded them, to the great scandal of the latter. They already had true notions of a representative government. The deputies of the people levied the necessary taxes, deliberated on the affairs of the community, and performed, in their simple and patriarchal manner, nearly all the functions of the representative assemblies of the present day. Finally, the Archbishop of Bremen, together with the Count of Oldenburgh and other neighbouring potentates, formed a league against that section of the Frieslanders known by the name of the Stedinger, and succeeded, after harassing them and sowing dissensions among them for many years, in bringing them under the yoke. But the Stedinger, devotedly attached to their ancient laws, by which they had attained a degree of civil and religious liberty very uncommon in that age, did not submit without a violent struggle. They arose in insurrection in the year 1204, in defence of the ancient customs of their country, refused to pay taxes to the feudal chiefs or tithes to the clergy—who had forced themselves into their peaceful retreats—and drove out many of their oppressors. For a period of eight-and-twenty years the brave Stedinger continued the struggle single-handed against the forces of the Archbishops of Bremen and the Counts of Oldenburg, and destroyed, in the year 1232, the strong castle of Slutterberg, near

* *Entstehungsgeschichte der freistädtlischen Bünde im Mittelalter,* von Dr. F. Kortüm. 1827.

Delmenhorst, built by the latter nobleman as a position from which he could send out his marauders to plunder and destroy the possessions of the peasantry.

The invincible courage of these poor people proving too strong for their oppressors to cope with by the ordinary means of warfare, the Archbishop of Bremen applied to Pope Gregory IX. for his spiritual aid against them. That prelate entered cordially into the cause, and launching forth his anathema against the Stedinger as heretics and witches, encouraged all true believers to assist in their extermination. A large body of thieves and fanatics broke into their country in the year 1233, killing and burning wherever they went, and not sparing either women or children, the sick or the aged, in their rage. The Stedinger, however, rallied in great force, routed their invaders, and killed in battle their leader, Count Burckhardt of Oldenburg, with many inferior chieftains.

Again the pope was applied to, and a crusade against the Stedinger was preached in all that part of Germany. The pope wrote to all the bishops and leaders of the faithful an exhortation to arm, to root out from the land those abominable witches and wizards. " The Stedinger," said his holiness, " seduced by the devil, have abjured all the laws of God and man, slandered the Church, insulted the holy sacraments, consulted witches to raise evil spirits, shed blood like water, taken the lives of priests, and concocted an infernal scheme to propagate the worship of the devil, whom they adore under the name of Asmodi. The devil appears to them in different shapes,—sometimes as a goose or a duck, and at others in the figure of a pale black-eyed youth, with a melancholy aspect, whose embrace fills their hearts with eternal hatred against the holy Church of Christ. This devil presides at their sabbaths, when they all kiss him and dance around him. He then envelopes them in total darkness, and they all, male and female, give themselves up to the grossest and most disgusting debauchery."

In consequence of these letters of the pope, the emperor of Germany, Frederic II., also pronounced his ban against them. The Bishops of Ratzebourg, Lubeck, Osnabrück, Munster, and Minden took up arms to exterminate them, aided by the Duke of Brabant, the Counts of Holland, of Clêves, of the Mark, of Oldenburg, of Egmond, of Diest, and many other powerful nobles. An army of forty thousand men was soon collected, which marched, under the command of the Duke of Brabant, into the country of the Stedinger. The latter mustered vigorously in defence of their lives and liberties, but could raise no greater force, including every man capable of bearing arms, than eleven thousand men, to cope against the overwhelming numbers of their foe. They fought with the energy of despair, but all in vain. Eight thousand of them were slain on the field of battle; the whole race was exterminated; and the enraged conquerors scoured the country in all directions, slew the women and children and old men, drove away the cattle, fired the woods and cottages, and made a total waste of the land.

Just as absurd and effectual was the charge brought against the Templars in 1307, when they had rendered themselves obnoxious to the potentates and prelacy of Christendom. Their wealth, their power, their pride, and their insolence had raised up enemies on every side; and every sort of accusation was made against them, but failed to work their overthrow, until the terrible cry of witchcraft was let loose upon them. This effected its object, and the Templars were extirpated. They were accused of having sold their souls to the devil, and of celebrating all the infernal mysteries of the witches' sabbath. It was pretended that, when they admitted a novice into their order, they forced him to renounce his salvation and curse

PHILIP IV

Jesus Christ; that they then made him submit to many unholy and disgusting ceremonies, and forced him to kiss the superior on the cheek, the navel, and the breech, and spit three times upon a crucifix; that all the members were forbidden to have connexion with women, but might give themselves up without restraint to every species of unmentionable debauchery; that when by any mischance a Templar infringed this order, and a child was born, the whole order met, and tossed it about like a shuttlecock from one to the other until it expired; that they then roasted it by a slow fire, and with the fat which trickled from it anointed the hair and beard of a large image of the devil. It was also said that when one of the knights died, his body was burnt into a powder, and then mixed with wine and drunk by every member of the order. Philip IV., who, to exercise his own implacable hatred, invented, in all probability, the greater part of these charges, issued orders for the immediate arrest of all the Templars in his dominions. The pope afterwards took up the cause with almost as much fervour as the king of France ; and in every part of Europe the Templars were thrown into prison, and their goods and estates confiscated. Hundreds of them, when put to the rack, confessed even the most preposterous of the charges against them, and by so doing increased the popular clamour and the hopes of their enemies. It is true that, when removed from the rack, they denied all they had previously confessed ; but this circumstance only increased the outcry, and was numbered as an additional crime against them. They were considered in a worse light than before, and condemned forthwith to the flames as relapsed heretics. Fifty-nine of these unfortunate victims were all burned together by a slow fire in a field in the suburbs of Paris, protesting to the very last moment of their lives their innocence of the crimes imputed to them, and refusing to accept of pardon upon condition of acknowledging themselves guilty. Similar scenes were enacted in the provinces ; and for four years hardly a month passed without witnessing the execution of one or more of these unhappy men. Finally, in 1313, the last scene of this tragedy closed by the burning of the Grand-Master, Jacques de Molay, and his companion Guy, the commander of Normandy. Any thing more atrocious it is impossible to conceive,—disgraceful alike to the monarch who originated, the pope who supported, and the age which tolerated the monstrous iniquity. That the malice of a few could invent such a charge is a humiliating thought for the lover of his species ; but that millions of mankind should credit it is still more so.

The execution of Joan of Arc is the next most notorious example which history affords us of the imputation of witchcraft against a political enemy. Instances of similar persecution, in which this crime was made the pretext for the gratification of political or religious hatred, might be multiplied to a great extent. But it is better to proceed at once to the consideration of the bull of Pope Innocent, the torch that set fire to the long-laid train, and caused so fearful an explosion over the Christian world. It will be necessary, however, to go back for some years anterior to that event, the better to understand the motives that influenced the Church in the promulgation of that fearful document.

Towards the close of the fourteenth and beginning of the fifteenth century, many witches were burned in different parts of Europe. As

a natural consequence of the severe persecution, the crime, or the
pretenders to it, increased. Those who found themselves accused and
threatened with the penalties, if they happened to be persons of a bad
and malicious disposition, wished they had the power imputed to
them, that they might be revenged upon their persecutors.   Numer-

JOAN OF ARC.

ous instances are upon record of half-crazed persons being found muttering the spells which were supposed to raise the evil one.   When
religion and law alike recognised the crime, it is no wonder that the
weak in reason and the strong in imagination, especially when they
were of a nervous temperament, fancied themselves endued with the
terrible powers of which all the world was speaking.   The belief of
their neighbours did not lag behind their own, and execution was the
speedy consequence.

As the fear of witchcraft increased, the Catholic clergy strove to
fix the imputation of it upon those religious sects, the pioneers of the
Reformation, who began about this time to be formidable to the
Church of Rome.   If a charge of heresy could not ensure their destruction, that of sorcery and witchcraft never failed.   In the year
1459, a devoted congregation of the Waldenses at Arras, who used to
repair at night to worship God in their own manner in solitary places,
fell victims to an accusation of sorcery.   It was rumoured in Arras
that in the desert places to which they retired the devil appeared before them in human form, and read from a large book his laws and
ordinances, to which they all promised obedience; that he then distributed money and food among them, to bind them to his service,
which done, they gave themselves up to every species of lewdness and

debauchery. Upon these rumours several creditable persons in Arras were seized and imprisoned, together with a number of decrepit and idiotic old women. The rack, that convenient instrument for making the accused confess any thing, was of course put in requisition. Monstrelet, in his chronicle, says that they were tortured until some of them admitted the truth of the whole accusations, and said, besides, that they had seen and recognised in their nocturnal assemblies many persons of rank; many prelates, seigneurs, governors of bailliages, and mayors of cities, being such names as the examiners had themselves suggested to the victims. Several who had been thus informed against were thrown into prison, and so horribly tortured, that reason fled, and in their ravings of pain they also confessed their midnight meetings with the devil, and the oaths they had taken to serve him. Upon these confessions judgment was pronounced. The poor old women, as usual in such cases, were hanged and burned in the marketplace; the more wealthy delinquents were allowed to escape upon payment of large sums. It was soon after universally recognised that these trials had been conducted in the most odious manner, and that the judges had motives of private vengeance against many of the more influential persons who had been implicated. The parliament of Paris afterwards declared the sentence illegal, and the judges iniquitous; but its *arrêt* was too late to be of service even to those who had paid the fine, or to punish the authorities who had misconducted themselves, for it was not delivered until thirty-two years after the executions had taken place.

In the mean time, accusations of witchcraft spread rapidly in France, Italy, and Germany. Strange to say, that although in the first instance chiefly directed against heretics, the latter were as firm believers in the crime as even the Catholics themselves. In after times we also find that the Lutherans and Calvinists became greater witch-burners than ever the Romanists had been, so deeply was the prejudice rooted. Every other point of belief was in dispute, but that was considered by every sect to be as well established as the authenticity of the Scriptures or the existence of a God.

But at this early period of the epidemic the persecutions were directed by the heads of the Catholic Church. The spread of heresy betokened, it was thought, the coming of Antichrist. Florimond, in his work concerning Antichrist, exposed the secret of these prosecutions. He says: "All who have afforded us some signs of the approach of Antichrist agree that the increase of sorcery and witchcraft is to distinguish the melancholy period of his advent; and was ever age so afflicted as ours? The seats destined for criminals in our courts of justice are blackened with persons accused of this guilt.

There are not judges enough to try them. Our dungeons are gorged
with them. No day passes that we do not render our tribunals bloody
by the dooms which we pronounce, or in which we do not return to
our homes discountenanced and terrified at the horrible confessions
which we have heard. And the devil is accounted so good a master,
that we cannot commit so great a number of his slaves to the flames
but what there shall arise from their ashes a sufficient number to supply their place."

Florimond here spoke the general opinion of the Church of Rome;
but it never suggested itself to the mind of any person engaged in
these trials, that if it were indeed a devil who raised up so many new
witches to fill the places of those consumed, it was no other than one
in their own employ—the devil of persecution. But so it was. The
more they burned, the more they found to burn, until it became a

GATE OF CONSTANCE.

common prayer with women in the humbler walks of life, that they
might never live to grow old. It was sufficient to be aged, poor, and
half-crazed, to ensure death at the stake or the scaffold.

In the year 1487 there was a severe storm in Switzerland, which laid waste the country for four miles around Constance. Two wretched old women, whom the popular voice had long accused of witchcraft, were arrested on the preposterous charge of having raised the tempest. The rack was displayed, and the two poor creatures were extended upon it. In reply to various questions from their tormentors, they owned in their agony that they were in the constant habit of meeting the devil; that they had sold their souls to him; and that at their command he had raised the tempest. Upon this insane and blasphemous charge they were condemned to die. In the criminal registers of Constance there stands against the name of each the simple but significant phrase, "*convicta et combusta.*"

This case and hundreds of others were duly reported to the ecclesiastical powers. There happened at that time to be a pontiff at the head of the Church who had given much of his attention to the subject of witchcraft, and who, with the intention of rooting out the supposed crime, did more to increase it than any other man that ever lived. John Baptist Cibo, elected to the papacy in 1485, under the designation of Innocent VIII., was sincerely alarmed at the number of witches, and launched forth his terrible manifesto against them. In his celebrated bull of 1488, he called the nations of Europe to the rescue of the Church of Christ upon earth, imperilled by the arts of Satan, and set forth the horrors that had reached his ears; how that numbers of both sexes had intercourse with the infernal fiends; how by their sorceries they afflicted both man and beast; how they blighted the marriage-bed, destroyed the births of women and the increase of cattle; and how they blasted the corn on the ground, the grapes of the vineyard, the fruits of the trees, and the herbs of the field. In order that criminals so atrocious might no longer pollute the earth, he appointed inquisitors in every country, armed with the apostolic power to convict and punish.

It was now that the *Witch Mania*, properly so called, may be said to have fairly commenced. Immediately a class of men sprang up in Europe, who made it the sole business of their lives to discover and burn the witches. Sprenger, in Germany, was the most celebrated of these national scourges. In his notorious work, the *Malleus Maleficarum*, he laid down a regular form of trial, and appointed a course of examination by which the inquisitors in other countries might best discover the guilty. The questions, which were always enforced by torture, were of the most absurd and disgusting nature. The inquisitors were required to ask the suspected whether they had midnight meetings with the devil? whether they attended the witches' sabbath on the Brocken? whether they had their familiar spirits? whether they could raise whirlwinds and call down the lightning? and whether they had had sexual intercourse with Satan?

Straightway the inquisitors set to work : Cumanus, in Italy, burned forty-one poor women in one province alone ; and Sprenger, in Germany, burned a number which can never be ascertained correctly, but which, it is agreed on all hands, amounted to more than five hundred in a year. The great resemblance between the confessions of the unhappy victims was regarded as a new proof of the existence of the crime. But this is not astonishing. The same questions from the *Malleus Maleficarum* were put to them all, and torture never failed to educe the answer required by the inquisitor. Numbers of people, whose imaginations were filled with these horrors, went further in the way of confession than even their tormentors anticipated, in the hope that they would thereby be saved from the rack, and put out of their misery at once. Some confessed that they had had children by the devil ; but no one who had ever been a mother gave utterance to such a frantic imagining, even in the extremity of her anguish. The childless only confessed it, and were burned instanter as unworthy to live.

For fear the zeal of the enemies of Satan should cool, successive popes appointed new commissions. One was appointed by Alexander VI. in 1494, another by Leo X. in 1521, and a third by Adrian VI. in 1522. They were all armed with the same powers to hunt out and destroy, and executed their fearful functions but too rigidly. In Geneva alone five hundred persons were burned in the years 1515 and 1516, under the title of Protestant witches. It would appear that their chief crime was heresy, and their witchcraft merely an aggravation. Bartolomeo de Spina has a list still more fearful. He informs us that in the year 1524 no less than a thousand persons suffered death for witchcraft in the district of Como, and that for several years afterwards the average number of victims exceeded a hundred annually. One inquisitor, Remigius, took great credit to himself for having, during fifteen years, convicted and burned nine hundred.

In France, about the year 1520, fires for the execution of witches blazed in almost every town. Danæus, in his *Dialogues of Witches*, says they were so numerous that it would be next to impossible to tell the number of them. So deep was the thraldom of the human mind, that the friends and relatives of the accused parties looked on and approved. The wife or sister of a murderer might sympathise in his fate, but the wives and husbands of sorcerers and witches had no pity. The truth is, that pity was dangerous, for it was thought no one could have compassion on the sufferings of a witch who was not a dabbler in sorcery : to have wept for a witch would have insured the stake. In some districts, however, the exasperation of the people broke out, in spite of superstition. The inquisitor of a rural township in Piedmont burned the victims so plentifully and so fast, that there was not a family in the place which did not lose a member. The people at last arose, and the inquisitor was but too happy to escape from the country with whole limbs. The archbishop of the diocese proceeded afterwards to the trial of such as the inquisitor had left in prison.

Some of the charges were so utterly preposterous that the poor wretches were at once liberated; others met a harder, but the usual fate. Some of them were accused of having joined the witches' dance at midnight under a blasted oak, where they had been seen by creditable people. The husbands of several of these women (two of whom were young and beautiful) swore positively that at the time stated their wives were comfortably asleep in their arms; but it was all in vain. Their word was taken, but the archbishop told them they had been deceived by the devil and their own senses. It was true they might have had the semblance of their wives in their beds, but the originals were far away at the devil's dance under the oak. The honest fellows were confounded, and their wives burned forthwith.

CHARLES IX.

In the year 1561, five poor women of Verneuil were accused of transforming themselves into cats, and in that shape attending the sabbath of the fiends—prowling around Satan, who presided over them in the form of a goat, and dancing, to amuse him, upon his back. They were found guilty, and burned.*

In 1564, three wizards and a witch appeared before the Presidents Salvert and D'Avanton: they confessed, when extended on the rack, that they anointed the sheep-pens with infernal unguents to kill the sheep; that they attended the sabbath, where they saw a great black goat,

* Bodin, p. 95; Garinet, p. 125; *Anti-demon de Serclier*, p. 346.

which spoke to them, and made them kiss him, each holding a lighted candle in his hand while he performed the ceremony. They were all executed at Poitiers.

In 1571 the celebrated sorcerer Trois Echelles was burned in the Place de Grêve in Paris. He confessed, in the presence of Charles IX., and of the Marshals de Montmorency, De Retz, and the Sieur du Mazille, physician to the king, that he could perform the most wonderful things by the aid of a devil to whom he had sold himself. He described at great length the saturnalia of the fiends, the sacrifices which they offered up, the debaucheries they committed with the young and handsome witches, and the various modes of preparing the infernal unguent for blighting cattle. He said he had upwards of twelve hundred accomplices in the crime of witchcraft in various parts of France, whom he named to the king, and many of whom were afterwards arrested and suffered execution.

At Dôle, two years afterwards, Gilles Garnier, a native of Lyons, was indicted for being a *loup-garou*, or man-wolf, and for prowling in that shape about the country at night to devour little children. The indictment against him, as read by Henri Camus, doctor of laws and counsellor of the king, was to the effect that he, Gilles Garnier, had seized upon a little girl, twelve years of age, whom he drew into a vineyard and there killed, partly with his teeth and partly with his hands, seeming like wolf's paws; that from thence he trailed her bleeding body along the ground with his teeth into the wood of La Serre, where he ate the greatest portion of her at one meal, and carried the remainder home to his wife; that upon another occasion, eight days before the festival of All Saints, he was seen to seize another child in his teeth, and would have devoured her had she not been rescued by the country people, and that the said child died a few days afterwards of the injuries he had inflicted; that fifteen days after the same festival of All Saints, being again in the shape of a wolf, he devoured a boy thirteen years of age, having previously torn off his leg and thigh with his teeth, and hid them away for his breakfast on the morrow. He was furthermore indicted for giving way to the same diabolical and unnatural propensities even in his shape of a man; and that he had strangled a boy in a wood with the intention of eating him, which crime he would have effected if he had not been seen by the neighbours and prevented.

Gilles Garnier was put to the rack after fifty witnesses had deposed against him. He confessed every thing that was laid to his charge. He was thereupon brought back into the presence of his judges, when Dr. Camus, in the name of the parliament of Dôle, pronounced the following sentence:

" Seeing that Gilles Garnier has, by the testimony of credible witnesses, and by his own spontaneous confession, been proved guilty of the abominable crimes of lycanthropy and witchcraft, this court condemns him, the said Gilles, to be this day taken in a cart from this spot to the place of execution, accompanied by the executioner (*mattre exécuteur de la haute justice*), where he, by the said executioner, shall be tied to a stake and burned alive, and that his ashes be then scattered to the winds. The court further condemns him, the said Gilles, to the costs of this prosecution.

" Given at Dôle, this 18th day of January, 1573."

In 1578, the parliament of Paris was occupied for several days with the trial of a man named Jacques Rollet. He also was found guilty of being a *loup-garou*, and in that shape devouring a little boy. He was burnt alive in the Place de Grêve.

In 1579, so much alarm was excited in the neighbourhood of Melun by the increase of witches and *loup-garous*, that a council was held to devise some measures to stay the evil. A decree was passed that all witches and consulters with witches should be punished with death ; and not only those, but fortune-tellers and conjurors of every kind. The parliament of Rouen took up the same question in the following year, and decreed that the possession of a *grimoire*, or book of spells, was sufficient evidence of witchcraft, and that all persons on whom such books were found should be burned alive. Three councils were held in different parts of France in the year 1583, all in relation to the same subject. The parliament of Bordeaux issued strict injunctions to all curates and clergy whatever to use redoubled efforts to root out the crime of witchcraft. The parliament of Tours was equally peremptory, and feared the judgments of an offended God, if all these dealers with the devil were not swept from the face of the land. The parliament of Rheims was particularly severe against the *noueurs d'aiguillette*, or " tyers of the knot"—people of both sexes who took pleasure in preventing the consummation of marriage, that they might counteract the command of God to our first parents to increase and multiply. This parliament held it to be sinful to wear amulets to preserve from witchcraft ; and that this practice might not be continued within its jurisdiction, drew up a form of exorcism, which would more effectually defeat the agents of the devil, and put them to flight.

A case of witchcraft, which created a great sensation in its day, occurred in 1588, at a village in the mountains of Auvergne, about two leagues from Apchon. A gentleman of that place being at his window, there passed a friend of his who had been out hunting, and who was then returning to his own house. The gentleman asked his

friend what sport he had had ; upon which the latter informed him
that he had been attacked in the plain by a large and savage wolf,
which he had shot at without wounding, and that he had then drawn
out his hunting-knife and cut off the animal's fore-paw as it sprang
upon his neck to devour him. The huntsman upon this put his hand
into his bag to pull out the paw, but was shocked to find that it was
a woman's hand, with a wedding-ring on the finger. The gentleman
immediately recognised his wife's ring, "which," says the indictment
against her, "made him begin to suspect some evil of her." He immediately went in search of her, and found her sitting by the fire in
the kitchen, with her arm hidden underneath her apron. He tore off
her apron with great vehemence, and found that she had no hand,
and that the stump was even then bleeding. She was given into
custody, and burnt at Riom, in presence of some thousands of spectators.*

In the midst of these executions, rare were the gleams of mercy.
Few instances are upon record of any acquittal taking place when the
crime was witchcraft. The discharge of fourteen persons by the parliament of Paris, in the year 1589, is almost a solitary example of a
return to reason. Fourteen persons condemned to death for witchcraft appealed against the judgment to the parliament of Paris, which
for political reasons had been exiled to Tours. The parliament named
four commissioners—Pierre Pigray, the king's surgeon, and Messieurs
Leroi, Renard, and Falaiseau, the king's physicians—to visit and
examine these witches, and see whether they had the mark of the
devil upon them. Pigray, who relates the circumstance in his work
on Surgery (book vii. chap. 10), says the visit was made in presence
of two counsellors of the court. The witches were all stripped
naked, and the physicians examined their bodies very diligently,
pricking them in all the marks they could find to see whether they
were insensible to pain, which was always considered a certain proof
of guilt. They were, however, very sensible of the pricking, and
some of them called out very lustily when the pins were driven into
them. " We found them," continues Pierre Pigray, " to be very
poor, stupid people, and some of them insane. Many of them were
quite indifferent about life, and one or two of them desired death as
a relief from their sufferings. Our opinion was, that they stood more
in need of medicine than of punishment; and so we reported to the
parliament. Their case was thereupon taken into further consideration ; and the parliament, after mature counsel amongst all the mem-

* Tabller. See also Boguet, _Discours sur les Sorciers ;_ and M. Jules Garinet, _Histoire
de la Magie,_ p. 150.

bers, ordered the poor creatures to be sent to their homes, without inflicting any punishment upon them."

Such was the dreadful state of Italy, Germany, and France during the sixteenth century, which was far from being the worst crisis of the popular madness with regard to witchcraft. Let us see what was the state of England during the same period. The Reformation, which in its progress had rooted out so many errors, stopped short at this, the greatest error of all. Luther and Calvin were as firm believers in witchcraft as Pope Innocent himself; and their followers shewed themselves more zealous persecutors than the Romanists. Dr. Hutchinson, in his work on Witchcraft, asserts that the mania manifested itself later in England, and raged with less virulence than on the continent. The first assertion only is true; for though the persecution began later both in England and Scotland, its progress was as fearful as elsewhere.

It was not until more than fifty years after the issuing of the bull of Innocent VIII. that the legislature of England thought fit to make any more severe enactments against sorcery than those already in operation. The statute of 1541 was the first that specified the particular crime of witchcraft. At a much earlier period many persons had suffered death for sorcery, in addition to other offences; but no executions took place for attending the witches' sabbath, raising tempests, afflicting cattle with barrenness, and all the fantastic trumpery of the continent. Two statutes were passed in 1551: the first relating to false prophecies, caused mainly, no doubt, by the impositions of Elizabeth Barton, the holy maid of Kent, in 1534; and the second against conjuration, witchcraft, and sorcery. But even this enactment did not consider witchcraft as penal in itself, and only condemned to death those who, by means of spells, incantations, or contracts with the devil, attempted the lives of their neighbours. The statute of Elizabeth, in 1562, at last recognised witchcraft as a crime of the highest magnitude, whether exerted or not to the injury of the lives, limbs, and possessions of the community. From that date the persecution may be fairly said to have commenced in England. It reached its climax in the early part of the seventeenth century, which was the hottest period of the mania all over Europe.

A few cases of witch persecution in the sixteenth century will enable the reader to form a more accurate idea of the progress of this great error than if he plunged at once into that busy period of its history when Matthew Hopkins and his coadjutors exercised their infernal calling. Several instances occur in England during the latter years of the reign of Elizabeth. At this time the public mind had become pretty familiar with the details of the crime. Bishop

Jewell, in his sermons before her majesty, used constantly to conclude them by a fervent prayer that she might be preserved from
witches.   Upon one occasion, in 1598, his words were, "It may

please your grace to understand
that witches and sorcerers within these last four years are mar-
vellously increased within this
your grace's realm. Your grace's
subjects pine away even unto the
death ; their colour fadeth—their
flesh rotteth—their speech is be-
numbed—their senses are bereft !
I pray God they may never practise further than upon the *subject !*"

By degrees, an epidemic terror
of witchcraft spread into the villages. In proportion as the doctrine of the Puritans took root,
this dread increased, and, of
course, brought persecution in
its train. The Church of England has claimed, and is entitled
to the merit, of having been less

JEWELL.

influenced in these matters than any other sect of Christians ; but
still they were tainted with the superstition of the age.   One of the
most flagrant instances of cruelty and delusion upon record was con-
summated under the authority of the Church, and commemorated
till a very late period by an annual lecture at the University of Cambridge.

This is the celebrated case of the witches of Warbois, who were
executed about thirty-two years after the passing of the statute of
Elizabeth.   Although in the interval but few trials are recorded,
there is, unfortunately, but too much evidence to shew the extreme
length to which the popular prejudice was carried.   Many women
lost their lives in every part of England without being brought to
trial at all, from the injuries received at the hands of the people.
The number of these can never be ascertained.

The case of the witches of Warbois merits to be detailed at
length, not only from the importance attached to it for so many
years by the learned of the University, but from the singular absurdity of the evidence upon which men, sensible in all other respects, could condemn their fellow-creatures to the scaffold.

The principal actors in this strange drama were the families of Sir Samuel Cromwell and a Mr. Throgmorton, both gentlemen of landed property near Warbois in the county of Huntingdon. Mr. Throgmorton had several daughters, the eldest of whom, Mistress Joan, was an imaginative and melancholy girl, whose head was filled with stories of ghosts and witches. Upon one occasion she chanced to pass the cottage of one Mrs., or, as she was called, Mother Samuel, a very aged, a very poor, and a very ugly woman. Mother Samuel was sitting at her door knitting, with a black cap upon her head, when this silly young lady passed, and taking her eyes from her work she looked stedfastly at her. Mistress Joan immediately fancied that she felt sudden pains in all her limbs, and from that day forth never ceased to tell her sisters, and every body about her, that Mother Samuel had bewitched her. The other children took up the cry, and actually frightened themselves into fits whenever they passed within sight of this terrible old woman.

Mr. and Mrs. Throgmorton, not a whit wiser than their children, believed all the absurd tales they had been told; and Lady Cromwell, a gossip of Mrs. Throgmorton, made herself very active in the business, and determined to bring the witch to the ordeal. The sapient Sir Samuel joined in the scheme; and the children, thus encouraged, gave loose reins to their imaginations, which seem to have been of the liveliest. They soon invented a whole host of evil spirits, and names for them besides, which they said were sent by Mother Samuel to torment them continually. Seven spirits especially, they said, were raised from hell by this wicked woman to throw them into fits; and as the children were actually subject to fits, their mother and her commeres gave the more credit to the story. The names of these spirits were, "First Smack," "Second Smack," "Third Smack," "Blue," "Catch," "Hardname," and "Pluck."

Throgmorton, the father, was so pestered by these idle fancies, and yet so well inclined to believe them, that he marched valiantly forth to the hut where Mother Samuel resided with her husband and daughter, and dragged her forcibly into his own grounds. Lady Cromwell, Mrs. Throgmorton, and the girls were in waiting, armed with long pins to prick the witch, and see if they could draw blood from her. Lady Cromwell, who seems to have been the most violent of the party, tore the old woman's cap off her head, and plucking out a handful of her grey hair, gave it to Mrs. Throgmorton to burn, as a charm which would preserve them all from her future machinations. It was no wonder that the poor creature, subjected to this rough usage, should give vent to an involuntary curse upon her tormentors. She did so, and her curse was never forgotten. Her hair, however, was supposed to be a grand specific, and she was allowed to depart, half dead with terror and ill-usage. For more than a year the families of Cromwell and Throgmorton continued to persecute her, and to assert that her imps afflicted them with pains and fits, turned the milk sour in their pans, and prevented their cows and ewes from bearing. In the midst of these fooleries, Lady Cromwell was taken ill and died. It was then remembered that her death had taken place exactly a year and a quarter since she was cursed by Mother Samuel, and that on several occasions she had dreamed of the witch and a black cat, the latter being of course the arch-enemy of mankind himself.

Sir Samuel Cromwell now conceived himself bound to take more energetic measures against the sorceress, since he had lost his wife by her means. The year and a quarter and the black cat were proofs positive. All the neighbours had taken up the cry of witchcraft against Mother Samuel; and her personal appearance, unfortunately for her the very ideal of what a witch ought to be, increased the popular suspicion. It would appear that at last the poor woman believed, even to her own disadvantage, that she was what every body represented her to be. Being forcibly brought into Mr. Throgmorton's house, when his daughter Joan was in one of her customary fits, she was commanded by him and Sir Samuel Cromwell to expel the devil from the young lady. She was told to repeat her exorcism, and to add, " As I am a witch, and the causer of Lady Cromwell's death, I charge thee, fiend, to come out of her !" She did as was required of her; and moreover confessed that her husband and daughter were leagued with her in witchcraft, and had, like her, sold their souls to the devil. The whole family were immediately arrested, and sent to Huntingdon to prison.

The trial was instituted shortly afterwards before Mr. Justice Fenner, when all the crazy girls of Mr. Throgmorton's family gave evidence against Mother Samuel and her family. They were all three put to the torture. The old woman confessed in her anguish that she was a witch; that she had cast her spells upon the young ladies; and that she had caused the death of Lady Cromwell. The father and daughter, stronger in mind than their unfortunate wife and parent, refused to confess any thing, and asserted their innocence to the last. They were all three condemned to be hanged, and their bodies burned. The daughter, who was young and good-looking, excited the pity of many persons, and she was advised to plead pregnancy, that she might gain at least a respite from death. The poor girl refused proudly, on the ground that she would not be accounted both a witch and a strumpet. Her half-witted old mother caught at the idea of a few weeks' longer life, and asserted that she was pregnant. The court was convulsed with laughter, in which the wretched victim herself joined; and this was accounted an additional proof that she was a witch. The whole family were executed on the 7th of April, 1593.

Sir Samuel Cromwell, as lord of the manor, received the sum of 40*l.* out of the confiscated property of the Samuels, which he turned into a rent-charge of 40*s.* yearly, for the endowment of an annual sermon or lecture upon the enormity of witchcraft, and this case in particular, to be preached by a doctor or bachelor of divinity of Queen's College, Cambridge. I have not been able to ascertain the exact date at which this annual lecture was discontinued; but it appears to have been preached so late as 1718, when Dr. Hutchinson published his work upon witchcraft.

To carry on in proper chronological order the history of the witch delusion in the British isles, it will be necessary to examine into what was taking place in Scotland during all that part of the sixteenth century anterior to the accession of James VI. to the crown of England. We naturally expect that the Scotch—a people renowned from the earliest times for their powers of imagination—should be more deeply imbued with this gloomy superstition than their neighbours of the south. The nature of their soil and climate tended to encourage the dreams of early ignorance. Ghosts, goblins, wraiths, kelpies, and a whole host of spiritual beings, were familiar to the dwellers by the misty glens of the Highlands and the romantic streams of the Lowlands. Their deeds, whether of good or ill, were enshrined in song, and took a greater hold upon the imagination because "verse had sanctified them." But it was not till the religious reformers began the practice of straining Scripture to the severest extremes that the arm of the law was called upon to punish witchcraft as a crime *per se.* What Pope Innocent VIII. had done for Germany and France, the preachers of the Reformation did for the Scottish people. Witchcraft, instead of being a mere article of faith, became enrolled in the statute-book, and all good subjects and true Christians were called upon to take arms against it. The ninth parliament of Queen Mary passed an act in 1563, which decreed the punishment of death against witches and consulters with witches; and immediately the whole bulk of the people were smitten with an epidemic fear of the devil and his mortal agents. Persons in the highest ranks of life shared and encouraged the delusion of the vulgar. Many were themselves accused of witchcraft; and noble ladies were shewn to have dabbled in mystic arts, and proved to the world that if they were not witches, it was not for want of the will.

Among the dames who became notorious for endeavouring to effect their wicked ends by the devil's aid may be mentioned the celebrated Lady Buccleugh of Branxholme (familiar to all the readers of Sir Walter Scott), the Countess of Lothian, the Countess of Angus, the Countess of Atholl, Lady Kerr, the Countess of Huntley, Euphemia Macalzean (the daughter of Lord Cliftonhall), and Lady Fowlis. Among the celebrated of the other sex who were accused of wizardism was Sir Lewis Ballantyne, the Lord Justice-Clerk for Scotland, who, if we may believe Scot of Scotstarvet, "dealt by curiosity with a warlock called Richard Grahame," and prayed him to raise the devil. The warlock consented, and raised him *in propriâ personâ* in the yard of his house in the Canongate, "at sight of him the Lord Justice-Clerk was so terrified, that he took sickness and thereof died." By such idle reports as these did the envious ruin the reputation of those they hated; though it would appear in this case that Sir Lewis had been fool enough to make the attempt of which he was accused, and that the success of the experiment was the only apocryphal part of the story.

JOHN KNOX.

The enemies of John Knox invented a similar tale, which found ready credence among the Roman Catholics, glad to attach any stigma to that grand scourge of the vices of their Church. It was reported that he and his secretary went into the churchyard of St. Andrew's with the intent to raise "some sanctes;" but that, by a mistake in their conjurations, they raised the great fiend himself instead of the saints they wished to consult. The popular rumour added, that Knox's secretary was so frightened at the great horns, goggle eyes, and long tail of Satan, that he went mad, and shortly afterwards died. Knox himself was built of sterner stuff, and was not to be frightened.

The first name that occurs in the records of the High Court of Justiciary of persons tried or executed for witchcraft, is that of Janet Bowman in 1572, nine years after the passing of the act of Mary. No particulars of her crimes are given, and against her name there only stands the words, "convict and brynt." It is not, however, to be inferred, that in this interval no trials or executions took place; for it appears, on the authority of documents of unquestioned authenticity in the Advocates' Library at Edinburgh,* that the Privy Council made a practice of granting commissions to resident gentlemen and ministers in every part of Scotland to examine, try, and execute witches within their own parishes. No records of those who suffered from the sentence of these tribunals have been preserved; but if popular tradition may be believed even to the amount of one-fourth of its assertions, their number was fearful. After the year 1572, the entries of executions for witchcraft in the records of the High Court become more frequent, but do not average more than one per annum,—another proof that trials for this offence were in general entrusted to the local magistracy. The latter appear to have ordered witches to the stake with as little compunction, and after as summary a mode, as modern justices of the peace order a poacher to the stocks.

As James VI. advanced in manhood, he took great interest in the witch trials. One of them especially—that of Gellie Duncan, Dr. Fian, and their accomplices, in the year 1591—engrossed his whole attention, and no doubt suggested in some degree the famous work on Demonology, which he wrote shortly afterwards. As these witches had made an attempt upon his own life, it is not surprising, with his habits, that he should have watched the case closely, or become strengthened in his prejudice and superstition by its singular details. No other trial that could be selected would give so fair an idea of the delusions of the Scottish people as this. Whether we consider the number of victims, the absurdity of the evidence, and the real villany of some of the persons implicated, it is equally extraordinary.

Gellie Duncan, the prime witch in these proceedings, was servant to the deputy bailiff of Tranent, a small town in Haddingtonshire,

* *Foreign Quarterly Review*, vol. vi. p. 41.

about ten miles from Edinburgh. Though neither old nor ugly (as witches usually were), but young and good-looking, her neighbours, from some suspicious parts of her behaviour, had long considered her a witch. She had, it appears, some pretensions to the healing art. Some cures which she effected were so sudden, that the worthy bailiff, her master, who, like his neighbours, mistrusted her, considered them no less than miraculous. In order to discover the truth, he put her to the torture; but she obstinately refused to confess that she had dealings with the devil. It was the popular belief that no witch would confess as long as the mark which Satan had put upon her remained undiscovered upon her body. Somebody present reminded the torturing bailie of this fact, and on examination, the devil's mark was found upon the throat of poor Gellie. She was put to the torture again, and her fortitude giving way under the extremity of her anguish, she confessed that she was indeed a witch— that she had sold her soul to the devil, and effected all her cures by his aid. This was something new in the witch creed, according to which, the devil delighted more in laying diseases on than in taking them off; but Gellie Duncan fared no better on that account. The torture was still applied, until she had named all her accomplices, among whom were one Cunningham, a reputed wizard, known by the name of Dr. Fian; a grave and matron-like witch, named Agnes Sampson; Euphemia Macalzean, the daughter of Lord Cliftonhall, already mentioned, and nearly forty other persons, some of whom were the wives of respectable individuals in the city of Edinburgh. Every one of these persons was arrested, and the whole realm of Scotland thrown into commotion by the extraordinary nature of the disclosures which were anticipated.

About two years previous to this time, James had suddenly left his kingdom, and proceeded gallantly to Denmark, to fetch over his bride, the Princess of Denmark, who had been detained by contrary weather in the harbour of Upslo. After remaining for some months in Copenhagen, he set sail with his young bride, and arrived safely in Leith on the 1st of May 1590, having experienced a most boisterous passage, and been nearly wrecked. As soon as the arrest of Gellie Duncan and Fian became known in Scotland, it was reported by every body who pretended to be well-informed, that these witches and their associates had, by the devil's means, raised the storms which had endangered the lives of the king and queen. Gellie, in her torture, had confessed that such was the fact, and the whole kingdom waited aghast and open-mouthed for the corroboration about to be furnished by the trial.

Agnes Sampson, the "grave and matron-like" witch implicated

by Gellie Duncan, was put to the horrible torture of the *pilliewinkis*. She laid bare all the secrets of the sisterhood before she had suffered an hour, and confessed that Gellie Duncan, Dr. Fian, Marian Lincup, Euphemia Macalzean, herself, and upwards of two hundred witches and warlocks, used to assemble at midnight in the kirk of North Berwick, where they met the devil; that they had plotted there to attempt the king's life ; that they were incited to this by the old fiend himself, who had asserted with a thundering oath that James was the greatest enemy he ever had, and that there would be no peace for the devil's children upon earth until he were got rid of ; that the devil upon these occasions always liked to have a little music, and that Gellie Duncan used to play a reel before him on a trump or Jew's harp, to which all the witches danced.

James was highly flattered at the idea that the devil should have said that he was the greatest enemy he ever had. He sent for Gellie Duncan to the palace, and made her play before him the same reel which she had played at the witches' dance in the kirk.

TORTURE OF THE BOOTS.

Dr. Fian, or rather Cunningham, a petty schoolmaster of Tranent, was put to the torture among the rest. He was a man who had led an infamous life, was a compounder of and dealer in poisons, and a pretender to magic. Though not guilty of the preposterous crimes laid to his charge, there is no doubt that he was a sorcerer in

will, though not in deed, and that he deserved all the misery he endured.   When put on the rack, he would confess nothing, and held
out so long unmoved, that the severe torture of the *boots* was resolved
upon.   He endured this till exhausted nature could bear no longer,
when insensibility kindly stepped in to his aid.   When it was seen
that he was utterly powerless, and that his tongue cleaved to the
roof of his mouth, he was released.   Restoratives were administered;
and during the first faint gleam of returning consciousness, he was
prevailed upon to sign, ere he well knew what he was about, a
full confession, in strict accordance with those of Gellie Duncan and
Agnes Sampson.   He was then remanded to his prison, from which,
after two days, he managed, some how or other, to escape.   He was
soon recaptured, and brought before the Court of Justiciary, James
himself being present.   Fian now denied all the circumstances of the
written confession which he had signed ; whereupon the king, enraged at his " stubborn wilfulness," ordered him once more to the
torture.   His finger-nails were riven out with pincers, and long needles thrust up to the eye into the quick ; but he did not wince.   He
was then consigned again to the *boots*, in which, to quote a pamphlet
published at the time,* he continued " so long, and abode so many
blows in them, that his legs were crushed and beaten together as
small as might be, and the bones and flesh so bruised, that the blood
and marrow spouted forth in great abundance, whereby they were
made unserviceable for ever."

The astonishing similarity of the confessions of all the persons
implicated in these proceedings has often been remarked.   It would
appear that they actually endeavoured to cause the king's death by
their spells and sorceries.   Fian, who was acquainted with all the
usual tricks of his profession, deceived them with pretended apparitions, so that many of them were really convinced that they had
seen the devil.   The sum of their confessions was to the following
effect :

Satan, who was, of course, a great foe of the reformed religion,
was alarmed that King James should marry a Protestant princess.
To avert the consequences to the realms of evil, he had determined
to put an end to the king and his bride by raising a storm on their
voyage home.   Satan, first of all, sent a thick mist over the waters,
in the hope that the king's vessel might be stranded on the coast
amid the darkness.   This failing, Dr. Fian, who, from his superior
scholarship, was advanced to the dignity of the devil's secretary, was
commanded to summon all the witches to meet their master, each
one sailing on a sieve on the high seas.

* *News from Scotland, declaring the Damnable Life of Dr. Fian.*

On All Hallowmas Eve, they assembled to the number of upwards
of two hundred, including Gellie Duncan, Agnes Sampson, Euphemia
Macalzean, one Barbara Napier, and several warlocks ; and each embarking in a riddle or sieve, they sailed "over the ocean very sub-
stantially." After cruising about for some time, they met with the
fiend, bearing in his claws a cat, which had been previously drawn
nine times through the fire. This he delivered to one of the warlocks,
telling him to cast it into the sea and cry "Hola!" This was done
with all solemnity, and immediately the ocean became convulsed, the
waters hissèd loudly, and the waves rose mountains high,

> " Twisting their arms to the dun-coloured heaven."

The witches sailed gallantly through the tempest they had raised, and
landing on the coast of Scotland, took their sieves in their hands and
marched on in procession to the haunted kirk of North Berwick, where
the devil had resolved to hold a preaching. Gellie Duncan, the musi-
cian of the party, tripped on before, playing on her Jew's harp and
singing,

> " Cummer, go ye before, cummer, go ye ;
> Gif ye will not go before, cummer, let me !"

Arrived at the kirk, they paced around it *withershins*, that is, in reverse
of the apparent motion of the sun. Dr. Fian then blew into the keyhole of the door, which opened immediately, and all the witches entered. As it was pitch-dark, Fian blew with his mouth upon the
candles, which immediately lighted, and the devil was seen occupying
the pulpit. He was attired in a black gown and hat, and the witches
saluted him by crying " All hail, master! " His body was hard, like
iron ; his face terrible ; his nose like the beak of an eagle ; he had
great burning eyes ; his hands and legs were hairy ; and he had long
claws upon his hands and feet, and spake with an exceedingly gruff
voice. Before commencing his sermon he called over the names of
his congregation, demanding whether they had been good servants,
and what success had attended their operations against the life of the
king and his bride.

Gray Meill, a crazy old warlock, who acted as beadle or door-
keeper, was silly enough to answer " that nothing ailed the king yet,
God be thanked ;" upon which the devil, in a rage, stepped down
from the pulpit and boxed his ears for him. He then remounted and
commenced the preaching, commanding them to be dutiful servants
to him and do all the evil they could. Euphemia Macalzean and
Agnes Sampson, bolder than the rest, asked him whether he had
brought the image or picture of King James, that they might, by
pricking it, cause pains and diseases to fall upon him. " The father

of lies" spoke truth for once, and confessed that he had forgotten it; upon which Euphemia Macalzean upbraided him loudly for his carelessness. The devil, however, took it all in good part, although Agnes Sampson and several other women let loose their tongues at him immediately. When they had done scolding, he invited them all to a grand entertainment. A newly-buried corpse was dug up and divided among them, which was all they had in the way of edibles. He was more liberal in the matter of drink, and gave them so much excellent wine that they soon became jolly. Gellie Duncan then played the old tune upon her trump, and the devil himself led off the dance with Euphemia Macalzean. Thus they kept up the sport till the cock crew.

Agnes Sampson, the wise woman of Keith, as she was called, added some other particulars in her confession. She stated that, on a previous occasion, she had raised an awful tempest in the sea by throwing a cat into it, with four joints of men tied to its feet. She said also, that on their grand attempt to drown King James, they did not meet with the devil after cruising about, but that he had accompanied them from the first, and that she had seen him dimly in the distance, rolling himself before them over the great waves, in shape and size not unlike a huge haystack. They met with a foreign ship richly laden with wines and other good things, which they boarded, and sunk after they had drunk all the wine and made themselves quite merry.

JAMES THE DEMONOLOGIST.

Some of these disclosures were too much even for the abundant faith of King James, and he more than once exclaimed, that the witches were like their master, "extreme lyars." But they confessed many other things of a less preposterous nature, and of which they were no doubt really guilty. Agnes Sampson said she was to have taken the king's life by anointing his linen with a strong poison. Gellie Duncan used to threaten her neighbours by saying she would send the devil after them; and many persons of weaker minds than usual were frightened into fits by her, and rendered subject to them for the remainder of their lives.   Dr. Fian also made no scruple in aiding and abetting murder, and would rid any person of an enemy by means of poison, who could pay him his fee for it.   Euphemia Macalzean also was far from being pure.   There is no doubt that she meditated the king's death, and used such means to compass it as the superstition of the age directed.   She was a devoted partisan of Bothwell, who was accused by many of the witches as having consulted them on the period of the king's death.   They were all found guilty, and sentenced to be hanged and burned.   Barbara Napier, though found guilty upon other counts, was acquitted upon the charge of having been present at the great witch meeting in Berwick kirk.   The king was highly displeased, and threatened to have the jury indicted for a wilful error upon an assize.   They accordingly reconsidered their verdict, and threw themselves upon the king's mercy for the fault they had committed.   James was satisfied, and Barbara Napier was hanged along with Gellie Duncan, Agnes Sampson, Dr. Fian, and five-and-twenty others.   Euphemia Macalzean met a harder fate.   Her connexion with the bold and obnoxious Bothwell, and her share in poisoning one or two individuals who had stood in her way, were thought deserving of the severest punishment the law could inflict.   Instead of the ordinary sentence, directing the criminal to be first strangled and then burned, the wretched woman was doomed " to be bound to a stake, and burned in ashes, *quick* to the death."   This cruel sentence was executed on the 25th of June, 1591.

These trials had the most pernicious consequences all over Scotland.   The lairds and ministers in their districts, armed with due power from the privy council, tried and condemned old women after the most summary fashion.   Those who still clung to the ancient faith of Rome were the severest sufferers, as it was thought, after the disclosures of the fierce enmity borne by the devil towards a Protestant king and his Protestant wife, that all the Catholics were leagued with the powers of evil to work woe on the realm of Scotland.   Upon a very moderate calculation, it is presumed that from the passing of the act of Queen Mary till the accession of James to the throne of England, a period of thirty-nine years, the average number of executions for witchcraft in Scotland was two hundred annually, or upwards of seventeen thousand altogether.   For the first nine years the number was not one quarter so great ; but towards the years 1590 to 1593, the number must have been more than four hundred.   The case last cited was one of an extraordinary character.   The general aspect of the trials will be better seen from that of Isabel Gowdie, which, as it would be both wearisome and disgusting to go through them all, is given as a

fair specimen, although it took place at a date somewhat later than
the reign of James. This woman, wearied of her life by the persecutions of her neighbours, voluntarily gave herself up to justice, and
made a confession, embodying the whole witch-creed of the period.
She was undoubtedly a monomaniac of the most extraordinary kind.
She said that she deserved to be stretched upon an iron rack, and
that her crimes could never be atoned for, even if she were to be
drawn asunder by wild horses. She named a long list of her associates, including nearly fifty women and a few warlocks. They dug
up the graves of unchristened infants, whose limbs were serviceable
in their enchantments. When they wanted to destroy the crops
of an enemy, they yoked toads to his plough, and on the following
night Satan himself ploughed the land with his team, and blasted it
for the season. The witches had power to assume almost any shape ;
but they generally chose either that of a cat or a hare, oftenest the
latter. Isabel said, that on one occasion, when she was in this dis-
guise, she was sore pressed by a pack of hounds, and had a very narrow escape with her life. She reached her own door at last, feeling
the hot breath of the pursuing dogs at her haunches. She managed,
however, to hide herself behind a chest, and got time to pronounce
the magic words that could alone restore her to her proper shape.
They were :

> " Hare ! hare !
> God send thee care !
>   I am in a hare's likeness now ;
>   But I shall be a woman e'en now !
> Hare ! hare !
> God send thee care !"

If witches, when in this shape, were bitten by the dogs, they always
retained the marks in their human form ; but she had never heard
that any witch had been bitten to death. When the devil appointed
any general meeting of the witches, the custom was that they should
proceed through the air mounted on broomsticks, or on corn or bean-
straws, pronouncing as they went :

> " Horse and pattock, horse and go,
> Horse and pellats, ho ! ho ! ho !"

They generally left behind them a broom or a three-legged stool,
which, when placed in their beds and duly charmed, assumed the
human shape till their return. This was done that the neighbours
might not know when they were absent.

She added that the devil furnished his favourite witches with servant imps to attend upon them. These imps were called, " The

Roaring Lion," "Thief of Hell," "Wait-upon-Herself," "Ranting Roarer," "Care-for-Naught," &c., and were known by their liveries, which were generally yellow, sad-dun, sea-green, pea-green, or grass-green. Satan never called the witches by the names they had received at baptism; neither were they allowed, in his presence, so to designate each other. Such a breach of the infernal etiquette assuredly drew down his most severe displeasure. But as some designation was necessary, he re-baptised them in their own blood by the names of "Able-and-Stout," "Over-the-dike-with-it," "Raise-the-wind," "Pickle-nearest-the-wind," "Batter-them-down-Maggy," "Blow-Kale," and such like. The devil himself was not very particular what name they called him, so that it was not "Black John." If any witch was unthinking enough to utter these words, he would rush out upon her and beat and buffet her unmercifully, or tear her flesh with a wool-card. Other names he did not care about; and once gave instructions to a noted warlock that whenever he wanted his aid, he was to strike the ground three times and exclaim, "Rise up, foul thief!"

Upon this confession many persons were executed. So strong was the popular feeling, that no one once accused of witchcraft was acquitted; at least, acquittals did not average one in a hundred trials. Witch-finding, or witch-pricking, became a trade, and a set of mercenary vagabonds roamed about the country provided with long pins to run into the flesh of supposed criminals. It was no unusual thing then, nor is it now, that in aged persons there should be some spot on the body totally devoid of feeling. It was the object of the witch-pricker to discover this spot, and the unhappy wight who did not bleed when pricked upon it was doomed to the death. If not immediately cast into prison, her life was rendered miserable by the persecution of her neighbours. It is recorded of many poor women, that the annoyances they endured in this way were so excessive, that they preferred death. Sir George Mackenzie, the Lord Advocate, at the time when witch trials were so frequent, and himself a devout believer in the crime, relates, in his *Criminal Law*, first published in 1678, some remarkable instances of it. He says, "I went, when I was a justice-depute, to examine some women who had confessed judicially; and one of them, who was a silly creature, told me, under secrecy, that she had not confessed because she was guilty, but being a poor creature, who wrought for her meat, and being defamed for a witch, she knew she should starve, for no person thereafter would either give her meat or lodging, and that all men would beat her and set dogs at her, and that, therefore, she desired to be out of the world; whereupon she wept most bitterly, and upon her knees called God to witness to what she said." Sir George, though not wholly elevated above the prejudices of his age upon this subject, was clear-sighted enough to see the danger to society of the undue encouragement given to the

SIR G. MACKENSIE.

witch prosecutions. He was convinced that three-fourths of them were unjust and unfounded. He says in the work already quoted, that the persons who were in general accused of this crime were poor ignorant men and women who did not understand the nature of the accusation, and who mistook their own superstitious fears for witchcraft. One poor wretch, a weaver, confessed that he was a warlock, and, being asked why, he replied, because "he had seen the devil dancing, like a fly, about the candle!" A simple woman, who, because she was called a witch, believed that she was, asked the judge upon the bench whether a person might be a witch and not know it? Sir George adds, that all the supposed criminals were subjected to severe torture in prison from their gaolers, who thought they did God good service by vexing and tormenting them; "and I know," says this humane and enlightened magistrate, "that this usage was the ground of all their confession; and albeit, the poor miscreants cannot prove this usage, the actors in it being the only witnesses; yet the judge should be jealous of it, as that which did at first elicit the confession, and for fear of which they dare not retract it." Another author,* also a firm believer in witchcraft, gives a still more lamentable instance of a woman who preferred execution as a witch to live on under the imputation. This woman, who knew that three others were to be strangled and burned on an early day, sent for the minister of the parish, and confessed that she had sold her soul to Satan. "Whereupon being called before the judges, she was condemned to die with the rest. Being carried forth to the place of execution, she remained silent during the first, second, and third prayer, and then, perceiving that there remained no more but to rise and go to the stake, she lifted up her body, and, with a loud voice, cried out, ' Now all you that see me this day, know that I am now to die as a witch, by

* *Satan's Invisible World Discovered*, by the Rev. G. Sinclair.

my own confession; and I free all men, especially the ministers and magistrates, of the guilt of my blood. I take it wholly upon myself. My blood be upon my own head. And, as I must make answer to the God of heaven presently, I declare I am as free of witchcraft as any child. But, being delated by a malicious woman, and put in prison under the name of a witch, disowned by my husband and friends, and seeing no ground of hope of ever coming out again, I made up that confession to destroy my own life, being weary of it, and choosing rather to die than to live.'" As a proof of the singular obstinacy and blindness of the believers in witches, it may be stated that the minister who relates this story only saw in the dying speech of the unhappy woman an additional proof that she was a witch. True, indeed, is it, that "none are so blind as those who will not see."

It is time, however, to return to James VI., who is fairly entitled to share with Pope Innocent, Sprenger, Bodinus, and Matthew Hopkins the glory or the odium of being at the same time a chief enemy and chief encourager of witchcraft. Towards the close of the sixteenth century, many learned men, both on the continent and in the isles of Britain, had endeavoured to disabuse the public mind on this subject. The most celebrated were Wierus, in Germany; Pietro d'Apone, in Italy; and Reginald Scot, in England. Their works excited the attention of the zealous James, who, mindful of the involuntary compliment which his merits had extorted from the devil, was ambitious to deserve it by still continuing " his greatest enemie." In the year 1597, he published in Edinburgh his famous treatise on Demonology. Its design may be gathered from the following passage in the introduction : " The fearful abounding," says the king, " at this time and in this country of these detestable slaves of the devil, the witches or enchanters, hath moved me, beloved reader, to despatch in post this following treatise of mine, not in any wise, as I protest, to serve for a show of mine own learning and in- gene [ingenuity], but only (moved of conscience) to press thereby, so far as I can, to resolve the doubting hearts of many, both that such assaults of Satan are most certainly practised, and that the instrument thereof merits most severely to be punished, against the damnable opinions of two, principally in our age; whereof the one called Scot, an Englishman, is not ashamed in public print to deny that there can be such thing as witchcraft, and so maintains the old error of the Sadducees in denying of spirits. The other, called Wierus, a German physician, sets out a public apology for all these crafts-folks, whereby procuring for them impunity, he plainly betrays himself to have been one of that profession." In other parts of this treatise, which the author had put into the form of a dialogue, to " make it more pleasant and facile," he says : " Witches ought to be put to death, according to the law of God, the civil and imperial law, and the municipal law of all Christian

PIETRO D'APONE.

nations: yea, to spare the life, and not strike whom God bids strike, and so severely punish in so odious a treason against God, is not only unlawful, but doubtless as great a sin in the magistrate as was Saul's sparing Agag." He says also that the crime is so abominable, that it may be proved by evidence which would not be received against any other offenders,—young children, who knew not the nature of an oath, and persons of an infamous character, being sufficient witnesses against them; but lest the innocent should be accused of a crime so difficult to be acquitted of, he recommends that in all cases the ordeal should be resorted to. He says, " Two good helps may be used : the one is the finding of their mark, and the trying the insensibleness thereof; the other is their floating on the water, — for, as in a secret murther, if the dead carcass be at any time thereafter handled by the murtherer, it will gush out of blood, as if the blood were crying to Heaven for revenge of the murtherer (God having appointed that secret supernatural sign for trial of that secret unnatural crime), so that it appears that God hath appointed (for a supernatural sign of the monstrous impiety of witches) that the water shall refuse to receive them in her bosom that have shaken off them the sacred water of baptism, and wilfully refused the benefit thereof;—no, not so much as their eyes are able to shed tears (threaten and torture them as you please), while first they repent (God not permitting them to dissemble their obstinacy in so horrible a crime); albeit, the womenkind especially, be able otherwise to shed tears at every light occasion when they will, yea, although it were dissembling like the crocodiles."

When such doctrines as these were openly promulgated by the highest authority in the realm, and who, in promulgating them, flattered, but did not force the public opinion, it is not surprising that the sad delusion should have increased and multiplied until the race of wizards and witches replenished the earth.   The reputation which he lost by being afraid of a naked sword, he more than regained by his courage in combating the devil.   The Kirk shewed itself a most zealous coadjutor, especially during those halcyon days when it was not at issue with the king upon other matters of doctrine and prerogative.

On his accession to the throne of England in 1603, James came amongst a people who had heard with admiration of his glorious deeds against the witches.   He himself left no part of his ancient prejudices behind him ; and his advent was the signal for the persecution to burst forth in England with a fury equal to that in Scotland.   It had languished a little during the latter years of the reign of Elizabeth ; but the very first parliament of King James brought forward the subject.   James was flattered by their promptitude, and the act passed in 1604.   On the second reading in the House of Lords, the bill passed into a committee, in which were twelve bishops.   By it was enacted, " That if any person shall use, practise, or exercise any conjuration of any wicked or evil spirit, or shall consult, covenant with, or feed any such spirit, the first offence to be imprisonment for a year, and standing in the pillory once a quarter; the second offence to be death."

The minor punishment seems but rarely to have been inflicted. Every record that has been preserved mentions that the witches were hanged and burned, or burned, without the previous strangling, " alive and quick."   During the whole of James's reign, amid the civil wars of his successor, the sway of the Long Parliament, the usurpation of Cromwell, and the reign of Charles II., there was no abatement of the persecution.   If at any time it raged with less virulence, it was when Cromwell and the Independents were masters.   Dr. Zachary Grey, the editor of an edition of " Hudibras," informs us, in a note to that work, that he himself perused a list of three thousand witches who were executed in the time of the Long Parliament alone. During the first eighty years of the seventeenth century, the number executed has been estimated at five hundred annually, making the frightful total of forty thousand.   Some of these cases deserve to be cited.   The great majority resemble closely those already mentioned ; but two or three of them let in a new light upon the popular superstition.

Every one has heard of the " Lancashire witches," a phrase now used to compliment the ladies of that county for their bewitching beauty; but it is not every one who has heard the story in which it originated. A villanous boy, named Robinson, was the chief actor in the tragedy. He confessed many years afterwards that he had been suborned by his father and other persons to give false evidence against the unhappy witches whom he brought to the stake. The time of this famous trial was about the year 1634. This boy Robinson, whose father was a wood-cutter, residing on the borders of Pendle Forest, in Lancashire, spread abroad many rumours against one Mother Dickenson, whom he accused of being a witch. These rumours coming to the ears of the local magistracy, the boy was sent for and strictly examined. He told the following extraordinary story without hesitation or prevarication, and apparently in so open and honest a manner, that no one who heard him doubted the truth of it. He said, that as he was roaming about in one of the glades of the forest, amusing himself by gathering blackberries, he saw two greyhounds before him, which he thought at the time belonged to some gentleman of the neighbourhood. Being fond of sport, he proposed to have a course; and a hare being started, he incited the hounds to run. Neither of them would stir. Angry at the beasts, he seized hold of a switch, with which he was about to punish them, when one of them suddenly started up in the form of a woman, and the other of a little boy. He at once recognised the woman to be the witch Mother Dickenson. She offered him some money to induce him to sell his soul to the devil; but he refused. Upon this she took a bridle out of her pocket, and shaking it over the head of the other little boy, he was instantly turned into a horse. Mother Dickenson then seized him in her arms, sprang upon the horse, and placing him before her, rode with the swiftness of the wind over forests, fields, bogs, and rivers, until they came to a large barn. The witch alighted at the door, and, taking him by the hand, led him inside. There he saw seven old women pulling at seven halters which hung from the roof. As they pulled, large pieces of meat, lumps of butter, loaves of bread, basins of milk, hot puddings, black-puddings, and other rural dainties, fell from the halters on to the floor. While engaged in this charm, they made such ugly faces, and looked so fiendish, that he was quite frightened. After they had pulled in this manner enough for an ample feast, they set-to, and shewed, whatever might be said of the way in which their supper was procured, that their epicurism was a little more refined than that of the Scottish witches, who, according to Gellie Duncan's confession, feasted upon dead men's flesh in the old kirk of Berwick. The boy added, that as soon as supper was ready, many other witches came to partake of it, several of whom he named.

In consequence of this story, many persons were arrested, and the boy Robinson was led about from church to church, in order that he might point out to the officers by whom he was accompanied the hags he had seen in the barn. Altogether, about twenty persons were thrown into prison; eight of them were condemned to die, including Mother Dickenson, upon this evidence alone, and executed accordingly. Among the wretches who concocted this notable story, not one was ever brought to justice for his perjury; and Robinson, the father, gained considerable sums by threatening persons who were rich enough to buy off exposure.

Among the ill-weeds which flourished amid the long dissensions of the civil war, Matthew Hopkins, the witch-finder, stands eminent in his sphere. This vulgar fellow resided, in the 'year 1644, at the town of Manningtree, in Essex, and made himself very conspicuous in discovering the devil's marks upon several unhappy witches. The credit he gained by his skill in this instance seems to have inspired him to renewed exertions. In the course of a very short time, whenever a witch was spoken of in Essex, Matthew Hopkins was sure to be present, aiding the judges with his knowledge of "such cattle," as he called them. As his reputation increased, he assumed the title of "Witch-finder General," and travelled through the counties of Norfolk, Essex, Huntingdon, and Sussex, for the sole purpose of finding out witches. In one year he brought sixty poor creatures to the stake. The test he commonly adopted was that of swimming, so highly recommended by King James in his *Demonologie*. The hands and feet of the suspected persons were tied together crosswise, the thumb of the right hand to the toe of the left foot, and *vice versa*. They were then wrapped up in a large sheet or blanket, and laid upon their backs in a pond or river. If they sank, their friends and relatives had the poor consolation of knowing they were innocent; but there was an end of them: if they floated, which, when laid carefully on the water, was generally the case, there was also an end of them; for they were deemed guilty of witchcraft, and burned accordingly.

Another test was to make them repeat the Lord's prayer and creed. It was affirmed that no witch could do so correctly. If she missed a word, or even pronounced one incoherently, which in her trepidation it was most probable she would, she was accounted guilty. It was thought that witches could not weep more than three tears, and those only from the left eye. Thus the conscious innocence of many persons, which gave them fortitude to bear unmerited torture without flinching, was construed by their unmerciful tormentors into proofs of guilt. In some districts the test resorted to was to weigh the culprit against the church Bible. If the suspected witch proved heavier than the Bible, she was set at liberty. This mode was far too humane for the witch-finders by profession. Hopkins always maintained that the most legitimate modes were pricking and swimming.

Hopkins used to travel through his counties like a man of consideration, attended by his two assistants, always putting up at the chief inn of the place, and always at the cost of the authorities. His charges were twenty shillings a town, his expenses of living while there, and his carriage thither and back. This he claimed whether he found witches or not. If he found any, he claimed twenty shillings a head in addition when they were brought to execution. For about three years he carried on this infamous trade, success making him so insolent and rapacious that high and low became his enemies. The Rev. Mr. Gaul, a clergyman of Houghton, in Huntingdonshire, wrote a pamphlet impugning his pretensions, and accusing him of being a common nuisance. Hopkins replied in an angry letter to the functionaries of Houghton, stating his intention to visit their town; but desiring to know whether it afforded many such sticklers for witchcraft as Mr. Gaul, and whether they were willing to receive and entertain him with the customary hospitality, if he so far honoured them. He added, by way of threat, that in case he did not receive a satisfactory reply, "he would waive their shire altogether, and betake himself to such places where he might do and punish, not only without control, but with thanks and recompense." The authorities of Houghton were not much alarmed at this awful threat of letting them alone. They very wisely took no notice either of him or his letter.

Mr. Gaul describes in his pamphlet one of the modes employed by Hopkins, which was sure to swell his revenues very considerably. It was a proof even more atrocious than the swimming. He says, that the "Witch-finder General" used to take the suspected witch and place her in the middle of a room, upon a stool or table, cross-legged, or in some other uneasy posture. If she refused to sit in this manner, she was bound with strong cords. Hopkins then placed persons to watch her for four-and-twenty hours, during which time she was to be kept without meat or drink. It was supposed that one of her imps would come during that interval and suck her blood. As the imp might come in the shape of a wasp, a moth, a fly, or other insect, a hole was made in the door or window to let it enter. The watchers were ordered to keep a sharp look out, and endeavour to kill any insect that appeared in the room. If any fly escaped, and they could not kill it, the woman was guilty; the fly was her imp, and she was sentenced to be burned, and twenty shillings went into the pockets of Master Hopkins. In this manner he made one old

MATTHEW HOPKINS.*

woman confess, because four flies had appeared in the room, that she was attended by four imps, named "Ilemazar," "Pye-wackett," "Peck-in-the-crown," and "Grizel-Greedigut."

* This illustration, representing Matthew Hopkins examining two witches who are confessing to him the names of their imps and familiars, is copied from Caulfield's *Memoirs of Remarkable Persons*, 1794, where it is taken from an extremely rare print.

It is consoling to think that this impostor perished in his own snare. Mr. Gaul's exposure and his own rapacity weakened his influence among the magistrates; and the populace, who began to find that not even the most virtuous and innocent were secure from his persecution, looked upon him with undisguised aversion. He was beset by a mob at a village in Suffolk, and accused of being himself a wizard. An old reproach was brought against him, that he had, by means of sorcery, cheated the devil out of a certain memorandum-book, in which he, Satan, had entered the names of all the witches in England. "Thus," said the populace, "you find out witches, not by God's aid, but by the devil's." In vain he denied his guilt. The populace longed to put him to his own test. He was speedily stripped, and his thumbs and toes tied together. He was then placed in a blanket, and cast into a pond. Some say that he floated, and that he was taken out, tried, and executed upon no other proof of his guilt. Others assert that he was drowned. This much is positive, that there was an end of him. As no judicial entry of his trial and execution is to be found in any register, it appears most probable that he expired by the hands of the mob. Butler has immortalised this scamp in the following lines of his *Hudibras* :

> " Hath not this present Parliament
> A lieger to the devil sent,
> Fully empower'd to treat about
> Finding revolted witches out ?
> And has he not within a year
> Hang'd threescore of them in one shire ?
> Some only for not being drown'd,
> And some for sitting above ground
> Whole days and nights upon their breeches,
> And feeling pain, were hang'd for witches ;
> And some for putting knavish tricks
> Upon green geese or turkey chicks ;
> Or pigs that suddenly deceased
> Of griefs unnatural, as he guess'd ;
> Who proved himself at length a witch,
> And made a rod for his own breech."

In Scotland also witch-finding became a trade. They were known under the designation of "common prickers," and, like Hopkins, received a fee for each witch they discovered. At the trial of Janet Peaston, in 1646, the magistrates of Dalkeith "caused John Kincaid of Tranent, the common pricker, to exercise his craft upon her. He found two marks of the devil's making; for she could not feel the pin when it was put into either of the said marks, nor did the marks bleed when the pin was taken out again. When she was asked where she thought the pins were put in her, she pointed to a part of her body distant from the real place. They were pins of three inches in length."*

These common prickers became at last so numerous that they were considered nuisances. The judges refused to take their evidence; and in 1678 the privy council of Scotland condescended to hear the complaint of an honest woman who had been indecently exposed by one of them, and expressed their opinion that common prickers were common cheats.

But such an opinion was not formed in high places before hundreds of innocent persons had fallen victims. The parliaments had encouraged the delusion both in England and Scotland; and by arming these fellows with a sort of authority, had in a manner forced the magistrates and ministers to receive their evidence. The fate of one poor old gentleman, who fell a victim to the arts of Hopkins in 1646, deserves to be recorded. Mr. Louis, a venerable clergyman, upwards of seventy years of age, and who had been rector of Framlingham, in Suffolk, for fifty years, excited suspicion that he was a wizard. Being a violent royalist, he was likely to meet with no sympathy at that time; and even his own parishioners, whom he had served so long and so faithfully, turned their backs upon him as soon as he was accused. Placed under the hands of Hopkins, who knew so well how to bring the refractory to confession, the old man, the light of whose intellect had become somewhat dimmed from age, confessed that he was a wizard. He said he had two imps that continually excited him to do evil; and that one day, when he was walking on the sea-coast, one of them prompted him to express a wish that a ship, whose sails were just visible in the distance, might sink. He consented, and saw the vessel sink before his eyes. He was, upon this confession, tried and condemned. On his trial, the flame of reason burned up as brightly as ever. He denied all that had been alleged against him, and cross-examined Hopkins with great tact and severity. After his condemnation, he begged that the funeral service of the Church might be read for him. The request was refused, and he repeated it for himself from memory as he was led to the scaffold.

A poor woman in Scotland was executed upon evidence even less strong than this. John Bain, a common pricker, swore that, as he passed her door, he heard her talking to the devil. She said, in defence, that it was a foolish practice she had of talking to herself, and several of her neighbours corroborated her statement; but the evidence of the pricker was received. He swore that none ever talked

* Pitcairn's *Records of Justiciary*.

to themselves who were not witches. The devil's mark being found upon her, the additional testimony of her guilt was deemed conclusive, and she was "convict and brynt."

From the year 1652 to 1682, these trials diminished annually in number, and acquittals were by no means so rare as they had been. To doubt in witchcraft was no longer dangerous. Before country justices, condemnations on the most absurd evidence still continued ; but when the judges of the land had to charge the jury, they took a more humane and philosophical view. By degrees, the educated classes (comprised in those days within very narrow limits) openly expressed their unbelief of modern witchcraft, although they were not bold enough to deny its existence altogether. Between them and the believers in the old doctrine fierce arguments ensued, and the sceptics were designated Sadducees. To convince them, the learned and Reverend Joseph Glanvil wrote his well-known work, *Sadducismus Triumphatus*, and *The Collection of Relations ;* the first part intended as a philosophical inquiry into witchcraft, and the power of the devil " to assume a mortal shape :" the latter containing what he considered a multitude of well-authenticated modern instances.

SIR MATTHEW HALE.

But though progress was made, it was slow. In 1664, the venerable Sir Matthew Hale condemned two women, named Amy Duny and Rose Cullender, to the stake at St. Edmondsbury, upon evidence the most ridiculous. These two old women, whose ugliness gave their neighbours the first idea that they were witches, went to a shop to purchase herrings, and were refused. Indignant at the prejudice against them, they were not sparing of their abuse. Shortly afterward, the daughter of the herring-dealer fell sick, and a cry was raised that she was bewitched by the old women who had been refused the herrings. This girl was subject to epileptic fits. To discover the guilt of Amy Duny and Rose Cullender, the girl's eyes were blinded closely with a shawl, and the witches were commanded to touch her. They did so, and she was immediately seized with a fit. Upon this evidence they were sent to prison. The girl was afterwards touched by an indifferent person, and the force of her imagination was so great, that, thinking it was again the witches, she fell down in a violent fit as before. This, however, was not received in favour of the accused.

The following extract, from the published reports of the trial, will shew the sort of evidence which was received :

"Samuel Pacey, of Leystoff (a good, sober man), being sworn, said that, on Thursday the 10th of October last, his younger daughter, Deborah, about nine years old, was suddenly taken so lame that she could not stand on her legs, and so continued till the 17th of the same month, when the child desired to be carried to a bank on the east side of the house, looking towards the sea; and, while she was sitting there, Amy Duny came to this examinant's house to buy some herrings, but was denied. Then she came twice more, but, being as often denied, she went away discontented and grumbling. At this instant of time, the child was taken with terrible fits, complaining of a pain in her stomach, as if she was pricked with pins, shrieking out with a voice like a whelp, and thus continued till the 30th of the same month. This examinant further saith, that Amy Duny, having long had the reputation of a witch, and his child having, in the intervals of her fits, constantly cried out on her as the cause of her disorder, saying, that the said Amy did appear to her and fright her; he himself did suspect the said Amy to be a witch, and charged her with being the cause of his child's illness, and set her in the stocks. Two days after, his daughter Elizabeth was taken with such strange fits, that they could not force open her mouth without a tap; and the younger child being in the same condition, they used to her the same remedy. Both children grievously complained that Amy Duny and another woman, whose habit and looks they described, did appear to them and torment them, and would cry out, 'There stands Amy Duny ! There stands Rose Cullender !' the other person who afflicted them. Their fits were not alike. Sometimes they were lame on the right side; sometimes on the left; and sometimes so sore, that they could not bear to be touched. Sometimes they were perfectly well in other respects, but they could not *hear ;* at other times they could not *see.* Sometimes they lost their speech for one, two, and once for eight days together. At times they had swooning fits, and, when they could speak, were taken with a fit of coughing, and vomited phlegm and crooked pins; and once a great twopenny nail, with above forty pins; which nail he, the examinant, saw vomited up, with many of the pins. The nail and pins were produced in the court. Thus the children continued for two months, during which time the examinant often made them read in the New Testament, and observed, when they came to the words *Lord Jesus,* or *Christ,* they could not pronounce them, but fell into a fit. When they came to the word *Satan,* or *devil,* they would point, and say, 'This bites, but makes me speak right well.' Finding his children thus tormented without hopes of recovery, he sent them to his sister, Margaret Arnold, at Yarmouth, being willing to try whether change of air would help them.

"Margaret Arnold was the next witness. Being sworn, she said, that about the 30th of November, Elizabeth and Deborah Pacey came to her house with her brother, who told her what had happened, and that he thought his children bewitched. She, this examinant, did not much regard it, supposing the children had played tricks, and put the pins into their mouths themselves. She therefore took all the pins from their clothes, sewing them with thread instead of pinning them. But, notwithstanding, they raised, at times, at least thirty pins in her presence, and had terrible fits; in which fits they would cry out upon Amy Duny and Rose Cullender, saying, that they saw them and heard them threatening, as before; that they saw things like mice running about the house; and one of them catched one, and threw it into the fire, which made a noise like a rat. Another time the younger child, being out of doors, a thing like a bee would have forced itself into her mouth, at which the child ran screaming into the house, and before this examinant could come at her, fell into a fit, and vomited a twopenny nail, with a broad head. After that, this examinant asked the child how she came by this nail, when she answered, 'The bee brought the nail, and forced it into my mouth.' At other times the eldest child told this examinant that she saw flies bring her crooked pins. She would then fall into a fit, and vomit such pins. One time the said child said she saw a mouse, and crept under the table to look for it; and afterwards, the child seemed to put something into her apron, saying, 'She had caught it.' She then ran to the fire, and threw it in, on which there did appear to this examinant something like a flash of gunpowder, although she does own she saw nothing in the child's hand. Once the child, being speechless, but otherwise very sensible, ran up and down the house crying, 'Hush! hush!' as if she had seen poultry; but this examinant saw nothing. At last the child catched at something, and threw it into the fire. Afterwards, when the child could speak, this examinant asked her what she saw at the time? She answered that she saw a duck. Another time the youngest child said, after a fit, that Amy Duny had been with her, and tempted her to drown herself, or cut her throat, or otherwise destroy herself. Another time they both cried out upon Amy Duny and Rose Cullender, saying, 'Why don't you come yourselves? Why do you send your imps to torment us?' "

The celebrated Sir Thomas Brown, the author of *Vulgar Errors,* was also examined as a witness upon the trial. Being desired to give his opinion of the three persons in court, he said he was clearly of opinion that they were bewitched. He said there had lately been a discovery of witches in Denmark, who used the same way of tormenting persons, by conveying crooked pins, needles, and nails into their bodies. That he thought, in such cases, the devil acted upon human bodies by natural means, namely, by exciting and stirring up the

SIR THOMAS BROWN

superabundant humours; he did afflict them in a more surprising manner by the same diseases their bodies were usually subject to; that these fits might be natural, only raised to a great degree by the subtlety of the devil, co-operating with the malice of these witches.

The evidence being concluded, Sir Matthew Hale addressed the jury. He said, he would waive repeating the evidence, to prevent any mistake, and told the jury there were two things they had to inquire into. First, Whether or not these children were bewitched; secondly, Whether these women did bewitch them. He said, he did not in the least doubt there were witches; first, Because the Scriptures affirmed it; secondly, Because the wisdom of all nations, particularly our own, had provided laws against witchcraft, which implied their belief of such a crime. He desired them strictly to observe the evidence, and begged of God to direct their hearts in the weighty concern they had in hand, since, to condemn the innocent and let the guilty go free are both an abomination to the Lord.

The jury then retired, and in about half an hour returned a verdict of guilty upon all the indictments, being thirteen in number. The next morning the children came with their father to the lodgings of Sir Matthew Hale, very well, and quite restored to their usual health. Mr. Pacey, being asked at what time their health began to improve, replied, that they were quite well in half an hour after the conviction of the prisoners.

Many attempts were made to induce the unfortunate women to confess their guilt; but in vain, and they were both hanged.

Eleven trials were instituted before Chief Justice Holt for witch-craft, between the years 1694 and 1701. The evidence was of the usual character ; but Holt appealed so successfully in each case to the common sense of the jury, that they were every one acquitted. A general feeling seemed to pervade the country that blood enough had been shed upon these absurd charges. Now and then the flame of persecution burnt up in a remote district ; but these instances were no longer looked upon as mere matters of course. They appear, on the contrary, to have excited much attention ; a sure proof, if no other were to be obtained, that they were becoming unfrequent.

A case of witchcraft was tried in 1711, before Lord Chief Justice Powell ; in which, however, the jury persisted in a verdict of guilty, though the evidence was of the usual absurd and contradictory cha-racter, and the enlightened judge did all in his power to bring them to a right conclusion. The accused person was one Jane Wenham, better known as the Witch of Walkerne ; and the persons who were alleged to have suffered from her witchcraft were two young women, named Thorne and Street. A witness, named Mr. Arthur Chauncy, deposed that he had seen Ann Thorne in several of her fits, and that she always recovered upon prayers being said, or if Jane Wenham came to her. He related, that he had pricked the prisoner several times in the arms, but could never fetch any blood from her; that he had seen her vomit pins, when there were none in her clothes or within her reach ; and that he had preserved several of them, whic he was ready to produce. The judge, however, told him that was needless, *as he supposed they were crooked pins.*

Mr. Francis Bragge, another witness, deposed, that strange " cakes" of bewitched feathers having been taken from Ann Thorne's pillow, he was anxious to see them. He went into a room where some of these feathers were, and took two of the cakes, and compared them together. They were both of a circular figure, something larger than a crown piece ; and he observed that the small feathers were placed in a nice and curious order, at equal distances from each other, making so many radii of the circle, in the centre of which the quill-ends of the feathers met. He counted the number of these feathers, and found them to be exactly thirty-two in each cake. He afterwards endeavoured to pull off two or three of them, and observed that they were all fastened together by a sort of viscous matter, which would stretch seven or eight times in a thread before it broke. Having taken off several of these feathers, he removed the viscous matter with his fingers, and found under it, in the centre, some short hairs, black and grey, matted together, which he verily believed to be cat's hair. He also said, that Jane Wenham confessed to him that she had bewitched the pillow, and had practised witchcraft for sixteen years.

The judge interrupted the witness at this stage, and said, he should very much like to see an enchanted feather, and seemed to wonder when he was told that none of these strange cakes had been preserved. His lordship asked the witness why he did not keep one or two of them, and was informed that they had all been burnt, in order to relieve the bewitched person of the pains she suffered, which could not be so well effected by any other means.

A man, named Thomas Ireland, deposed, that hearing several times a great noise of cats crying and screaming about his house, he went out and frightened them away, and they all ran towards the cottage of Jane Wenham. One of them he swore positively had a face very like Jane Wenham's. Another man, named Burville, gave similar evidence, and swore that he had often seen a cat with Jane Wenham's face. Upon one occasion he was in Ann Thorne's chamber, when several cats came in, and among them the cat above stated. This witness would have favoured the court with a much longer statement, but was stopped by the judge, who said he had heard quite enough.

The prisoner, in her defence, said nothing, but that " she was a clear woman." The learned judge then summed up, leaving it to the jury to determine whether such evidence as they had heard was sufficient to take away the prisoner's life upon the indictment. After a long deliberation they brought in their verdict, that she was guilty upon the evidence. The judge then asked them whether they found her guilty upon the indictment of conversing with the devil in the shape of a cat? The sapient foreman very gravely answered, " We find her guilty of *that*." The learned judge then very reluctantly proceeded to pass sentence of death ; but, by his persevering exertions, a pardon was at last obtained, and the wretched old woman was set at liberty.

In the year 1716, a woman and her daughter—the latter only nine years of age—were hanged at Huntingdon for selling their souls to the devil, and raising a storm by pulling off their stockings and making a lather of soap. This appears to have been the last judicial execution in England. From that time to the year 1736, the populace raised at intervals the old cry, and more than once endangered the lives of poor women by dragging them through ponds on suspicion; but the philosophy of those who, from their position, sooner or later give the tone to the opinions and morals of the poor, was silently working a cure for the evil. The fear of witches ceased to be epidemic, and became individual, lingering only in minds fettered by inveterate prejudice or brutalising superstition. In the year 1736, the penal statute of James I. was finally blotted from the statute-book, and suffered no longer to disgrace the advancing intelligence of the country. Pretenders to witchcraft, fortune-tellers, conjurors, and all their train, were liable only to the common punishment of rogues and impostors—imprisonment and the pillory.

In Scotland, the delusion also assumed the same phases, and was gradually extinguished in the light of civilisation. As in England, the progress of improvement was slow. Up to the year 1665, little or no diminution of the mania was perceptible. In 1643, the General Assembly recommended that the privy council should institute a standing commission, composed of any " understanding gentlemen or magistrates," to try the witches, who were stated to have increased enormously of late years. In 1649, an act was passed, confirmatory of the original statute of Queen Mary, explaining some points of the latter which were doubtful, and enacting severe penalties, not only against witches themselves, but against all who covenanted with them, or sought by their means to pry into the secrets of futurity, or cause any evil to the life, lands, or limbs of their neighbours. For the next ten years, the popular madness upon this subject was perhaps more furious than ever; upwards of four thousand persons suffered for the crime during that interval. This was the consequence of the act of parliament and the unparalleled severity of the magistrates; the latter frequently complained that for two witches they burned one day, there were ten to burn the next: they never thought that they themselves were the cause of the increase. In a single circuit, held at Glasgow, Ayr, and Stirling, in 1659, seventeen unhappy creatures were burned by judicial sentence for trafficking with Satan. In one day (November 7, 1661), the privy council issued no less than fourteen commissions for trials in the provinces. Next year, the violence of the persecution seems to have abated. From 1662 to 1668, although "the understanding gentlemen and magistrates" already mentioned continued to try and condemn, the High Court of Justiciary had but one offender of this class to deal with, and she was acquitted. James Welsh, a common pricker, was ordered to be publicly whipped through the streets of Edinburgh for falsely accusing a woman of witchcraft; a fact which alone proves that the superior court sifted the evidence in these cases with much more care and severity than it had done a few years previously. The enlightened Sir George Mackenzie, styled by Dryden "the noble wit of Scotland," laboured hard to introduce this rule into court, that the confessions of the witches should be held of little worth, and that the evidence of the prickers and other interested persons should be received with distrust and jealousy. This was reversing the old practice, and saved many innocent lives. Though a firm believer both in ancient and modern witchcraft, he could not shut his eyes to the atrocities daily committed under the name of justice. In his work on the Criminal Law of Scotland, published in 1678, he says, "From the horridness of this crime, I do conclude that, of all others, it requires the clearest relevancy and most convincing probature; and I condemn, next to the witches themselves, those cruel and too forward judges who burn persons by thousands as guilty of this crime." In the same year, Sir John Clerk plumply refused to serve as a commissioner on trials for witchcraft, alleging, by way of excuse, "that he was not himself good conjuror enough to be duly qualified." The views entertained by Sir George Mackenzie were so favourably received by the Lords of Session, that he was deputed, in 1680, to report to them on the cases of a number of poor women who were then in prison awaiting their trial. Sir George stated that there was no evidence against them whatever but their own confessions, which were absurd and contradictory, and drawn from them by severe torture. They were immediately discharged.

For the next sixteen years the Lords of Session were unoccupied with trials for witchcraft. Not one is entered upon the record. But in 1697 a case occurred which equalled in absurdity any of those that signalised the dark reign of King James. A girl named Christiana Shaw, eleven years of age, the daughter of John Shaw of Bargarran, was subject to fits; and being of a spiteful temper, she accused her maid-servant, with whom she had frequent quarrels, of bewitching her. Her story unfortunately was believed. Encouraged to tell all the persecutions of the devil which the maid had sent to torment her, she in the end concocted a romance that involved twenty-one persons. There was no other evidence against them but the fancies of this lying child, and the confessions which pain had extorted from them; but upon this no less than five women were condemned before Lord Blantyre and the rest of the commissioners, appointed specially by the privy council to try this case. They were burned on the Green at Paisley. The warlock of the party, one John Reed, who was also condemned, hanged himself in prison. It was the general belief in Paisley that the devil had strangled him lest he should have revealed in his last moments too many of the unholy secrets of witchcraft. This trial excited considerable disgust in Scotland. The Rev. Mr. Bell, a contemporary writer, observed that, in this business, "persons of more goodness and esteem than most of their calumniators were defamed for witches." He adds, that the persons chiefly to blame were "certain ministers of too much forwardness and absurd credulity, and some topping professors in and about Glasgow'."*

After this trial, there again occurs a lapse of seven years, when the subject was painfully forced upon public attention by the brutal cruelty of the mob at Pittenween. Two women were accused of having bewitched a strolling beggar who was subject to fits, or who pretended to be so, for the purpose of exciting commiseration. They were cast into prison, and tortured until they confessed. One of them, named Janet Cornfoot, contrived to escape, but was brought back to Pittenween next day by a party of soldiers. On her approach to the town she was unfortunately met by a furious mob, composed principally of fishermen and their wives, who seized upon her with the intention of swimming her. They forced her away to the sea-shore, and tying a rope around her body, secured the end of it to the mast of a fishing-boat lying alongside. In this manner they ducked her several times. When she was half dead, a sailor in the boat cut away the rope, and the mob dragged her through the sea to the beach. Here, as she lay quite insensible, a brawny ruffian took down the door of his hut, close by, and placed it on her back. The mob gathered large stones from the beach and piled them upon her till the wretched woman was pressed to death. No magistrate made the slightest attempt to interfere; and the soldiers looked on, delighted spectators. A great outcry was raised against this culpable remissness, but no judicial inquiry was set on foot. This happened in 1704.

The next case we hear of is that of Elspeth Rule, found guilty of witchcraft before Lord Anstruther, at the Dumfries circuit, in 1708. She was sentenced to be marked in the cheek with a red-hot iron, and banished the realm of Scotland for life.

Again there is a long interval. In 1718, the remote county of Caithness, where the delusion remained in all its pristine vigour for years after it had ceased elsewhere, was startled from its propriety by the cry of witchcraft. A silly fellow, named William Montgomery, a carpenter, had a mortal antipathy to cats; and somehow or other these animals generally chose his back-yard as the scene of their cat-

* Preface to *Law's Memorials*, edited by Sharpe.

terwaulings. He puzzled his brains for a long time to know why he, above all his neighbours, should be so pestered. At last he came to the sage conclusion that his tormentors were no cats, but witches. In this opinion he was supported by his maid-servant, who swore a round oath that she had often heard the aforesaid cats talking together in human voices. The next time the unlucky tabbies assembled in his back-yard, the valiant carpenter was on the alert. Arming himself with an axe, a dirk, and a broadsword, he rushed out among them. One of them he wounded in the back, a second in the hip, and the leg of a third he maimed with his axe; but he could not capture any of them. A few days afterwards, two old women of the parish died; and it was said, that when their bodies were laid out, there appeared upon the back of one the mark as of a recent wound, and a similar scar upon the hip of the other. The carpenter and his maid were convinced that they were the very cats, and the whole county repeated the same story. Every one was upon the look-out for proofs corroborative; a very remarkable one was soon discovered. Nanny Gilbert, a wretched old creature of upwards of seventy years of age, was found in bed with her leg broken. As she was ugly enough for a witch, it was asserted that she also was one of the cats that had fared so ill at the hands of the carpenter. The latter, when informed of the popular suspicion, asserted that he distinctly remembered to have struck one of the cats a blow with the back of his broadsword, which ought to have broken her leg. Nanny was immediately dragged from her bed and thrown into prison. Before she was put to the torture, she explained in a very natural and intelligible manner how she had broken her limb; but this account did not give satisfaction. The professional persuasions of the torturer made her tell a different tale, and she confessed that she was indeed a witch, and had been wounded by Montgomery on the night stated; that the two old women recently deceased were witches also, besides about a score of others whom she named. The poor creature suffered so much by the removal from her own home, and the tortures inflicted upon her, that she died the next day in prison. Happily for the persons she had named in her confession, Dundas of Arniston, at that time the king's advocate-general, wrote to the sheriff-depute, one Captain Ross of Littledean, cautioning him not to proceed to trial, the "thing being of too great difficulty, and beyond the jurisdiction of an inferior court." Dundas himself examined the precognition with great care, and was so convinced of the utter folly of the whole case, that he quashed all further proceedings.

We find this same sheriff-depute of Caithness very active four years afterwards in another trial for witchcraft. In spite of the warning he had received that all such cases were to be tried in future by the superior courts, he condemned to death an old woman at Dornoch, upon the charge of bewitching the cows and pigs of her neighbours. This poor creature was insane, and actually laughed and clapped her hands at sight of "the bonnie fire" that was to consume her. She had a daughter who was lame both of her hands and feet, and one of the charges brought against her was, that she had used this daughter as a pony in her excursions to join the devil's sabbath, and that the devil himself had shod her, and produced lameness.

This was the last execution that took place in Scotland for witchcraft. The penal statutes were repealed in 1736; and, as in England, whipping, the pillory, or imprisonment, were declared the future punishments of all pretenders to magic or witchcraft.

Still for many years after this the superstition lingered both in England and Scotland, and in some districts is far from being extinct even at this day. But before we proceed to trace it any further than to its legal extinction, we have yet to see the frightful havoc it made in continental Europe from the commencement of the seventeenth to the middle of the eighteenth century. France, Germany, and Switzerland were the countries which suffered most from the epidemic. The number of victims in these countries during the sixteenth century has already been mentioned; but at the early part of the seventeenth, the numbers are so great, especially in Germany, that were they not to be found in the official records of the tribunals, it would be almost impossible to believe that mankind could ever have been so maddened and deluded. To use the words of the learned and indefatigable Horst,* " the world seemed to be like a large madhouse for witches and devils to play their antics in." Satan was believed to be at every body's call to raise the whirlwind, draw down the lightning, blight the productions of the earth, or destroy the health and paralyse the limbs of man. This belief, so insulting to the majesty and beneficence of the Creator, was shared by the most pious ministers of religion. Those who in their morning and evening prayers acknowledged the one true God, and praised him for the blessings of the seed-time and the harvest, were convinced that frail humanity could enter into a compact with the spirits of hell to subvert his laws and thwart all his merciful intentions. Successive popes, from Innocent VIII. downwards, promulgated this degrading doctrine, which spread so rapidly, that society seemed to be divided into two great factions, the bewitching and the bewitched.

The commissioners named by Innocent VIII. to prosecute the witch-trials in Germany were, Jacob Sprenger, so notorious for his

* _Zauberbibliothek_, Thiel 5.

work on demonology, entitled the *Malleus Malleficarum, or Hammer to knock down Witches;* Henry Institor, a learned jurisconsult; and the Bishop of Strasburgh. Bamberg, Trèves, Cologne, Paderborn, and Würzburg, were the chief seats of the commissioners, who, during their lives alone, condemned to the stake, on a very moderate calculation, upwards of three thousand victims. The number of witches so increased, that new commissioners were continually appointed in Germany, France, and Switzerland. In Spain and Portugal the Inquisition alone took cognisance of the crime. It is impossible to search the records of those dark, but now happily non-existing tribunals; but the mind recoils with affright even to form a guess of the multitudes who perished.

The mode of trial in the other countries is more easily ascertained. Sprenger in Germany, and Bodinus and Delrio in France, have left but too ample a record of the atrocities committed in the much-abused names of justice and religion. Bodinus, of great repute and authority in the seventeenth century, says, "The trial of this offence must not be conducted like other crimes. Whoever adheres to the ordinary course of justice perverts the spirit of the law, both divine and human. He who is accused of sorcery should never be acquitted, unless the malice of the prosecutor be clearer than the sun; for it is so difficult to bring full proof of this secret crime, that out of a million of witches not one would be convicted if the usual course were followed!" Henri Boguet, a witch-finder, who styled himself "The Grand Judge of Witches for the Territory of St. Claude," drew up a code for the guidance of all persons engaged in the witch-trials, consisting of seventy articles, quite as cruel as the code of Bodinus. In this document he affirms, that a mere suspicion of witchcraft justifies the immediate arrest and torture of the suspected person. If the prisoner muttered, looked on the ground, and did not shed any tears, all these were proofs positive of guilt! In all cases of witchcraft, the evidence of the child ought to be taken against its parent; and persons of notoriously bad character, although not to be believed upon their oaths on the ordinary occasions of dispute that might arise between man and man, were to be believed, if they swore that any person had bewitched them! Who, when he hears that this diabolical doctrine was the universally received opinion of the ecclesiastical and civil authorities, can wonder that thousands upon thousands of unhappy persons should be brought to the stake? that Cologne should for many years burn its three hundred witches annually? the district of Bamberg its four hundred? Nuremberg, Geneva, Paris, Toulouse, Lyons, and other cities, their two hundred?

A few of these trials may be cited, taking them in the order of

priority, as they occurred in different parts of the Continent. In 1595,
an old woman residing in a village near Constance, angry at not being
invited to share the sports of the country people on a day of public

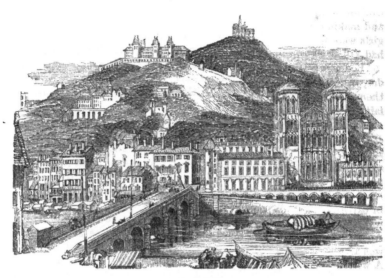

CITY OF LYONS.

rejoicing, was heard to mutter something to herself, and'was afterwards seen to proceed through the fields towards a hill, where she was
lost sight of. A violent thunder-storm arose about two hours afterwards, which wet the dancers to the skin, and did considerable damage
to the plantations. This woman, suspected before of witchcraft, was
seized and imprisoned, and accused of having raised the storm, by
filling a hole with wine, and stirring it about with a stick. She was
tortured till she confessed, and was burned alive the next evening.

About the same time two sorcerers in Toulouse were accused of
having dragged a crucifix about the streets at midnight, stopping
at times to spit upon and kick it, and uttering at intervals an exorcism to raise the devil. The next day a hail-storm did considerable
damage to the crops ; and a girl, the daughter of a shoemaker in the
town, remembered to have heard in the night the execrations of the
wizards. Her story led to their arrest. The usual means to produce
confession were resorted to. The wizards owned that they could raise
tempests whenever they pleased, and named several persons who possessed similar powers. They were hanged, and then burned in the

market-place, and seven of the persons they had mentioned shared the same fate.

Hoppo and Stadlin, two noted wizards of Germany, were executed in 1599. They implicated twenty or thirty witches, who went about causing women to miscarry, bringing down the lightning of heaven, and making maidens bring forth toads. To this latter fact several girls were found to swear most positively! Stadlin confessed that he had killed seven infants in the womb of one woman.

Bodinus highly praises the exertions of a witch-finder named Nider, in France, who prosecuted so many that he could not calculate them. Some of these witches could, by a single word, cause people to fall down dead; others made women go with child three years instead of nine months; while others, by certain invocations and ceremonies, could turn the faces of their enemies upside down, or twist them round to their backs. Although no witness was ever procured who saw persons in this horrible state, the witches confessed that they had the power and exercised it. Nothing more was wanting to ensure the stake.

At Amsterdam a crazy girl confessed that she could cause sterility in cattle, and bewitch pigs and poultry, by merely repeating the magic words *Turius und Shurius Inturius!* She was hanged and burned. Another woman in the same city, named Kornelis van Purmerund, was arrested in consequence of some disclosures the former had made. A witness came forward and swore that she one day looked through the window of her hut, and saw Kornelis sitting before a fire muttering something to the devil. She was sure it was to the devil, because she heard him answer her. Shortly afterwards twelve black cats ascended out of the floor, and danced on their hind legs around the witch for the space of about half an hour. They then vanished with a horrid noise, and leaving a disagreeable smell behind them. She also was hanged and burned.

At Bamberg, in Bavaria, the executions from the year 1610 to 1640 were at the rate of about a hundred annually. One woman, suspected of witchcraft, was seized because, having immoderately praised the beauty of a child, it had shortly afterwards fallen ill and died. She confessed upon the rack that the devil had given her the power to work evil upon those she hated, by speaking words in their praise. If she said with unwonted fervour, " What a strong man !" " What a lovely woman !" " What a sweet child !" the devil understood her, and afflicted them with diseases immediately. It is quite unnecessary to state the end of this poor creature. Many women were executed for causing strange substances to lodge in the bodies of those who offended them. Bits of wood, nails, hair, egg-shells, bits of glass, shreds of linen and woollen cloth, pebbles, and even hot cinders and knives, were the articles generally chosen. These were believed to remain in the body till the witches confessed or were executed, when they were voided from the bowels, or by the mouth,

BAMBERG.

nostrils, or ears. Modern physicians have often had cases of a similar description under their care, where girls have swallowed needles, which have been voided on the arms, legs, and other parts of the body. But the science of that day could not account for these phenomena otherwise than by the power of the devil; and every needle swallowed by a servant-maid cost an old woman her life. Nay, if no more than one suffered in consequence, the district might think itself fortunate. The commissioners seldom stopped short at one victim. The revelations of the rack in most cases implicated half a score.

Of all the records of the witch-trials preserved for the wonder of succeeding ages, that of Würzburg, from 1627 to 1629, is the most frightful. Hauber, who has preserved this list in his *Acta et Scripta Magica*, says, in a note at the end, that it is far from complete, and that there were a great many other burnings too numerous to specify. This record, which relates to the city only, and not to the province of Würzburg, contains the names of one hundred and fifty-seven persons who were burned in two years in twenty-nine burnings, averaging from five to six at a time. The list comprises three play-actors, four innkeepers, three common councilmen of Würzburg, fourteen vicars of the cathedral, the burgomaster's lady, an apothecary's wife and daughter, two choristers of the cathedral, Göbel Babelin, the prettiest girl in the town, and the wife, the two little sons, and the daughter of the councillor Stolzenberg. Rich and poor, young and old, suffered alike. At the seventh of these recorded burnings, the victims are described as a wandering boy, twelve years of age, and four strange men and women found sleeping in the market-place. Thirty-two of the whole number appear to have been vagrants, of both sexes, who, failing to give a satisfactory account of themselves, were accused and found guilty of witchcraft. The number of children on the list is horrible to think upon. The thirteenth and fourteenth burnings comprised four persons, who are stated to have been a little maiden nine years of age, a maiden still less, her sister, their mother, and their aunt, a pretty young woman of twenty-four. At the eighteenth burning, the victims were two boys of twelve, and a girl of fifteen; at the nineteenth, the young heir of the noble house of Rotenhahn, aged nine, and two other boys, one aged ten, and the other twelve. Among other entries appear the names of Baunach, the fattest, and Steinacher, the richest burgher in Würzburg. What tended to keep up the delusion in this unhappy city, and, indeed, all over Europe, was the number of hypochondriac and diseased persons who came voluntarily forward and made confession of witchcraft. Several of the victims in the foregoing list had only themselves to blame for their fate. Many, again, including the apothecary's wife and daughter already mentioned, pretended to sorcery, and sold poisons, or attempted, by means of charms and incantations, to raise the devil. But throughout all this fearful period the delusion of the criminals was as great as that of the judges. Depraved persons, who in ordinary times would have been thieves or murderers, added the desire of sorcery to their depravity, sometimes with the hope of acquiring power over their fellows, and sometimes with the hope of securing impunity in this world by the protection of Satan. One of the persons executed at the first burning, a prostitute, was heard repeating the exorcism which was supposed to have the power of raising the arch enemy in the form of a goat.

This precious specimen of human folly has been preserved by Horst in his *Zauberbibliothek*. It ran as follows, and was to be repeated slowly, with many ceremonies and wavings of the hand:

> " Lalle, Bachera, Magotte, Baphia, Dajam,
> Vagoth Heneche Ammi Nagaz, Adomator
> Raphael Immanuel Christus, Tetragrammaton
> Agra Jod Loi. König ! König !"

The last two words were uttered quickly, and with a sort of scream, and were supposed to be highly agreeable to Satan, who loved to be called a king. If he did not appear immediately, it was necessary to repeat a further exorcism. The one in greatest repute was as follows, and was to be read backwards, with the exception of the last two words:

> " Anion, Lalle, Sabolos, Sado, Pater, Aziel
> Adonai Sado Vagoth Agra, Jod,
> Baphra ! Komm ! Komm !"

When the witch wanted to get rid of the devil, who was sometimes in the habit of prolonging his visits to an unconscionable length, she had only to repeat the following, also backwards, when he generally disappeared, leaving behind him a suffocating smell:

> "Zellianelle Heotti Bonus Vagotha
> Plisos sother osech unicus Beelzebub
> Dax ! Komm ! Komm !"

This nonsensical jargon soon became known to all the idle and foolish boys of Germany. Many an unhappy urchin, who in a youthful frolic had repeated it, paid for his folly the penalty of his life. Three, whose ages varied from ten to fifteen, were burned alive at Würzburg for no other offence. Of course every other boy in the city became still more convinced of the power of the charm. One boy confessed that he would willingly have sold himself to the devil, if he could have raised him, for a good dinner and cakes every day of his life, and a pony to ride upon. This luxurious youngster, instead of being horsewhipped for his folly, was hanged and burned.

The small district of Lindheim was, if possible, even more notorious than Würzburg for the number of its witch-burnings. In the year 1633 a famous witch, named Pomp Anna, who could cause her foes to fall sick by merely looking at them, was discovered and burned, along with three of her companions. Every year in this parish, consisting at most of a thousand persons, the average number of executions was five. Between the years 1660 and 1664, the number consumed was thirty. If the executions all over Germany had been in this frightful proportion, hardly a family could have escaped losing one of its members.

In 1627, a ballad entitled the *Druten Zeitung*, or the *Witches'
Gazette*, was very popular in Germany. It detailed, according to the
title-page of a copy printed at Smalcald in 1627, " An account of the
remarkable events which took place in Franconia, Bamberg, and
Würzburg, with those wretches who, from avarice or ambition, have
sold themselves to the devil, and how they had their reward at last :
set to music, and to be sung to the tune of Dorothea." The sufferings of the witches at the stake are explained in it with great minute-
ness, the poet waxing extremely witty when he describes the horrible
contortions of pain upon their countenances, and the shrieks that rent
the air when any one of more than common guilt was burned alive.
A trick resorted to in order to force one witch to confess, is told in
this doggrel as an excellent joke. As she obstinately refused to own
that she was in league with the powers of evil, the commissioners
suggested that the hangman should dress himself in a bear's skin,
with the horns, tail, and all the et-ceteras, and in this form penetrate
into her dungeon. The woman, in the darkness of her cell, could
not detect the imposture, aided as it was by her own superstitious
fears. She thought she was actually in the presence of the prince of
hell; and when she was told to keep up her courage, and that she
should be relieved from the power of her enemies, she fell on her
knees before the supposed devil, and swore to dedicate herself hereafter, body and soul, to his service. Germany is perhaps the only
country in Europe where the delusion was so great as to have made
such detestable verses as these the favourites of the people :

" Man shickt ein Henkersknecht
Zu ihr in Gefängniss n'unter,
    Den man hat kleidet recht,
Mit einer Bärnhaute,
    Als wenns der Teufel wär ;
Als ihm die Drut anschaute
    Meints ihr Buhl kam daher.

Sie sprach zu ihm behende,
    Wie lässt du mich so lang
In der Obrigkeit Hände ?
    Hilf mir aus ihren Zwang,
Wie du mir hast verheissen,
    Ich bin ja eben dein,
Thu mich aus der Angst entreissen
    O liebster Buhle mein !"*

* They sent a hangman's assistant down to her in her prison; they clothed him properly in a bear's skin, as if he were the devil. Him, when the witch saw, she thought
he was her familiar. She said to him quickly, " Why hast thou left me so long in the
magistrates' hands? Help me out of their power, as thou hast promised, and I will be
thine alone. Help me from this anguish, O thou dearest devil [or lover] mine!"

This rare poet adds, that in making such an appeal to the hangman, the witch never imagined the roast that was to be made of her,
and puts in, by way of parenthesis, "was not that fine fun!—*was das
war für ein Spiel!*" As feathers thrown into the air shew how the
wind blows, so this trumpery ballad serves to shew the current of
popular feeling at the time of its composition.

All readers of history are familiar with the celebrated trial of the
Maréchale d'Ancre, who was executed in Paris in the year 1617.
Although witchcraft was one of the accusations brought against her,
the real crime for which she suffered was her ascendency over the
mind of Mary of Medicis, and the consequent influence she exercised
indirectly over the unworthy king, Louis XIII. Her coachman gave
evidence that she had sacrificed a cock at midnight in one of the
churches, and others swore they had seen her go secretly into the
house of a noted witch named Isabella. When asked by what means
she had acquired so extraordinary an influence over the mind of the
Queen Mother, she replied boldly that she exercised no other power
over her than that which a strong mind can always exercise over the
weak. She died with great firmness.

In two years afterwards, scenes far more horrible than any that
had yet taken place in France were enacted at Labourt, at the foot of
the Pyrenees. The parliament of Bourdeaux, scandalised at the
number of witches who were said to infest Labourt and its neighbourhood, deputed one of its own members, the noted Pierre de
l'Ancre, and its president, Espaignel, to inquire into the matter, with
full powers to punish the offenders. They arrived at Labourt in
May 1619. De l'Ancre wrote a book setting forth all his great
deeds in this battle against the powers of evil. It is full of obscenity
and absurdity, but the facts may be relied on as far as they relate to
the number of trials and executions, and the strange confessions
which torture forced from the unhappy criminals.

De l'Ancre states as a reason why so many witches were to be found
at Labourt, that the country was mountainous and sterile! He discovered many of them from their partiality to smoking tobacco. It
may be inferred from this that he was of the opinion of King James,
that tobacco was the "devil's weed." When the commission first
sat, the number of persons brought to trial was about forty a day.
The acquittals did not average so many as five per cent. All the
witches confessed that they had been present at the great Domdaniel,
or Sabbath. At these saturnalia the devil sat upon a large gilded
throne, sometimes in the form of a goat; sometimes as a gentleman,
dressed all in black, with boots, spurs, and sword; and very often as
a shapeless mass, resembling the trunk of a blasted tree, seen indis-

tinctly amid the darkness. They generally proceeded to the Domdaniel, riding on spits, pitchforks, or broomsticks, and on their arrival indulged with the fiends in every species of debauchery. Upon one occasion they had had the audacity to celebrate this festival in the very heart of the city of Bourdeaux. The throne of the arch fiend was placed in the middle of the Place de Gallienne, and the whole space was covered with the multitude of witches and wizards who flocked to it from far and near, some arriving even from distant Scotland.

After two hundred poor wretches had been hanged and burned, there seemed no diminution in the number of criminals to be tried. Many of the latter were asked upon the rack what Satan had said when he found that the commissioners were proceeding with such severity? The general reply was, that he did not seem to care much about it. Some of them asserted that they had boldly reproached him for suffering the execution of their friends, saying, " *Out upon thee, false fiend! thy promise was that they should not die! Look, how thou hast kept thy word! They have been burned, and are a heap of ashes!* " Upon these occasions he was never offended: he would give orders that the sports of the Domdaniel should cease, and producing illusory fires that did not burn, he encouraged them to walk through, assuring them that the fires lighted by the executioner gave no more pain than those. They would then ask him, where their friends were, since they had not suffered; to which the " Father of Lies" invariably replied, that they were happy in a far country, and could see and hear all that was then passing; and that, if they called by name those they wished to converse with, they might hear their voices in reply. Satan then imitated the voices of the defunct witches so successfully that they were all deceived. Having answered all objections, the orgies recommenced and lasted till the cock crew.

De l'Ancre was also very zealous in the trial of unhappy monomaniacs for the crime of lycanthropy. Several who were arrested confessed, without being tortured, that they were *weir-wolves*, and that at night they rushed out among the flocks and herds killing and devouring. One young man at Besançon, with the full consciousness of the awful fate that awaited him, voluntarily gave himself up to the Commissioner Espaignel, and confessed that he was the servant of a strong fiend, who was known by the name of "Lord of the ·Forests:" by his power he was transformed into the likeness of a wolf. The "Lord of the Forests" assumed the same shape; but was much larger, fiercer, and stronger. They prowled about the pastures together at midnight, strangling the watch-dogs that defended the

folds, and killing more sheep than they could devour. He felt, he
said, a fierce pleasure in these excursions, and howled in excess of
joy as he tore with his fangs the warm flesh of the sheep asunder.
This youth was not alone in this horrid confession; many others
voluntarily owned that they were *weir-wolves*, and many more were
forced by torture to make the same avowal. Such criminals were
thought to be too atrocious to be hanged first and then burned: they
were generally sentenced to be burned alive, and their ashes to be
scattered to the winds.   Grave and learned doctors of divinity openly
sustained the possibility of these transformations, relying mainly
upon the history of Nebuchadnezzar. They could not imagine why,
if he had been an ox, modern men could not become wolves by
Divine permission and the power of the devil. They also contended
that, if men should confess, it was evidence enough, if there had
been no other. Delrio mentions that one gentleman accused of
lycanthropy was put to the torture no less than twenty times; but
still he would not confess. An intoxicating draught was then given
him, and under its influence he confessed that he was a *weir-wolf*.
Delrio cites this to shew the extreme equity of the commissioners.
They never burned any body till he confessed; and if one course of
torture would not suffice, their patience was not exhausted, and they
tried him again and again, even to the twentieth time! Well may
we exclaim, when such atrocities have been committed in the name
of religion,

> " Quel lion, quel tigre égale en cruauté,
> Une injuste fureur qu'arme la piété ?"

The trial of the unhappy Urbain Grandier, the curate of Loudun,
for bewitching a number of girls in the convent of the Ursulines in
that town, was, like that of the Maréchale d'Ancre, an accusation
resorted to by his enemies to ruin one against whom no other charge
could be brought so readily. This noted affair, which kept France
in commotion for months, and the true character of which was
known even at that time, merits no more than a passing notice in
this place. It did not spring from the epidemic dread of sorcery then
so prevalent, but was carried on by wretched intriguers, who had
sworn to have the life of their foe. Such a charge could not be
refuted in 1634; the accused could not, as Bodinus expresses it,
" make the malice of the prosecutors more clear than the sun ;" and
his own denial, however intelligible, honest, and straightforward,
was held as nothing in refutation of the testimony of the crazy
women who imagined themselves bewitched. The more absurd and
contradictory their assertions, the stronger the argument employed

by his enemies that the devil was in them. He was burned alive, under circumstances of great cruelty.*

A singular instance of the epidemic fear of witchcraft occurred at Lille, in 1639. A pious but not very sane lady, named Antoinette Bourignon, founded a school, or *hospice*, in that city. One day, on entering the schoolroom, she imagined that she saw a great number of little black angels flying about the heads of the children. In great alarm she told her pupils of what she had seen, warning them to beware of the devil, whose imps were hovering about them. The foolish woman continued daily to repeat the same story, and Satan and his power became the only subject of conversation, not only between the girls themselves, but between them and their instructors. One of them at this time ran away from the school. On being brought back and interrogated, she said she had not run away, but had been carried away by the devil; she was a witch, and had been one since the age of seven. Some other little girls in the school went into fits at this announcement, and, on their recovery, confessed that they also were witches. At last the whole of them, to the number of fifty, worked upon each other's imaginations to such a degree that they also confessed that they were witches—that they attended the Domdaniel, or meeting of the fiends—that they could ride through the air on broomsticks, feast on infants' flesh, or creep through a keyhole.

The citizens of Lille were astounded at these disclosures. The clergy hastened to investigate the matter; many of them, to their credit, openly expressed their opinion that the whole affair was an imposture—not so the majority; they strenuously insisted that the confessions of the children were valid, and that it was necessary to make an example by burning them all for witches. The poor parents, alarmed for their offspring, implored the examining Capuchins with tears in their eyes to save their young lives, insisting that they were bewitched, and not bewitching. This opinion also gained ground in the town. Antoinette Bourignon, who had put these absurd notions into the heads of the children, was accused of witchcraft, and examined before the council. The circumstances of the case seemed so unfavourable towards her that she would not stay for a second examination. Disguising herself as she best could, she hastened out of Lille and escaped pursuit. If she had remained four hours longer, she

* A very graphic account of the execution of this unfortunate gentleman is to be found in the excellent romance of M. Alfred de Vigny, entitled *Cinq Mars;* but if the eader wishes for a full and accurate detail of all the circumstances of one of the most extraordinary trials upon record, he is referred to a work published anonymously, at Amsterdam, in 1693, entitled *Histoire des Diables de Loudun, ou de la Possession des Religieuses Ursulines, et de la Condemnation et du Supplice d'Urbain Grandier.*

would have been burned by judicial sentence as a witch and a heretic. It is to be hoped that, wherever she went, she learned the danger of tampering with youthful minds, and was never again entrusted with the management of children.

The Duke of Brunswick and the Elector of Menz were struck with the great cruelty exercised in the torture of suspected persons, and convinced, at the same time, that no righteous judge would consider a confession extorted by pain, and contradictory in itself, as sufficient evidence to justify the execution of any accused person. It is related of the Duke of Brunswick that he invited two learned Jesuits to his house, who were known to entertain strong opinions upon the subject of witchcraft, with a view of shewing them the cruelty and absurdity of such practices. A woman lay in the dungeon of the city accused of witchcraft, and the duke, having given previous instructions to the officiating torturers, went with the two Jesuits to hear her confession. By a series of artful leading questions the poor creature, in the extremity of her anguish, was induced to confess that she had often attended the sabbath of the fiends upon the Brocken ; that she had seen two Jesuits there, who had made themselves notorious, even among witches, for their abominations ; that she had seen them assume the form of goats, wolves, and other animals ; and that many noted witches had born them five, six, and seven children at a birth, who had heads like toads, and legs like spiders. Being asked if the Jesuits were far from her, she replied that they were in the room beside her. The Duke of Brunswick led his astounded friends away, and explained the stratagem. This was convincing proof to both of them that thousands of persons had suffered unjustly ; they knew their own innocence, and shuddered to think what their fate might have been if an enemy instead of a friend had put such a confession into the mouth of a criminal. One of these Jesuits was Frederick Spee, the author of the *Cautio Criminalis*, published in 1631. This work, exposing the horrors of the witch-trials, had a most salutary effect in Germany : Schonbrunn, Archbishop and Elector of Menz, abolished the torture entirely within his dominions, and his example was imitated by the Duke of Brunswick and other potentates. The number of supposed witches immediately diminished, and the violence of the mania began to subside. The Elector of Brandenburg issued a rescript, in 1654, with respect to the case of Anna of Ellerbrock, a supposed witch, forbidding the use of torture, and stigmatising the swimming of witches as an unjust, cruel, and deceitful test.

This was the beginning of the dawn after the long-protracted darkness. The tribunals no longer condemned witches to execution by hundreds in a year. Würzburg, the grand theatre of the burnings, burned but one where, forty years previously, it had burned three score. From 1660 to 1670 the electoral chambers, in all parts of Germany, constantly commuted the sentence of death passed by the provincial tribunals into imprisonment for life, or burning on the cheek.

ROUEN.

A truer philosophy had gradually disabused the public mind. Learned men freed themselves from the trammels of a debasing superstition, and governments, both civil and ecclesiastical, repressed the popular delusion they had so long encouraged. The parliament of Normandy condemned a number of women to death, in the year 1670, on the old charge of riding on broomsticks to the Domdaniel; but Louis XIV. commuted the sentence into banishment for life. The parliament remonstrated, and sent the king the following remarkable request. The reader will perhaps be glad to see this document at length. It is of importance, as the last effort of a legislative assembly to uphold this great error; and the arguments they used and the instances they quoted are in the highest degree curious. It reflects honour upon the memory of Louis XIV. that he was not swayed by it.

"SIRE,—Emboldened by the authority which your majesty has committed into our hands in the province of Normandy, to try and punish offences, and more particularly those offences of the nature of witchcraft, which tend to the destruction of religion and the ruin of nations, we, your parliament, remonstrate humbly with your majesty upon certain cases of this kind which have been lately brought before us. We cannot permit the letter addressed by your majesty's command to the attorney-general of this district, for the reprieve of certain persons condemned to death for witchcraft, and for the staying of proceedings in several other cases, to remain unnoticed, and without remarking upon the consequences which may ensue. There is also a letter from your secretary of state, declaring your majesty's intention to commute the punishment of these criminals into one of perpetual banishment, and to submit to the opinion of the procureur-general, and of the most learned members of the parliament of Paris, whether, in the matter of witchcraft, the jurisprudence of the parliament of Rouen is to be followed in preference to that of the parliament of Paris, and of the other parliaments of the kingdom which judge differently.

" Although by the ordinances of the kings your predecessors, parliaments have been forbidden to pay any attention to *lettres de cachet ;* we, nevertheless, from the knowledge which we have, in common with the whole kingdom, of the care bestowed by your majesty for the good of your subjects, and from the submission and obedience to your commandments which we have always manifested, have stayed all proceedings, in conformity to your orders ; hoping that your majesty, considering the importance of the crime of witchcraft, and the consequences likely to ensue from its impunity, will be graciously pleased to grant us once more your permission to continue the trials, and execute judgment upon those found guilty. And as, since we received the letter of your secretary of state, we have also been made acquainted with the determination of your majesty, not only to commute the sentence of death passed upon these witches into one of perpetual banishment from the province, but to re-establish them in the possession of their goods and chattels, and of their good fame and character, your parliament have thought it their duty, on occasion of these crimes, the greatest which men can commit, to make you acquainted with the general and uniform feelings of the people of this province with regard to them ; it being, moreover, a question in which are concerned the glory of God and the relief of your suffering subjects, who groan under their fears from the threats and menaces of this sort of persons, and who feel the effects of them every day in the mortal and extraordinary maladies which attack them, and the surprising damage and loss of their possessions.

'Your majesty knows well that there is no crime so opposed to the commands of God as witchcraft, which destroys the very foundation of religion, and draws strange abominations after it. It is for this reason, sire, that the Scriptures pronounce the punishment of death against offenders, and that the Church and the holy fathers have fulminated their anathemas, and that canonical decisions have one and all decreed the most severe punishments, to deter from this crime; and that the Church of France, animated by the piety of the kings your predecessors, has expressed so great a horror at it, that, not judging the punishment of perpetual imprisonment, the highest it has the power to inflict, sufficiently severe, it has left such criminals to be dealt with by the secular power.

" It has been the general feeling of all nations that such criminals ought to be condemned to death, and all the ancients were of the same opinion. The law of the ' Twelve Tables,' which was the principal of the Roman laws, ordains the same punishment. All jurisconsults agreed in it, as well as the constitutions of the emperors, and more especially those of Constantine and Theodosius, who, enlightened by the Gospel, not only renewed the same punishment, but also deprived, expressly, all persons found guilty of witchcraft of the right of appeal, and declared them to be unworthy of a prince's mercy. And Charles VIII., sire, inspired by the same sentiments, passed that beautiful and severe ordinance (*cette belle et sévère ordonnance*), which enjoined the judges to punish witches according to the exigencies of the case, under a penalty of being themselves fined or imprisoned, or dismissed from their office ; and decreed, at the same time, that all persons who refused to denounce a witch, should be punished as accomplices; and that all, on the contrary, who gave evidence against one should be rewarded.

" From these considerations, sire, and in the execution of so holy an ordinance, your parliaments, by their decrees, proportion their punishments to the guilt of the offenders; and your parliament of Normandy has never, until the present time, found that its practice was different from that of other courts ; for all the books which treat upon this matter cite an infinite number of decrees condemning witches to be burnt, or broken on the wheel, or to other punishments. The following are examples :—In the time of Chilperic, as may be seen in Gregory of Tours, b. vi. c. 35 of his *History of France*, all the decrees of the parliament of Paris passed according to, and in conformity with, this ancient jurisprudence of the kingdom, cited by

Imbert, in his *Judicial Practice;* all those cited by Monstrelet, in 1459, against the witches of Artois; the decrees of the same parliament, of the 13th of October 1573, against Mary le Fief, native of Saumur; of the 21st of October 1596, against the Sieur de Beaumont, who pleaded, in his defence, that he had only sought the aid of the devil for the purpose of unbewitching the afflicted and of curing diseases; of the 4th of July 1606, against Francis du Bose; of the 20th of July 1582, against Abel de la Rue, native of Coulommiers; of the 2d of October 1593, against Rousseau and his daughter; of 1608, against another Rousseau and one Peley, for witchcraft and adoration of the devil at the Sabbath, under the figure of a he-goat, as confessed by them; the decree of 4th of February 1615, against Leclerc, who appealed from the sentence of the parliament of Orleans, and who was condemned for having attended the Sabbath, and confessed, as well as two of his accomplices, who died in prison, that he had adored the devil, renounced his baptism and his faith in God, danced the witches' dance, and offered up unholy sacrifices; the decrees of the 6th of May 1616, against a man named Leger, on a similar accusation; the pardon granted by Charles IX. to Trois Echelles, upon condition of revealing his accomplices, but afterwards revoked for renewed sorcery on his part; the decree of the parliament of Paris, cited by Mornac in 1595; the judgments passed in consequence of the commission given by Henry IV. to the Sieur de l'Ancre, councillor of the parliament of Bourdeaux; of the 20th of March 1619, against Etienne Audibert; those passed by the chamber of Nerac, on the 26th of June 1620, against several witches; those passed by the parliament of Toulouse in 1577, as cited by Gregory Tolosanus, against four hundred persons accused of this crime, and who were all marked with the sign of the devil. Besides all these, we might recal to your majesty's recollection the various decrees of the parliament of Provence, especially in the case of Gaufrédy in 1611; the decrees of the parliament of Dijon, and those of the parliament of Rennes, following the example of the condemnation of the Marshal de Rays, who was burned in 1441, for the crime of witchcraft, in presence of the Duke of Brittany;—all these examples, sire, prove that the accusation of witchcraft has always been punished with death by the parliaments of your kingdom, and justify the uniformity of their practice.

" These, sire, are the motives upon which your parliament of Normandy has acted in decreeing the punishment of death against the persons lately brought before it for this crime. If it has happened that, on any occasion, these parliaments, and the parliament of Normandy among the rest, have condemned the guilty to a less punishment than that of death, it was for the reason that their guilt was not of the deepest dye ; your majesty, and the kings your predecessors, having left full liberty to the various tribunals to whom they delegated the administration of justice, to decree such punishment as was warranted by the evidence brought before them.

" After so many authorities, and punishments ordained by human and divine laws, we humbly supplicate your majesty to reflect once more upon the extraordinary results which proceed from the malevolence of this sort of people ; on the deaths from unknown diseases, which are often the consequences of their menaces, on the loss of the goods and chattels of your subjects, on the proofs of guilt continually afforded by the insensibility of the marks upon the accused, on the sudden transportation of bodies from one place to another, on the sacrifices and nocturnal assemblies, and other facts, corroborated by the testimony of ancient and modern authors, and verified by so many eye-witnesses, composed partly of accomplices, and partly of people who had no interest in the trials beyond the love of truth, and confirmed, moreover, by the confessions of the accused parties themselves ; and that, sire, with so much agreement and conformity between the different cases, that the most ignorant persons convicted of this crime have spoken to the same circumstances, and in nearly the same words, as the most celebrated authors who have written about it, all of which may be easily proved to your majesty's satisfaction by the records of various trials before your parliaments.

" These, sire, are truths so intimately bound up with the principles of our religion, that, extraordinary although they be, no person has been able to this time to call them in question. If some have cited, in opposition to these truths, the pretended canon of the Council of Ancyre, and a passage from St. Augustin, in a treatise upon the *Spirit and the Soul*, it has been without foundation ; and it would be easy to convince your majesty that neither the one nor the other ought to be accounted of any authority ; and besides that the canon, in this sense, would be contrary to the opinion of all succeeding councils of the Church, Cardinal Baronius and all learned commentators agree that it is not to be found in any old edition. In effect, in those editions wherein it is found, it is in another language, and is in direct contradiction to the twenty-third canon of the same council, which condemns sorcery, according to all preceding constitutions. Even supposing that this canon was really promulgated by the Council of Ancyre, we must observe that it was issued in the second century, when the principal attention of the Church was directed to the destruction of paganism. For this reason, it condemns that class of women who said they could pass through the air, and over immense regions, with Diana and Herodias, and enjoins all

reachers to teach the falsehood of such an opinion, in order to deter'
people from the worship of these false divinities; but it does not
question the power of the devil over the human body, which is, in
fact, proved by the holy Gospel of Jesus Christ himself.   And with
regard, sire, to the pretended passage of St. Augustin, every body
knows that it was not written by him, because the writer, whoever
he was, cites Bœtius, who died more than eighty years after the time
of St. Augustin.   Besides, there is still more convincing proof in the
act, that the same father establishes the truth of witchcraft in all
his writings, and more particularly in his *City of God;* and in his
first volume, question the 25th, wherein he states that sorcery is a
communion between man and the devil, which all good Christians
ought to look upon with horror.

" Taking all these things into consideration, sire, the officers of
your parliament hope, from the justice of your majesty, that you will
be graciously pleased to receive the humble remonstrances they have
taken the liberty to make.   They are compelled, for the acquittal of
their own consciences and in discharge of their duty, to make known
to your majesty, that the decrees they passed against the sorcerers
and witches brought before them were passed after a mature deliberation on the part of all the judges present, and that nothing has been
done therein which is not conformable to the universal jurisprudence
of the kingdom, and for the general welfare of your majesty's subjects, of whom there is not one who can say that he is secure from
the malevolence of such criminals.   We therefore supplicate your
majesty to suffer us to carry into effect the sentences we passed, and
to proceed with the trial of the other persons accused of the same
crime ; and that the piety of your majesty will not suffer to be introduced during your reign an opinion contrary to the principles of that
holy religion for which you have always employed so gloriously both
your cares and your arms."

Louis, as we have already mentioned, paid no attention to this
appeal.   The lives of the old women were spared, and prosecutions
for mere witchcraft, unconnected with other offences, were discontinued throughout France.   In 1680 an act was passed for the punishment, not of witches, but of pretenders to witchcraft, fortune-tellers,
divineresses, and poisoners.

Thus the light broke in upon Germany, France, England, and
Scotland about the same time, gradually growing clearer and clearer
till the middle of the eighteenth century, when witchcraft was finally
reckoned amongst exploded doctrines, and the belief in it confined to
the uttermost vulgar.   Twice, however, did the madness burst forth

again as furious, while it lasted, as ever it had been. The first time in Sweden, in 1669, and the second in Germany so late as 1749. Both these instances merit particular mention. The first is one of the most extraordinary upon record, and for atrocity and absurdity is unsurpassed in the annals of any nation.

It having been reported to the king of Sweden that the little village of Mohra, in the province of Dalecarlia, was troubled exceedingly with witches, he appointed a commission of clergy and laymen to trace the rumour to its source, with full powers to punish the guilty. On the 12th of August 1669, the commissioners arrived in the bewitched village, to the great joy of the credulous inhabitants. On the following day the whole popula- tion, amounting to three

LOUIS XIV

thousand persons, assembled in the church. A sermon was preached, " declaring the miserable case of those people that suffered themselves to be deluded by the devil," and fervent prayer was offered up that God would remove the scourge from among them.

The whole assembly then adjourned to the rector's house, filling all the street before it, when the king's commission was read, charg- ing every person who knew any thing of the witchery to come for- ward and declare the truth. A passion of tears seized upon the mul- titude ; men, women, and children began to weep and sob, and all promised to divulge what they had heard or knew. In this frame of mind they were dismissed to their homes. On the following day they were again called together, when the depositions of several persons were taken publicly before them all. The result was that seventy persons, including fifteen children, were taken into custody. Numbers also were arrested in the neighbouring district of Elfdale. Being put to the torture, they all confessed their guilt. They said they used to go to a gravel-pit, that lay hard by the cross-way, where they put a vest upon their heads, and danced "round and round and round about." They then went to the cross-way, and called three times upon the devil; the first time in a low still voice; the second, some-what louder; and the third, very loudly, with these words, "Ante-cessor, come, and carry us to Blockula!" This invocation never failed to bring him to their view. He generally appeared as a little old man, in a grey coat, with red and blue stockings, with exceedingly long garters. He had besides a very high-crowned hat, with bands of many-coloured linen enfolded about it, and a long red beard that hung down to his middle.

The first question he put to them was, whether they would serve him soul and body? On their answering in the affirmative, he told them to make ready for the journey to Blockula. It was necessary to procure, in the first place, "some scrapings of altars and filings of church clocks." Antecessor then gave them a horn with some salve in it, wherewith they anointed themselves. These preparations ended, he brought beasts for them to ride upon,—horses, asses, goats, and monkeys; and giving them a saddle, a hammer, and a nail, uttered the word of command, and away they went. Nothing stopped them. They flew over churches, high walls, rocks, and mountains, until they came to the green meadow where Blockula was situated. Upon these occasions they carried as many children with them as they could; for the devil, they said, "did plague and whip them if they did not pro-cure him children, insomuch that they had no peace or quiet for him."

Many parents corroborated a part of this evidence, stating that their children had repeatedly told them that they had been carried away in the night to Blockula, where the devil had beaten them black and blue. They had seen the marks in the morning, but they soon disappeared. One little girl was examined, who swore positively that she was carried through the air by the witches, and when at a great height she uttered the holy name of Jesus. She immediately fell to the ground, and made a great hole in her side. " The devil, however, picked her up, healed her side, and carried her away to Blockula." She added (and her mother confirmed her statement), that she had till that day "an exceeding great pain in her side." This was a clencher, and the nail of conviction was driven home to the hearts of the judges.

The place called Blockula, whither they were carried, was a large house, with a gate to it, "in a delicate meadow, whereof they could see no end." There was a very long table in it, at which the witches sat down; and in other rooms "there were very lovely and delicate beds for them to sleep upon."

After a number of ceremonies had been performed, by which they bound themselves body and soul to the service of Antecessor, they sat down to a feast composed of broth, made of colworts and bacon, oatmeal, bread and butter, milk and cheese. The devil always took the chair, and sometimes played to them on the harp or the fiddle while they were eating. After dinner they danced in a ring, sometimes naked and sometimes in their clothes, cursing and swearing all the time. Some of the women added particulars too horrible and too obscene for repetition.

Once the devil pretended to be dead, that he might see whether his people regretted him. They instantly set up a loud wail, and wept three tears each for him; at which he was so pleased, that he jumped up among them, and hugged in his arms those who had been most obstreperous in their sorrow.

Such were the principal details given by the children, and corroborated by the confessions of the full-grown witches. Any thing more absurd was never before stated in a court of justice. Many of the accused contradicted themselves most palpably; but the commissioners gave no heed to discrepancies. One of them, the parson of the district, stated in the course of the inquiry, that on a particular night, which he mentioned, he had been afflicted with a headache so agonising, that he could not account for it otherwise than by supposing he was bewitched. In fact, he thought a score of witches must have been dancing on the crown of his head. This announcement excited great horror among the pious dames of the auditory, who loudly expressed their wonder that the devil should have power to hurt so good a man. One poor witch, who lay in the very jaws of death, confessed that she knew too well the cause of the minister's headache. The devil had sent her with a sledge-hammer and a large nail to drive into the good man's skull. She had hammered at it for some time, but the skull was so enormously *thick*, that she made no impression upon it. Every hand was held up in astonishment. The pious minister blessed God that his skull was so solid, and he became renowned for his thick head all the days of his life. Whether the witch intended a joke does not appear, but she was looked upon as a criminal more than usually atrocious. Seventy persons were condemned to death on these so awful, yet so ridiculous confessions. Twenty-three of them were burned together in one fire in the village of Mohra, in the presence of thousands of delighted spectators. On the following day fifteen children were murdered in the same manner, offered up in sacrifice to the bloody Moloch of superstition. The remaining thirty-two were executed at the neighbouring town of Fahluna. Besides these, fifty-six children were found guilty of witchcraft in a minor degree, and sentenced to various punishments, such as running the gauntlet, imprisonment, and public whipping once a week for a twelvemonth.

Long after the occurrence of this case, it was cited as one of the most convincing proofs upon record of the prevalence of witchcraft. When men wish to construct or support a theory, how they torture facts into their service! The lying whimsies of a few sick children, encouraged by foolish parents, and drawn out by superstitious neighbours, were sufficient to set a country in a flame. If, instead of commissioners as deeply sunk in the slough of ignorance as the people they were sent amongst, there had been deputed a few men firm in courage and clear in understanding, how different would have been the result! Some of the poor children who were burned would have been sent to an infirmary; others would have been well flogged; the credulity of the parents would have been laughed at; and the lives of seventy persons spared. The belief in witchcraft remains in Sweden to this day; but happily the annals of that country present no more such instances of lamentable aberration of intellect as the one just cited.

In New England, about the same time, the colonists were scared by similar stories of the antics of the devil. All at once a fear seized upon the multitude, and supposed criminals were arrested day after day in such numbers, that the prisons were found too small to contain them. A girl named Goodwin, the daughter of a mason, who was hypochondriac and subject to fits, imagined that an old Irish woman, named Glover, had bewitched her. Her two brothers, in whose constitutions there was apparently a predisposition to similar fits, went off in the same way, crying out that the devil and dame Glover were tormenting them. At times their joints were so stiff that they could not be moved; while at others, said the neighbours, they were so flexible, that the bones appeared softened into sinews. The supposed witch was seized, and as she could not repeat the Lord's Prayer without making a mistake in it, she was condemned and executed.

But the popular excitement was not allayed. One victim was not enough; the people waited agape for new disclosures. Suddenly two hysteric girls in another family fell into fits daily, and the cry of witchcraft resounded from one end of the colony to the other. The feeling of suffocation in the throat, so common in cases of hysteria, was said by the patients to be caused by the devil himself, who had stuck balls in the windpipe to choke them. They felt the pricking of thorns in every part of the body, and one of them vomited needles. The case of these girls, who were the daughter and niece of a Mr. Parvis, the minister of a Calvinist chapel, excited so much attention, that all the weak women in the colony began to fancy themselves similarly afflicted. The more they brooded on it, the more convinced they became. The contagion of this mental disease was as great as

if it had been a pestilence. One after the other the women fainted
away, asserting on their recovery that they had seen the spectres of
witches. Where there were three or four girls in a family, they so
worked each upon the diseased imagination of the other, that they
fell into fits five or six times in a day. Some related that the devil
himself appeared to them, bearing in his hand a parchment-roll, and
promising that if they would sign an agreement, transferring to him
their immortal souls, they should be immediately relieved from fits
and all the ills of the flesh. Others asserted that they saw witches
only, who made them similar promises, threatening that they should
never be free from aches and pains till they had agreed to become the
devil's. When they refused, the witches pinched, or bit, or pricked
them with long pins and needles. More than two hundred persons
named by these mischievous visionaries were thrown into prison.
They were of all ages and conditions of life, and many of them of
exemplary character. No less than nineteen were condemned and
executed before reason returned to the minds of the colonists. The
most horrible part of this lamentable history is, that among the victims there was a little child only five years old. Some women swore
that they had seen it repeatedly in company with the devil, and that
it had bitten them often with its little teeth for refusing to sign a
compact with the evil one. It can hardly increase our feelings of
disgust and abhorrence when we learn that this insane community
actually tried and executed a dog for the same offence !

One man, named Cory, stoutly refused to plead to the preposterous indictment against him. As was the practice in such cases, he
was pressed to death. It is told of the Sheriff of New England, who
superintended the execution, that when this unhappy man thrust out
his tongue in his mortal agony, he seized hold of a cane, and crammed
it back again into the mouth. If ever there were a fiend in human
form, it was this sheriff : a man who, if the truth were known, perhaps plumed himself upon his piety—thought he was doing God good
service, and

"Hoped to merit heaven by making earth a hell."

Arguing still in the firm belief of witchcraft, the bereaved people
began to inquire, when they saw their dearest friends snatched away
from them by these wide-spreading accusations, whether the whole
proceedings were not carried on by the agency of the devil. Might
not the great enemy have put false testimony into the mouths of the
witnesses, or might not the witnesses be witches themselves? Every
man who was in danger of losing his wife, his child, or his sister,
embraced this doctrine with avidity. The revulsion was as sudden as
the first frenzy. All at once, the colonists were convinced of their

error. The judges put a stop to the prosecutions, even of those who had confessed their guilt. The latter were no sooner at liberty than they retracted all they had said, and the greater number hardly remembered the avowals which agony had extorted from them. Eight persons, who had been tried and condemned, were set free; and gradually girls ceased to have fits and to talk of the persecutions of the devil. The judge who had condemned the first criminal executed on this charge, was so smitten with sorrow and humiliation at his folly, that he set apart the anniversary of that day as one of solemn penitence and fasting. He still clung to the belief in witchcraft; no new light had broken in upon him on that subject, but, happily for the community, the delusion had taken a merciful turn. The whole colony shared the feeling; the jurors on the different trials openly expressed their penitence in the churches; and those who had suffered were regarded as the victims, and not as the accomplices of Satan.

It is related that the Indian tribes in New England were sorely puzzled at the infatuation of the settlers, and thought them either a race inferior to, or more sinful than the French colonists in the vicinity, amongst whom, as they remarked, "the Great Spirit sent no witches."

Returning again to the continent of Europe, we find that, after the year 1680, men became still wiser upon this subject. For twenty years the populace were left to their belief, but governments in general gave it no aliment in the shape of executions. The edict of Louis XIV. gave a blow to the superstition, from which it never recovered. The last execution in the Protestant cantons of Switzerland was at Geneva, in 1652. The various potentates of Germany, although they could not stay the trials, invariably commuted the sentence into imprisonment, in all cases where the pretended witch was accused of pure witchcraft, unconnected with any other crime. In the year 1701, Thomasius, the learned professor at the University of Halle, delivered his inaugural thesis *De Crimine Magiæ*, which struck another blow at the falling monster of popular error. But a faith so strong as that in witchcraft was not to be eradicated at once; the arguments of learned men did not penetrate to the villages and hamlets: but still they achieved great things; they rendered the belief an unworking faith, and prevented the supply of victims, on which for so many ages it had battened and grown strong.

Once more the delusion broke out; like a wild beast wounded to the death, it collected all its remaining energies for the final convulsion, which was to shew how mighty it had once been. Germany, which had nursed the frightful error in its cradle, tended it on its death-ded, and Würzburg, the scene of so many murders on the same pretext, was destined to be the scene of the last. That it might lose no portion of its bad renown, the last murder was as atrocious as the first. This case offers a great resemblance to that of the witches of Mohra and New England, except in the number of its victims. It happened so late as the year 1749, to the astonishment and disgust of the rest of Europe.

VIEW IN WURZBURG.

A number of young women in a convent at Würzburg fancied themselves bewitched; they felt, like all hysteric subjects, a sense of

suffocation in the throat. They went into fits repeatedly; and one
of them, who had swallowed needles, evacuated them at abscesses,
which formed in different parts of the body. The cry of sorcery was
raised, and a young woman, named Maria Renata Sänger, was arrested on the charge of having leagued with the devil to bewitch five
of the young ladies. It was sworn on the trial that Maria had been
frequently seen to clamber over the convent-walls in the shape of a
pig—that, proceeding to the cellar, she used to drink the best wine
till she was intoxicated, and then start suddenly up in her own form.
Other girls asserted that she used to prowl about the roof like a cat,
and often penetrate into their chamber, and frighten them by her
dreadful howlings. It was also said that she had been seen in the
shape of a hare, milking the cows dry in the meadows belonging to
the convent; that she used to perform as an actress on the boards of
Drury Lane Theatre in London, and, on the very same night, return
upon a broomstick to Würzburg, and afflict the young ladies with
pains in all their limbs. Upon this evidence she was condemned, and
burned alive in the market-place of Würzburg.

Here ends this frightful catalogue of murder and superstition.
Since that day, the belief in witchcraft has fled from the populous
abodes of men, and taken refuge in remote villages and districts too
wild, rugged, and inhospitable to afford a resting-place for the foot
of civilisation. Rude fishers and uneducated labourers still attribute
every phenomenon of nature which they cannot account for, to the
devil and witches. Catalepsy, that wondrous disease, is still thought
by ignorant gossips to be the work of Satan; and hypochondriacs,
uninformed by science of the nature of their malady, devoutly believe
in the reality of their visions. The reader would hardly credit the
extent of the delusion upon this subject in the very heart of England
at this day. Many an old woman leads a life of misery from the un-
feeling insults of her neighbours, who raise the scornful finger and
hooting voice at her, because in her decrepitude she is ugly, spiteful,
perhaps insane, and realises in her personal appearance the description preserved by tradition of the witches of yore. Even in the neighbourhood of great towns the taint remains of this once widely-spread
contagion. If no victims fall beneath it, the enlightenment of the
law is all that prevents a recurrence of scenes as horrid as those of
the seventeenth century. Hundreds upon hundreds of witnesses
could be found to swear to absurdities as great as those asserted by
the infamous Matthew Hopkins.

In the *Annual Register* for 1760, an instance of the belief in witchcraft is related, which shews how superstition lingers. A dispute arose
in the little village of Glen, in Leicestershire, between two old women,

each of whom vehemently accused the other of witchcraft. The quarrel at last ran so high that a challenge ensued, and they both agreed to be tried by the ordeal of swimming. They accordingly stripped to their shifts—procured some men, who tied their thumbs and great toes together, cross-wise, and then, with a cart-rope about their middle, suffered themselves to be thrown into a pool of water. One of them sank immediately, but the other continued struggling a short time upon the surface of the water, which the mob deeming an infallible sign of her guilt, pulled her out, and insisted that she should immediately impeach all her accomplices in the craft. She accordingly told them that, in the neighbouring village of Burton, there were several old women as "much witches as she was." Happily for her, this negative information was deemed sufficient, and a student in astrology, or "white-witch," coming up at the time, the mob, by his direction, proceeded forthwith to Burton in search of all the delinquents. After a little consultation on their arrival, they went to the old woman's house on whom they had fixed the strongest suspicion. The poor old creature on their approach locked the outer door, and from the window of an upstairs room asked what they wanted. They informed her that she was charged with being guilty of witchcraft, and that they were come to duck her; remonstrating with her at the same time upon the necessity of submission to the ordeal, that, if she were innocent, all the world might know it. Upon her persisting in a positive refusal to come down, they broke open the door and carried her out by force, to a deep gravel-pit full of water. They tied her thumbs and toes together and threw her into the water, where they kept her for several minutes, drawing her out and in two or three times by the rope round her middle. Not being able to satisfy themselves whether she were a witch or no, they at last let her go, or, more properly speaking, they left her on the bank to walk home by herself, if she ever recovered. Next day they tried the same experiment upon another woman, and afterwards upon a third; but fortunately, neither of the victims lost her life from this brutality. Many of the ringleaders in the outrage were apprehended during the week, and tried before the justices at quarter-sessions. Two of them were sentenced to stand in the pillory and to be imprisoned for a month; and as many as twenty more were fined in small sums for the assault, and bound over to keep the peace for a twelvemonth.

"So late as the year 1785," says Arnot, in his collection and abridgment of *Criminal Trials in Scotland*, "it was the custom among the sect of Seceders to read from the pulpit an annual confession of sins, national and personal; amongst the former of which was particularly mentioned the 'Repeal by parliament of the penal statute against witches, contrary to the express laws of God.' "

Many houses are still to be found in England with the horse-shoe (the grand preservative against witchcraft) nailed against the threshold. If any over-wise philosopher should attempt to remove them, the chances are that he would have more broken bones than thanks

LADY HATTON'S HOUSE, CROSS STREET, HATTON GARDEN.

for his interference. Let any man walk into Cross Street, Hatton Garden, and from thence into Bleeding-heart Yard, and learn the tales still told and believed of one house in that neighbourhood, and he will ask himself in astonishment if such things can be in the nineteenth century. The witchcraft of Lady Hatton, the wife of the famous Sir Christopher, so renowned for his elegant dancing in the days of Elizabeth, is as devoutly believed as the Gospels. The room is to be seen where the devil seized her after the expiration of the contract he had made with her, and bore her away bodily to the pit of Tophet : the pump against which he dashed her is still pointed out, and the spot where her heart was found, after he had torn it out of her bosom with his iron claws, has received the name of Bleeding-heart Yard, in confirmation of the story. Whether the horse-shoe still remains upon the door of the haunted house, to keep away other witches, is uncertain. A former inmate relates that, " about twenty years ago, more than one old woman begged for admittance repeatedly, to satisfy themselves that it was in its proper place. One poor creature, apparently insane, and clothed in rags, came to the door with a tremendous double-knock, as loud as that of a fashionable footman, and walked straight along the passage to the horse-shoe. Great was the wonderment of the inmates, especially when the woman spat upon the horse-shoe, and expressed her sorrow that she could do no harm while it remained there. After spitting upon, and kicking it again and again, she coolly turned round and left the house, without saying a word to any body. This poor creature perhaps intended a joke, but the probability is that she imagined herself a witch. In Saffron Hill, where she resided, her ignorant neighbours gave her that character, and looked upon her with no little fear and aversion."

More than one example of the popular belief in witchcraft occurred in the neighbourhood of Hastings so lately as the year 1830. An aged woman, who resided in the Rope-walk of that town, was so repulsive in her appearance, that she was invariably accused of being a witch by all the ignorant people who knew her. She was bent completely double; and though very old, her eye was unusually bright and malignant. She wore a red cloak, and supported herself on a crutch; she was, to all outward appearance, the very *beau ideal* of a witch. So dear is power to the human heart, that this old woman actually encouraged the popular superstition; she took no pains to remove the ill impression, but seemed to delight that she, old and miserable as she was, could keep in awe so many happier and stronger fellow-creatures. Timid girls crouched with fear when they met her, and many would go a mile out of their way to avoid her. Like the witches of the olden time, she was not sparing of her curses against those who offended her. The child of a woman who resided within two doors of her was afflicted with lameness, and the mother constantly asserted that the old woman had bewitched her. All the neighbours credited the tale. It was believed, too, that she could assume the form of a cat. Many a harmless puss has been hunted almost to the death by mobs of men and boys, upon the supposition that the animal would start up before them in the true shape of Mother ———.

In the same town there resided a fisherman, who was the object of unceasing persecution, because it was said that he had sold himself to the devil. It was currently reported that he could creep through a keyhole, and that he had made a witch of his daughter, in order that he might have the more power over his fellows. It was also believed that he could sit on the points of pins and needles and feel no pain. His brother fishermen put him to this test whenever they had an opportunity. In the alehouses which he frequented, they often placed long needles in the cushions of the chairs in such a manner that he could not fail to pierce himself when he sat down. The result of these experiments tended to confirm their faith in his supernatural powers. It was asserted that he never flinched. Such was the popular feeling in the fashionable town of Hastings a few years ago ; very probably it is the same now.

In the north of England, the superstition lingers to an almost inconceivable extent. Lancashire abounds with witch-doctors, a set of quacks who pretend to cure diseases inflicted by the devil. The practices of these worthies may be judged of by the following case, reported in the *Hertford Reformer* of the 23d of June 1838. The witch-doctor alluded to is better known by the name of the *cunning man*, and has a large practice in the counties of Lincoln and Nottingham. According to the writer in the *Reformer*, the dupe, whose name is not mentioned, had been for about two years afflicted with a painful abscess, and had been prescribed for without relief by more than one medical gentleman. He was urged by some of his friends, not only in his own village but in neighbouring ones, to consult the witch-doctor, as they were convinced he was under some evil influence. He agreed, and sent his wife to the *cunning man*, who lived in New St. Swithin's, in Lincoln. She was informed by this ignorant impostor that her husband's disorder was an infliction of the devil, occasioned by his next-door neighbours, who had made use of certain charms for that purpose. From the description he gave of the process, it appears to be the same as that employed by Dr. Fian and Gellie Duncan to work woe upon King James. He stated that the neighbours, instigated by a witch, whom he pointed out, took some wax and moulded it before the fire into the form of her husband, as near as they could represent him ; they then pierced the image with pins on all sides, repeated the Lord's Prayer backwards, and offered prayers to the devil that he would fix his stings into the person whom that figure represented, in like manner as they pierced *it* with pins. To counteract the effects of this diabolical process, the witch-doctor prescribed a certain medicine, and a charm to be worn next the body, on that part where the disease principally lay. The patient was to repeat the 109th and 119th Psalms every day, or the cure would not be effectual. The fee which he claimed for this advice was a guinea.

So efficacious is faith in the cure of any malady, that the patient actually felt much better after a three weeks' course of this prescription. The notable charm which the quack had given was afterwards opened, and found to be a piece of parchment covered with some cabalistic characters and signs of the planets.

The next-door neighbours were in great alarm that the witch-doctor would, on the solicitation of the recovering patient, employ some means to punish them for their pretended witchcraft. To escape the infliction, they feed another cunning man, in Nottinghamshire, who told them of a similar charm, which would preserve them from all the malice of their enemies. The writer concludes by saying, that " the doctor, not long after he had been thus consulted, wrote to say, that he had discovered that his patient was not afflicted by Satan, as he had imagined, but by God, and would continue more or less in the same state till his life's end."

An impostor carried on a similar trade in the neighbourhood of Tunbridge Wells about the year 1830. He had been in practice for several years, and charged enormous fees for his advice. This fellow pretended to be the seventh son of a seventh son, and to be endowed in consequence with miraculous powers for the cure of all diseases, but especially of those resulting from witchcraft. It was not only the poor who employed him, but ladies who rode in their carriages. He was often sent for from a distance of sixty or seventy miles by these people, who paid all his expenses to and fro, besides rewarding him handsomely. He was about eighty years of age, and his extremely venerable appearance aided his imposition in no slight degree. His name was Okey or Oakley.

In France the superstition at this day is even more prevalent than it is in England. Garinet, in his history of Magic and Sorcery in that country, cites upwards of twenty instances which occurred between the years 1805 and 1818. In the latter year no less than three tribunals were occupied with trials originating in this humiliating belief: we shall cite only one of them. Julian Desbourdes, aged fifty-three, a mason, and inhabitant of the village of Thilouze, near Bourdeaux, was taken suddenly ill, in the month of January 1818. As he did not know how to account for his malady, he suspected at last that he was bewitched. He communicated this suspicion to his son-in-law Bridier, and they both went to consult a sort of idiot, named Baudouin, who passed for a conjuror or *white-witch*. This man told them that Desbourdes was certainly bewitched, and offered to accompany them to the house of an old man named Renard, who, he said, was undoubtedly the criminal. On the night of the 23d of January all three proceeded stealthily to the dwelling of Renard, and accused him of afflicting persons with diseases by the aid of the devil. Desbourdes fell on his knees and earnestly entreated to be restored to his former health, promising that he would take no measures against him for the evil he had done. The old man denied in the strongest terms that he was a wizard ; and when Desbourdes still pressed him to remove the spell from him, he said he knew nothing about the spell, and refused to remove it. The idiot Boudouin, the *white-witch*, now interfered, and told his companions that no relief for the malady could ever be procured until the old man confessed his guilt. To force him to confession they lighted some sticks of sulphur which they had brought with them for the purpose, and placed them under the old man's nose. In a few moments he fell down suffocated and apparently lifeless. They were all greatly alarmed ; and thinking that they had killed the man, they carried him out and threw him into a neighbouring pond, hoping to make it appear that he had fallen in accidentally. The pond, however, was not very deep, and the coolness of the water reviving the old man, he opened his eyes and sat up. Desbourdes and Bridier, who were still waiting on the bank, were now more alarmed than before, lest he should recover and inform against them. They therefore waded into the pond, seized their victim by the hair of the head, beat him severely, and then held him under water till he was drowned.

They were all three apprehended on the charge of murder a few days afterwards. Desbourdes and Bridier were found guilty of aggravated manslaughter only, and sentenced to be burnt on the back, and to work in the galleys for life. The *white-witch* Boudouin was acquitted on the ground of insanity.

M. Garinet further informs us that France, at the time he wrote (1818), was overrun by a race of fellows who made a trade of casting out devils and finding out witches. He adds also, that many of the priests in the rural districts encouraged the superstition of their parishioners by resorting frequently to exorcisms whenever any foolish persons took it into their heads that a spell had been thrown over them. He recommended, as a remedy for the evil, that all these exorcists, whether lay or clerical, should be sent to the galleys, and felt assured that the number of witches would then very sensibly diminish.

Many other instances of this lingering belief might be cited both in France and Great Britain, and indeed in every other country in Europe. So deeply rooted are some errors, that ages cannot remove them. The poisonous tree that once overshadowed the land may be cut down by the sturdy efforts of sages and philosophers; the sun may shine clearly upon spots where venomous things once nestled in security and shade; but still the entangled roots are stretched beneath the surface, and may be found by those who dig. Another king like James I. might make them vegetate again ; and more mischievous still, another Pope like Innocent VIII. might raise the decaying roots to strength and verdure.   Still it is consoling to think that the delirium has passed away; that the raging madness has given place to a milder folly; and that we may now count by units the votaries of a superstition which in former ages numbered its victims by tens of thousands, and its votaries by millions.

FLOATING A WITCH.

One of the first in point of date, and hardly second to any in point of atrocity, is the murder by this means of Sir Thomas Overbury, which disgraced the court of James I. in the year 1613. A slight sketch of it will be a fitting introduction to the history of the poisoning mania, which was so prevalent in France and Italy fifty years later.

Robert Kerr, a Scottish youth, was early taken notice of by James I., and loaded with honours, for no other reason that the world could ever discover than the beauty of his person. James, even in his own day, was suspected of being addicted to the most abominable of all offences; and the more we examine his history now, the stronger the suspicion becomes. However that may be, the handsome Kerr, lending his smooth cheek even in public to the disgusting kisses of his royal master, rose rapidly in favour. In the year 1613, he was made Lord High Treasurer of Scotland, and created an English peer by the style and title of Viscount Rochester. Still further honours were in store for him.

In this rapid promotion he had not been without a friend. Sir Thomas Overbury, the king's secretary — who appears, from some threats in his own letters, to have been no better than a pander to the vices of the king, and privy to his dangerous secrets—exerted all his backstair influence to forward the promotion of Kerr, by whom he was doubtless repaid in some way or other. Overbury did not confine his friendship to this—if friendship ever could exist between two such men—but acted the part of an *entremetteur*, and assisted Rochester to carry on an adulterous intrigue with the Lady Frances Howard, the wife of the Earl of Essex. This woman was a person of violent passions, and lost to all sense of shame. Her husband was in her way, and to be freed from him she instituted proceedings for a divorce, on grounds which a woman of any modesty or delicacy of feeling would die rather than avow. Her scandalous suit was successful, and was no sooner decided than preparations on a scale of the greatest magnificence were made for her marriage with Lord Rochester.

Sir Thomas Overbury, who had willingly assisted his patron to intrigue with the Countess of Essex, seems to have imagined that his marriage with so vile a woman might retard his advancement. He accordingly employed all his influence to dissuade him from it; but Rochester was bent on the match, and his passions were as violent as those of the countess. On one occasion, when Overbury and the viscount were walking in the gallery of Whitehall, Overbury was overheard to say, " Well, my lord, if you do marry that base woman, you will utterly ruin your honour and yourself. You shall never do it with my advice or consent ; and if you do, you had best look to stand

an apothecary named Franklin. Both these persons knew for what purposes the poisons were needed, and employed their skill in mixing them in the pastry and other edibles, in such small quantities as gradually to wear out the constitution of their victim. Mrs. Turner regularly furnished the poisoned articles to the under-keeper, who placed them before Overbury. Not only his food but his drink was

SIR THOMAS OVERBURY.

poisoned. Arsenic was mixed with the salt he ate, and cantharides with the pepper. All this time his health declined sensibly. Daily he grew weaker and weaker ; and with a sickly appetite craved for sweets and jellies. Rochester continued to condole with him, and anticipated all his wants in this respect, sending him abundance of pastry, and occasionally partridges and other game, and young pigs. With the sauce for the game, Mrs. Turner mixed a quantity of cantharides, and poisoned the pork with lunar-caustic. As stated on the trial

come to light by the judgment of physicians, the foul play that had been offered him, consented to stifle him with the bedclothes, which accordingly was performed ; and so ended his miserable life, with the assurance of the conspirators that he died by the poison ; none thinking otherwise than these two murderers."

The sudden death, the indecent haste of the funeral, and the non-holding of an inquest upon the body, strengthened the suspicions that were afloat. Rumour, instead of whispering, began to speak out ; and the relatives of the deceased openly expressed their belief that their kinsman had been murdered. But Rochester was still all powerful at court, and no one dared to utter a word to his discredit. Shortly afterwards, his marriage with the Countess of Essex was celebrated with the utmost splendour, the king himself being present at the ceremony.

It would seem that Overbury's knowledge of James's character was deeper than Rochester had given him credit for, and that he had been a true prophet when he predicted that his marriage would eventually estrange James from his minion. At this time, however, Rochester stood higher than ever in the royal favour ; but it did not last long—conscience, that busy monitor, was at work. The tongue of rumour was never still ; and Rochester, who had long been a guilty, became at last a wretched man. His cheeks lost their colour —his eyes grew dim ; and he became moody, careless, and melancholy. The king, seeing him thus, took at length no pleasure in his society, and began to look about for another favourite. George Villiers, Duke of Buckingham, was the man to his mind : quick-witted, handsome, and unscrupulous. The two latter qualities alone were sufficient to recommend him to James I. In proportion as the influence of Rochester declined, that of Buckingham increased. A falling favourite has no friends ; and rumour wagged her tongue against Rochester louder and more pertinaciously than ever. A new favourite, too, generally endeavours to hasten by a kick the fall of the old one ; and Buckingham, anxious to work the complete ruin of his forerunner in the king's good graces, encouraged the relatives of Sir Thomas Overbury to prosecute their inquiries into the strange death of their kinsman.

James was rigorous enough in the punishment of offences when he was not himself involved. He piqued himself, moreover, on his dexterity in unravelling mysteries. The affair of Sir Thomas Overbury found him congenial occupation. He set to work by ordering the arrest of Sir Jervis Elwes. James, at this early stage of the proceedings, does not seem to have been aware that Rochester was so deeply implicated. Struck with horror at the atrocious system of slow poison-

two or three, or more, as they list, which they four manner of ways do execute, viz. *haustu, gustu, odore,* and *contactu.*"

When the indictment was read over, Weston made no other reply than "Lord have mercy upon me! Lord have mercy upon me!" On being asked how he would be tried, he refused to throw himself upon a jury of his country, and declared that he would be tried by God alone. In this he persisted for some time. The fear of the dreadful punishment for contumacy* induced him at length to plead "Not guilty," and take his trial in due course of law.

LORD COKE.

All the circumstances against him were fully proved, and he was found guilty and executed at Tyburn. Mrs. Turner, Franklin, and Sir Jervis Elwes were also brought to trial, found guilty, and executed between the 19th of October and the 4th of December 1615; but the grand trial of the Earl and Countess of Somerset did not take place till the month of May following.

On the trial of Sir Jervis Elwes, circumstances had transpired, shewing a guilty knowledge of the poisoning on the part of the Earl of Northampton, the uncle of Lady Somerset, and the chief falconer Sir Thomas Monson. The former was dead; but Sir Thomas Monson was arrested and brought to trial. It appeared, however, that he was too dangerous a man to be brought to the scaffold. He knew too many of the odious secrets of James I., and his dying speech might contain disclosures which would compromise the king. To conceal old guilt it was necessary to incur new: the trial of Sir Thomas Monson was brought to an abrupt conclusion, and himself set at liberty.

---

* The punishment for the contumacious was expressed by the words *onere, frigore, et fame.* By the first was meant, that the culprit should be extended on his back on the ground, and weights placed over his body, gradually increased, until he expired. Sometimes the punishment was not extended to this length, and the victim being allowed to recover, underwent the second portion, the *frigore,* which consisted in his standing naked in the open air, for a certain space, in the sight of all the people. The third, or *fame,* was more dreadful, the statute saying, "That he was to be preserved with the coarsest bread that could be got, and water out of the next sink, or puddle, to the place of execution; and that day he had water he should have no bread, and that day he had bread he should have no water;" and in this torment he was to linger as long as nature would hold out.

eleven hours, he was found guilty, and condemned to the felon's death.

Whatever may have been the secrets between the criminal and the king, the latter, notwithstanding his terrific oath, was afraid to sign the death-warrant. It might, perchance, have been his own. The earl and countess were committed to the Tower, where they remained for nearly five years. At the end of this period, to the surprise and scandal of the community, and the disgrace of its chief magistrate, they both received the royal pardon, but were ordered to reside at a distance from the court. Having been found guilty of felony, the estates of the earl had become forfeited; but James granted him out of their revenues an income of 4000*l.* per annum ! Shamelessness could go no further.

THE COUNTESS OF SOMERSET.

Of the after-life of these criminals nothing is known, except that the love they had formerly borne each other was changed into aversion, and that they lived under the same roof for months together without the interchange of a word.

The exposure of their atrocities did not put a stop to the practice of poisoning. On the contrary, as we shall see hereafter, it engendered that insane imitation which is so strange a feature of the human character. James himself is supposed, with great probability, to have fallen a victim to it. In the notes to Harris's *Life and Writings of James I.*, there is a good deal of information on the subject. The guilt of Buckingham, although not fully established, rests upon circumstances of suspicion stronger than have been sufficient to lead hundreds to the scaffold. His motives for committing the crime are stated to have been a desire of revenge for the coldness with which the king, in the latter years of his reign, began to regard him ; his fear that James intended to degrade him ; and his hope that the great influence he possessed over the mind of the heir apparent would last through a new reign, if the old one were brought to a close.

In the second volume of the *Harleian Miscellany*, there is a tract, entitled the *Forerunner of Revenge*, written by George Eglisham, doctor of medicine, and one of the physicians to King James. Harris, in quoting it, says that it is full of rancour and prejudice. It is evidently exaggerated, but forms nevertheless a link in the chain of

stones, calling out, "The poisoner! the poisoner! Down with the wizard! down with him!" A mob very soon collected, and the doctor took to his heels and ran for his life. He was pursued and seized in Wood Street, and from thence dragged by the hair through the mire to St. Paul's Cross; the mob beating him with sticks and stones, and calling out, "Kill the wizard! kill the poisoner!"

Charles I., on hearing of the riot, rode from Whitehall to quell it; but he arrived too late to save the victim. Every bone in his body was broken, and he was quite dead. Charles was excessively indignant, and fined the city six hundred pounds for its inability to deliver up the ring-leaders to justice.

But it was in Italy that poisoning was most prevalent. From a very early period, it seems to have been looked upon in that country as a perfectly justifiable means of

PAUL'S CROSS; SEVENTEENTH CENTURY.

getting rid of an enemy. The Italians of the sixteenth and seventeenth centuries poisoned their opponents with as little compunction as an Englishman of the present day brings an action at law against any one who has done him an injury. The writings of contemporary authors informs us that, when La Spara and La Tophania carried on their infernal trade, ladies put poison-bottles on their dressing-tables as openly, and used them with as little scruple upon others, as modern dames use *eau de Cologne* or lavender-water upon themselves. So powerful is the influence of fashion, it can even cause murder to be regarded as a venial peccadillo.

In the memoirs of the last Duke of Guise, who made a Quixotic attempt, in 1648, to seize upon the government of Naples, we find some curious particulars relative to the popular feeling with regard to poisoning. A man named Gennaro Annese, who, after the short and extraordinary career of Masaniello the fisherman, had established himself as a sort of captain-general of the populace, rendered himself so obnoxious to the Duke of Guise, that the adherents of the latter de-

whom, it was afterwards ascertained, belonged to the first families of Rome.

In order to have positive evidence of the practices of this female conclave, a lady was employed by the government to seek an interview with them. She dressed herself out in the most magnificent style; and having been amply provided with money, she found but little difficulty, when she had stated her object, of procuring an audience of La Spara and her sisterhood. She pretended to be in extreme distress of mind on account of the infidelities and ill-treatment of her husband, and implored La Spara to furnish her with a few drops of the wonderful elixir, the efficacy of which in sending cruel husbands to "their last long sleep" was so much vaunted by the ladies of Rome. La Spara fell into the snare, and sold her some of her "drops" at a price commensurate with the supposed wealth of the purchaser.

The liquor thus obtained was subjected to an analysis, and found to be, as was suspected, a slow poison; clear, tasteless, and limpid, like that spoken of by the Duke of Guise. Upon this evidence, the house was surrounded by the police, and La Spara and her companions taken into custody. La Spara, who is described as having been a little ugly old woman, was put to the torture, but obstinately refused to confess her guilt. Another of the women, named La Gratiosa, had less firmness, and laid bare all the secrets of the infernal sisterhood. Taking a confession extorted by anguish on the rack at its true value (nothing at all), there is still sufficient evidence to warrant posterity in a belief of their guilt. They were found guilty, and condemned, according to their degrees of culpability, to various punishments. La Spara, Gratiosa, and three young women, who had poisoned their husbands, were hanged together at Rome. Upwards of thirty women were whipped publicly through the streets; and several, whose high rank screened them from more degrading punishment, were banished from the country, and mulcted in heavy fines. In a few months afterwards, nine women more were hanged for poisoning; and another bevy, including many young and beautiful girls, were whipped half naked through the streets of Rome.

This severity did not put a stop to the practice, and jealous women and avaricious men, anxious to step into the inheritance of fathers, uncles, or brothers, resorted to poison. As it was quite free from taste, colour, and smell, it was administered without exciting suspicion. The skilful vendors compounded it of different degrees of strength, so that the poisoners had only to say whether they wanted their victims to die in a week, a month, or six months, and they were suited with corresponding doses. The vendors were chiefly women,

:eedingly well taken ; for she contrived to elude the vigilance of the :horities for several years. What is still more extraordinary, as ?wing the ramifications of her system, her trade was still carried on as great an extent as before. Lebat informs us that she had so eat a sympathy for poor wives who hated their husbands and anted to get rid of them, but could not afford to buy her wonderful ∙7ua, that she made them presents of it.

She was not allowed, however, to play at this game for ever ; she ⁀as at length discovered in a nunnery, and her retreat cut off. The ∙iceroy made several representations to the superior to deliver her 1p, but without effect. The abbess, supported by the archbishop of the diocese, constantly refused. The public curiosity was in consequence so much excited at the additional importance thus thrust upon the criminal, that thousands of persons visited the nunnery in order to catch a glimpse of her.

The patience of the viceroy appears to have been exhausted by these delays. Being a man of sense, and not a very zealous Catholic, he determined that even the Church should not shield a criminal so atrocious. Setting the privileges of the nunnery at defiance, he sent a troop of soldiers, who broke over the walls, and carried her away, *vi et armis*. The archbishop, Cardinal Pignatelli, was highly indignant, and threatened to excommunicate and lay the whole city under interdict. All the inferior clergy, animated by the *esprit du corps*, took up the question, and so worked upon the superstitious and bigoted people, that they were ready to rise in a mass to storm the palace of the viceroy and rescue the prisoner.

These were serious difficulties ; but the viceroy was not a man to be daunted. Indeed he seems to have acted throughout with a rare union of astuteness, coolness, and energy. To avoid the evil consequences of the threatened excommunication, he placed a guard round the palace of the archbishop, judging that the latter would not be so foolish as to launch out an anathema which would cause the city to be starved, and himself in it. The market-people would not have dared to come to the city with provisions so long as it remained under the ban. There would have been too much inconvenience to himself and his ghostly brethren in such a measure ; and, as the viceroy anticipated, the good cardinal reserved his thunders for some other occasion.

Still there was the populace. To quiet their clamour and avert the impending insurrection, the agents of the government adroitly mingled with the people, and spread abroad a report that Tophania had poisoned all the wells and fountains of the city. This was enough. The popular feeling was turned against her immediately. Those who,

at once into the gulf of sin. She was drawn to its most loathsome depths ere retribution overtook her.

She had as yet shewn a fair outside to the world, and found but little difficulty in effecting a legal separation from her husband, who had not the art to conceal his vices. The proceeding gave great offence to her family. She appears, after this, to have thrown off the mask completely, and carried on her intrigues so openly with her lover, Sainte Croix, that her father, M. D'Aubray, scandalised at her conduct, procured a *lettre de cachet*, and had him imprisoned in the Bastille for a twelvemonth.

THE BASTILLE.

Sainte Croix, who had been in Italy, was a dabbler in poisons. He knew something of the secrets of the detestable La Spara, and improved himself in them from the instructions of Exili, with whom he speedily contracted a sort of friendship. By him he was shewn how to prepare, not only the liquid poisons employed in Italy, but that known as *succession-powder*, which afterwards became so celebrated in France. Like his mistress, he appeared amiable, witty, and intelligent, and shewed no signs to the world of the two fierce pas-

VOL. II. P

nistering the poisons; and in less than six weeks time they had both gone to their long home.

Suspicion was now excited ; but so cautiously had all been done, that it found no one upon whom to attach itself. The marquise had a sister, and she was entitled, by the death of her relatives, to half the property. Less than the whole would not satisfy Sainte Croix, and he determined that she should die the same death as her father and brothers. She was too distrustful, however; and, by quitting Paris, she escaped the destruction that was lurking for her.

The marquise had undertaken these murders to please her lover. She was now anxious to perpetrate another on her own account. She wished to marry Sainte Croix; but, though separated from her husband, she was not divorced. She thought it would be easier to poison him than to apply to the tribunals for a divorce, which might, perhaps, be refused. But Sainte Croix had no longer any love for his guilty instrument. Bad men do not admire others who are as bad as themselves. Though a villain himself, he had no desire to marry one, and was not at all anxious for the death of the marquis. He seemed, however, to enter into the plot, and supplied her with poison for her husband; but he took care to provide a remedy. La Brinvilliers poisoned him one day, and Sainte Croix gave him an antidote the next. In this manner he was buffeted about between them for some time, and finally escaped, with a ruined constitution and a broken heart.

But the day of retribution was at hand, and a terrible mischance brought the murders to light. The nature of the poisons compounded by Sainte Croix was so deadly, that, when working in his laboratory, he was obliged to wear a mask, to preserve himself from suffocation. One day, the mask slipped off, and the miserable wretch perished in his crimes. His corpse was found, on the following morning, in the obscure lodging where he had fitted up his laboratory. As he appeared to be without friends or relatives, the police took possession of his effects. Among other things, was found a small box, to which was affixed the following singular document :

" I humbly beg, that those into whose hands this box may fall, will do me the favour to deliver it into the hands only of the Marchioness de Brinvilliers, who resides in the Rue Neuve St. Paul, as every thing it contains concerns her, and belongs to her alone ; and as, besides, there is nothing in it that can be of use to any person but her. In case she shall be dead before me, it is my wish that it be burned, with every thing it contains, without opening or altering any thing. In order that no one may plead ignorance, I swear by the God that I adore, and by all that is held most sacred, that I assert nothing but the truth : and if my intentions, just and reasonable as

rtunes were so celebrated. Her vanity was flattered by the com-
nt. Desgrais saw, to use a vulgar but forcible expression, "that
ıd got on the blind side of her;" and he adroitly continued to
out the language of love and admiration till the deluded mar-
ess was completely thrown off her guard. She agreed, without
 solicitation, to meet him outside the walls of the convent,
: their amorous intrigue might be carried on more conveniently
within. Faithful to her appointment with her supposed new
 she came, and found herself, not in the embrace of a gallant,
. the custody of a policeman.
:r trial was not long delayed. The proofs against her were
ant. The dying declaration of La Chaussée would have been
enough to convict her; but besides that, there were the myste-
document attached to the box of Sainte Croix, her flight from
ı, and, stronger and more damning proof than all, a paper, in her
andwriting, found among the effects of Sainte Croix, in which
tailed to him the misdeeds of her life, and spoke of the murder
 father and brothers in terms that left no doubt of her guilt.
; the trial, all Paris was in commotion. La Brinvilliers was the
ıbject of conversation. All the details of her crimes were pub-
 and greedily devoured; and the idea of secret poisoning first
:o the heads of hundreds, who afterwards became guilty of it.
the 16th of July, 1676, the Superior Criminal Court of Paris
nced a verdict of guilty against her, for the murder of her
ınd brothers, and the attempt upon the life of her sister. She
ndemned to be drawn on a hurdle, with her feet bare, a rope
ıer neck, and a burning torch in her hand, to the great entrance
:athedral of Notre Dame, where she was to make the *amende*
Je in sight of all the people; to be taken from thence to the
e Grève, and there to be beheaded. Her body was afterwards
ırned, and her ashes scattered to the winds.
: her sentence, she made a full confession of her guilt. She seems
 looked upon death without fear; but it was recklessness, not
, that supported her. Madame de Sevigné says, that when on
ıle, on her way to the scaffold, she entreated her confessor to
s influence with the executioner to place himself next to her,
 body might hide from her view " that scoundrel Desgrais,
1 entrapped her." She also asked the ladies, who had been
o their windows to witness the procession, what they were
at? adding, "A pretty sight you have come to see, truly!"
;hed when on the scaffold, dying as she had lived, impenitent
rtless. On the morrow, the populace came in crowds to col-
 ashes, to preserve them as relics. She was regarded as a

'wo women, especially, made themselves notorious at this time,
were instrumental to the deaths of hundreds of individuals. They
resided in Paris, and were named Lavoisin and Lavigoreux.
Spara and Tophania, of whom they were imitators, they chiefly
their poisons to women who wanted to get rid of their husbands;
in some few instances, to husbands who wanted to get rid of
wives. Their ostensible occupation was that of midwives. They
pretended to be fortune-tellers, and were visited by persons of
· class of society. The rich and poor thronged alike to their
ardes to learn the secrets of the future. Their prophecies were
ipally of death. They foretold to women the approaching dis-
on of husbands, and to needy heirs the end of rich relatives,
had made them, as Byron expresses it, "wait too, too long
ly." They generally took care to be instrumental in fulfilling
own predictions. They used to tell their wretched employers
ome sign of the approaching death would take place in the house,
ıs the breaking of glass or china; and they paid servants consi-
le fees to cause a breakage, as if by accident, exactly at the ap-
:d time. Their occupation as midwives made them acquainted
the secrets of many families, which they afterwards turned to
ful account.
is not known how long they had carried on this awful trade
: they were discovered. Detection finally overtook them at the
of the year 1679. They were both tried, found guilty, and
d alive on the Place de Grève, on the 22d of February, 1680,
their hands had been bored through with a red-hot iron, and
ut off. Their numerous accomplices in Paris and· in the pro-
were also discovered and brought to trial. According to some
·s, thirty, and to others, fifty of them, chiefly women, were
l in the principal cities.
voisin kept a list of the visitors who came to her house to pur-
ɔoisons. This paper was seized by the police on her arrest, and
ıed by the tribunals. Among the names were found those of
arshal de Luxembourg, the Countess de Soissons, and the
ss de Bouillon. The marshal seems only to have been guilty
ece of discreditable folly in visiting a woman of this descrip-
ut the popular voice at the time imputed to him something
han folly. The author of the *Memoirs of the Affairs of Europe*
le *Peace of Utrecht*, says, "The miserable gang who dealt in
and prophecy alleged that he had sold himself to the devil,
ıt a young girl of the name of Dupin had been poisoned by his
Among other stories, they said he had made a contract with
il, in order to marry his son to the daughter of the Marquis

PALACE OF WOODSTOCK.

HAUNTED HOUSES.

Here's a knocking indeed! . . . . Knock! knock! knock! . . . ,
ho's there, i' the name o' Beelzebub? . . . . Who's there, i' the devil's
he? Knock! knock! knock!—Never at quiet?—*Macbeth.*

has not either seen or heard of some house, shut up and un-
table, fallen into decay, and looking dusty and dreary, from
, at midnight, strange sounds have been heard to issue—aerial
ings—the rattling of chains, and the groaning of perturbed spi-
-a house that people have thought it unsafe to pass after dark,
hich has remained for years without a tenant, and which no
would occupy, even were he paid to do so? There are hun-
of such houses in England in the present day; hundreds in
, Germany, and almost every country of Europe, which are
d with the mark of fear—places for the timid to avoid, and the
to bless themselves at, and ask protection from, as they pass—
odes of ghosts and evil spirits. There are many such houses in
a; and if any vain boaster of the march of intellect would but
he trouble to find them out and count them, he would be con-
that intellect must yet make some enormous strides before
d superstitions can be eradicated.
idea that such houses exist is a remnant of the witch creed,
merits separate notice from its comparative harmlessness, and

was so strong that it blew the door to with some violence. There
1g no latch, it swung open again; and when there was a fresh
t, was again blown to. The new proprietor lost no time in send-
for a glazier, and the mysterious noises ceased for ever. The
.se was replastered and repainted, and once more regained its lost
d name. It was not before two or three years, however, that it
thoroughly established in popular favour; and many persons,
1 then, would always avoid passing it, if they could reach their
ination by any other street.

1 similar story is narrated by Sir Walter Scott, in his *Letters on*
onology and Witchcraft, the hero of which was a gentleman of
1 and distinction, well known in the political world. Shortly
· he succeeded to his title and estates, there was a rumour among
servants concerning a strange noise that used to be heard at night
he family mansion, and the cause of which no one could ascer-
The gentleman resolved to discover it himself, and to watch
hat purpose with a domestic who had grown old in the family,
who, like the rest, had whispered strange things about the
king having begun immediately upon the death of his old mas-
These two watched until the noise was heard, and at last traced
a small store-room, used as a place for keeping provisions of
us kinds for the family, and of which the old butler had the
They entered this place, and remained for some time without
ng the noises which they had traced thither. At length the
l was heard, but much lower than it seemed to be while they
farther off, and their imaginations were more excited. They
discovered the cause without difficulty. A rat, caught in an
shioned trap, had occasioned the noise by its efforts to escape,
ich it was able to raise the trap-door of its prison to a certain
t, but was then obliged to drop it. The noise of the fall re-
ing through the house had occasioned the mysterious rumours,
but for the investigation of the proprietor, would in all pro-
:y have acquired so bad a name for the dwelling that no ser-
would have inhabited it. The circumstance was told to Sir
r Scott by the gentleman to whom it happened.

t in general, houses that have acquired this character have
aore indebted for it to the roguery of living men than to acci-
like these. Six monks played off a clever trick of the kind
hat worthy king, Louis, whose piety has procured him in the
of his own country the designation of "the Saint." Having
his confessor speak in terms of warm eulogy of the goodness
arning of the monks of the order of St. Bruno, he expressed
h to establish a community of them near Paris. Bernard de

liately, the lights disappeared, and the green ghost (so said the
ıks) was laid at rest for ever under the waves of the Red Sea.*

In the year 1580, one Gilles Blacre had taken the lease of a house
he suburbs of Tours, but repenting him of his bargain with the
llord, Peter Piquet, he endeavoured to prevail upon him to can-
the agreement. Peter, however, was satisfied with his tenant
his terms, and would listen to no compromise. Very shortly
rwards, the rumour was spread all over Tours that the house of
es Blacre was haunted. Gilles himself asserted that he verily
eved his house to be the general rendezvous of all the witches and
spirits of France. The noise they made was awful, and quite
/ented him from sleeping. They knocked against the wall, howled
he chimneys, broke his window-glass, scattered his pots and pans
)ver his kitchen, and set his chairs and tables a-dancing the whole
ıt through. Crowds of persons assembled round the house to hear
mysterious noises; and the bricks were observed to detach them-
es from the wall, and fall into the streets upon the heads of those
had not said their paternoster before coming out in the morning.
se things having continued for some time, Gilles Blacre made his
plaint to the Civil Court of Tours, and Peter Piquet was sum-
ıed to shew cause why the lease should not be annulled. Poor
ır could make no defence, and the court unanimously agreed that
ease could hold good under such circumstances, and annulled it
rdingly, condemning the unlucky owner to all the expenses of
suit. Peter appealed to the parliament of Paris; and after a
examination, the parliament confirmed the lease. "Not," said
judge, "because it has not been fully and satisfactorily proved
the house is troubled by evil spirits, but that there was an in-
ality in the proceedings before the Civil Court of Tours, that
ered its decision null and of no effect."

similar cause was tried before the parliament of Bourdeaux, in
/ear 1595, relative to a house in that city which was sorely trou-
by evil spirits. The parliament appointed certain ecclesiastics
camine and report to them, and on their report in the affirmative
the house was haunted, the lease was annulled, and the tenant
lved from all payment of rent and taxes.†

)ne of the best stories of a haunted house is that of the royal
;e of Woodstock, in the year 1649, when the commissioners sent
London by the Long Parliament to take possession of it, and
e all the emblems of royalty about it, were fairly driven out by
fear of the devil, and the annoyances they suffered from a
ish cavalier, who played the imp to admiration. The commis-

* Garinet, *Histoire de la Magie en France*, p.75.　　† Ibid. p. 156.

security. When, on the succeeding night, they heard no noises,
began to flatter themselves that the devil was driven out, and
ared accordingly to take up their quarters for the whole winter
ae palace. These symptoms on their part became the signal for
wed uproar among the fiends. On the 1st of November, they
d something walking with a slow and solemn pace up and down
withdrawing-room, and immediately afterwards a shower of stones,
cs, mortar, and broken glass pelted about their ears. On the
he steps were again heard in the withdrawing-room, sounding to
r fancy very much like the treading of an enormous bear, which
inued for about a quarter of an hour. This noise having ceased,
rge warming-pan was thrown violently upon the table, followed
, number of stones and the jawbone of a horse. Some of the
est walked valiantly into the withdrawing-room, armed with
·ds and pistols; but could discover nothing. They were afraid
 night to go to sleep, and sat up, making fires in every room,
burning candles and lamps in great abundance; thinking that,
he fiends loved darkness, they would not disturb a company sur-
ıded with so much light. They were deceived, however: buckets
ater came down the chimneys and extinguished the fires; and the
lles were blown out, they knew not how. Some of the servants
had betaken themselves to bed were drenched with putrid ditch-
·r as they lay, and arose in great fright, muttering incoherent
ers, and exposing to the wondering eyes of the commissioners
· linen all dripping with green moisture, and their knuckles red
the blows they had at the same time received from some invi-
tormentors. While they were still speaking, there was a noise
the loudest thunder, or the firing of a whole park of artillery,
ı which they all fell down upon their knees and implored the
ection of the Almighty. One of the commissioners then arose, the
rs still kneeling, and asked in a courageous voice, and in the name
od, who was there, and what they had done that they should be
bled in that manner. No answer was returned, and the noises
ed for a while. At length, however, as the commissioners said,
e devil came again, and brought with it seven devils worse than
f." Being again in darkness, they lighted a candle and placed it
ıe doorway, that it might throw a light upon the two chambers
ıce; but it was suddenly blown out, and one commissioner said
he had "seen the similitude of a horse's hoof striking the candle
candlestick into the middle of the chamber, and afterwards mak-
,hree scrapes on the snuff to put it out." Upon this, the same
ın was so bold as to draw his sword; but he asserted positively
he had hardly withdrawn it from the scabbard before an invisible

ns for a long time, and searched every corner of the house; but
overing nothing, he went to bed again. He was no sooner snug
er the clothes than the noise began again more furiously than
, sounding very much like a "thumping and drumming on the
of his house, and then by degrees going off into the air."

These things continued for several nights, when it came to the
lection of Mr. Mompesson that some time before he had given
rs for the arrest and imprisonment of a wandering drummer, who
; about the country with a large drum, disturbing quiet people and
iting alms, and that he had detained the man's drum, and that
ably the drummer was a wizard, and had sent evil spirits to
it his house to be revenged of him. He became strengthened in
opinion every day, especially when the noises assumed, to his
r, a resemblance to the beating of a drum, "like that at the
cing up of a guard." Mrs. Mompesson being brought to bed, the
, or the drummer, very kindly and considerately refrained from
ng the usual riot; but, as soon as she recovered strength, began
i "in a ruder manner than before, following and vexing the
g children, and beating their bedsteads with so much violence
every one expected they would fall in pieces." For an hour to-
er, as the worthy Mr. Mompesson repeated to his wondering
ibours, this infernal drummer "would beat ' Roundheads and
olds,' the 'Tat-too,' and several other points of war, as cleverly
y soldier." When this had lasted long enough, he changed his
es, and scratched with his iron talons under the children's bed.
the 5th of November," says the Rev. Joseph Glanvil, "it made
ghty noise; and a servant observing two boards in the children's
seeming to move, he bid it give him one of them. Upon which
oard came (nothing moving it that he saw) within a yard of him.
nan added, ' Nay, let me have it in my hand;' upon which the
, devil, or drummer pushed it towards him so close that he might
. it." "This," continues Glanvil, "was in the day-time, and
een by a whole roomful of people. That morning it left a
ureous smell behind it, which was very offensive. At night the
ter, one Mr. Cragg, and several of the neighbours came to the
on a visit. Mr. Cragg went to prayers with them, kneeling at
hildren's bedside, where it then became very troublesome and
During prayer-time, the spirit withdrew into the cock-loft, but
ned as soon as prayers were done; and then, in sight of the com-
the chairs walked about the room of themselves, the children's
were hurled over their heads, and every loose thing moved about
iamber. At the same time, a bed-staff was thrown at the mi-
, which hit him on the leg, but so favourably, that a lock of

L. II.   Q

into his mother's; filled the porringers with ashes; hid a Bible
· the grate; and turned the money black in people's pockets.
night," said Mr. Mompesson in a letter to Mr. Glanvil, "there
seven or eight of these devils in the shape of men, who, as soon
gun was fired, would shuffle away into an arbour;" a circum-
₃ which might have convinced Mr. Mompesson of the mortal
e of his persecutors, if he had not been of the number of those
than blind, who shut their eyes and refuse to see.

₁ the mean time the drummer, the supposed cause of all the mis-
passed his time in Gloucester gaol, whither he had been com-
d as a rogue and a vagabond. Being visited one day by some
₁ from the neighbourhood of Tedworth, he asked what was the
in Wiltshire, and whether people did not talk a great deal about
mming in a gentleman's house there? The visitor replied that
ard of nothing else; upon which the drummer observed, "I
done it; I have thus plagued him; and he shall never be quiet
he hath made me satisfaction for taking away my drum." No
the fellow, who seems to have been a gipsy, spoke the truth,
₁at the gang of which he was a member knew more about the
₁ at Mr. Mompesson's house than any body else. Upon these
, however, he was brought to trial at Salisbury for witchcraft;
₁eing found guilty, was sentenced to transportation; a sentence
, for its leniency, excited no little wonder in that age, when
an accusation, whether proved or not, generally insured the
or the gibbet. Glanvil says that the noises ceased immediately
₁ummer was sent beyond the seas; but that, somehow or other,
naged to return from transportation—"by raising storms and
₁ting the seamen, it was said,"—when the disturbances were
₁ith renewed, and continued at intervals for several years. Cer-
, if the confederates of this roving gipsy were so pertinacious in
₁ting poor weak Mr. Mompesson, their pertinacity is a most
₁rdinary instance of what revenge is capable of. It was believed
ny, at the time, that Mr. Mompesson himself was privy to the
matter, and permitted and encouraged these tricks in his house
₁ sake of notoriety; but it seems more probable that the gipsies
₁he real delinquents, and that Mr. Mompesson was as much
₁d and bewildered as his credulous neighbours, whose excited
₁ations conjured up no small portion of these stories,

"Which roll'd, and as they roll'd grew larger visibly."

₁ny instances of a similar kind, during the seventeenth cen-
night be gleaned from Glanvil and other writers of that period;
₁ey do not differ sufficiently from these to justify a detail of

hile this matter was yet pending, Miss Fanny was suddenly
 ill of the small-pox; and, notwithstanding every care and
:ion, she died in a few days, and was buried in a vault under
:nwell church. Parsons now began to hint that the poor lady
ome unfairly by her death, and that Mr. Kent was accessory to
m his too great eagerness to enter into possession of the pro-
she had bequeathed him. Nothing further was said for nearly
'ears; but it would appear that Parsons was of so revengeful
racter, that he had never forgotten or forgiven his differences
Mr. Kent, and the indignity of having been sued for the bor-
l money. The strong passions of pride and avarice were silently
rk during all that interval, hatching schemes of revenge, but
ssing them one after the other as impracticable, until, at last, a
le one suggested itself. About the beginning of the year 1762,
larm was spread over all the neighbourhood of Cock Lane, that
ouse of Parsons was haunted by the ghost of poor Fanny, and
the daughter of Parsons, a girl about twelve years of age, had
al times seen and conversed with the spirit, who had, moreover,
med her, that she had not died of the small-pox, as was cur-
y reported, but of poison, administered by Mr. Kent. Parsons,
originated, took good care to countenance these reports; and
ıswer to numerous inquiries, said his house was every night,
ıad been for two years, in fact, ever since the death of Fanny,
led by a loud knocking at the doors and in the walls. Having
prepared the ignorant and credulous neighbours to believe or
;erate for themselves what he had told them, he sent for a gen-
ın of a higher class in life, to come and witness these extraordi-
occurrences. The gentleman came accordingly, and found the
hter of Parsons, to whom the spirit alone appeared, and whom
 it answered, in bed, trembling violently, having just seen the
:, and been again informed that she had died from poison. A
knocking was also heard from every part of the chamber, which
ystified the not very clear understanding of the visitor, that he
rted, afraid to doubt and ashamed to believe, but with a promise
ing the clergyman of the parish and several other gentlemen on
ollowing day to report upon the mystery.
'n the following night he returned, bringing with him three
ymen, and about twenty other persons, including two negroes,
, upon a consultation with Parsons, they resolved to sit up the
e night, and await the ghost's arrival. It was then explained by
ıns, that although the ghost would never render itself visible to
ody but his daughter, it had no objection to answer the ques-
 that might be put to it by any person present, and that it ex-

[ow long was that before your death ?"—"About three hours."
Jan your former servant, Qarrots, give any information about
ison ?"—" Yes."
Are you Kent's wife's sister ?"—" Yes."
Were you married to Kent after your sister's death ?"—" No."
Was any body else, besides Kent, concerned in your murder ?"
o."
Jan you, if you like, appear visibly to any one ?"—" Yes."
Will you do so ?"—" Yes."
Jan you go out of this house ?"—" Yes."
Is it your intention to follow this child about every where ?"—
."
Are you pleased in being asked these questions ?"—"Yes."
Does it ease your troubled soul ?"—" Yes."
[ere there was heard a mysterious noise, which some wiseacre
it compared to the fluttering of wings.]
How long before your death did you tell your servant, Carrots,
ou were poisoned ? An hour ?"—" Yes."
arrots, who was present, was appealed to ; but she stated posi-
that such was not the fact, as the deceased was quite speechless
ur before her death. This shook the faith of some of the spec-
s, but the examination was allowed to continue.]
 How long did Carrots live with you ?"—" Three or four days."
Jarrots was again appealed to, and said that this was true.]
 If Mr. Kent is arrested for this murder, will he confess ?"—
s."
 Would your soul be at rest if he were hanged for it ?"—" Yes."
 Will he be hanged for it ?"—" Yes."
 How long a time first ?"—"Three years."
 How many clergymen are there in this room ?"—"Three."
 How many negroes ?"—" Two."
 Is this watch (held up by one of the clergymen) white ?"—" No."
 Is it yellow ?"—"No."
 Is it blue ?"—" No."
 Is it black ?"—" Yes."
The watch was in a black shagreen case.]
 At what time this morning will you take your departure ?"
he answer to this question was four knocks, very distinctly heard
very person present ; and accordingly, at four o'clock precisely
ghost took its departure to the Wheatsheaf public-house close by,
re it frightened mine host and his lady almost out of their wits,
nocking in the ceiling right above their bed.
The rumour of these occurrences very soon spread over London,

'here was now a considerable pause, and one of the clergymen
; downstairs to interrogate the father of the girl, who was wait-
the result of the experiment. He positively denied that there
any deception, and even went so far as to say that he himself,
ι one occasion, had seen and conversed with the awful ghost.
having been communicated to the company, it was unanimously
ved to give the ghost another trial; and the clergyman called
in a loud voice to the supposed spirit, that the gentleman to
n it had promised to appear in the vault was about to repair to
place, where he claimed the fulfilment of its promise. At one
after midnight they all proceeded to the .church, and the gen-
ιn in question, with another, entered the vault alone, and took
ιeir position alongside of the coffin of poor Fanny. The ghost was
summoned to appear, but it appeared not; it was summoned
ιock, but it knocked not; it was summoned to scratch, but it
ched not; and the two retired from the vault, with a firm be-
hat the whole business was a deception practised by Parsons and
laughter. There were others, however, who did not wish to
so hastily to a conclusion, and who suggested that they were
ιps trifling with this awful and supernatural being, which, be-
ffended with them for their presumption, would not condescend
swer them. Again, after serious consultation, it was agreed on
ιnds that if the ghost answered any body at all, it would answer
Kent, the supposed murderer; and he was accordingly requested
down into the vault. He went with several others, and sum-
ιd the ghost to answer whether he had indeed poisoned her.
ə being no answer, the question was put by Mr. Aldritch, who
ιred it, if it were indeed a spirit, to end their doubts, make a
of its presence, and point out the guilty person. There being
ιo answer for the space of half an hour, during which time all
boobies waited with the most praiseworthy perseverance, they
ned to the house of Mr. Aldritch, and ordered the girl to get
ιd dress herself. She was strictly examined, but persisted in
tatement that she used no deception, and that the ghost had
ʹ appeared to her.
ɔ many persons had, by their openly expressed belief of the re-
of the visitation, identified themselves with it, that Parsons and
mily were far from being the only persons interested in the con-
nce of the delusion. The result of the experiment convinced
people; but these were not to be convinced by any evidence, how-
ɔositive, and they therefore spread abroad the rumour, that the
had not appeared in the vault because Mr. Kent had taken care
əhand to have the coffin removed. That gentleman, whose pɔ-

ɔus and inexplicable, that the neighbours, dreading that the house
lf would next be seized with a fit of motion, and tumble about
r ears, left poor Mrs. Golding to bear the brunt of it by herself.
ghost in this case was solemnly remonstrated with, and urged to
ə its departure; but the demolition continuing as great as before,
ι. Golding finally made up her mind to quit the house altogether.
took refuge with Anne Robinson in the house of a neighbour;
his glass and crockery being immediately subjected to the same
secution, he was reluctantly compelled to give her notice to quit.
ɔ old lady thus forced back to her own house, endured the disturb-
e for some days longer, when suspecting that Anne Robinson was
cause of all the mischief, she dismissed her from her service. The
raordinary appearances immediately ceased, and were never after-
ʼds renewed; a fact which is of itself sufficient to point out the
disturber. A long time afterwards, Anne Robinson confessed
whole matter to the Reverend Mr. Brayfield. This gentleman
fided the story to Mr. Hone, who has published an explanation
ʒhe mystery. Anne, it appears, was anxious to have a clear house,
carry on an intrigue with her lover, and resorted to this trick to
ɔct her purpose. She placed the china on the shelves in such a
nner that it fell on the slightest motion, and attached horse-hairs
other articles, so that she could jerk them down from an adjoining
ʼm without being perceived by any one. She was exceedingly dex-
ous at this sort of work, and would have proved a formidable rival
many a juggler by profession. A full explanation of the whole
ıir may be found in the *Every-day Book*.

The latest instance of the popular panic occasioned by a house
ɔposed to be haunted, occurred in Scotland, in the winter of the
ır 1838. On the 5th of December, the inmates of the farm-house
Baldarroch, in the district of Banchory, Aberdeenshire, were
ırmed by observing a great number of sticks, pebble-stones, and
ɔds of earth flying about their yard and premises. They endea-
ured, but in vain, to discover who was the delinquent; and the
ɔwer of stones continuing for five days in succession, they came at
t to the conclusion that the devil and his imps were alone the
ıse of it. The rumour soon spread over all that part of the coun-
ʼ, and hundreds of persons came from far and near to witness the
tics of the devils of Baldarroch. After the fifth day, the shower of
ɔds and stones ceased on the outside of the premises, and the scene
ifted to the interior. Spoons, knives, plates, mustard-pots, roll-
ʒ-pins, and flat-irons appeared suddenly endued with the power of
f-motion, and were whirled from room to room, and rattled down
e chimneys in a manner which nobody could account for. The lid

l lost their specific gravity, and could harm nobody, even though
· fell upon a person's head.

Among the persons drawn to Baldarroch by these occurrences
ə the heritor, the minister, and all the elders of the Kirk, under
·se superintendence an investigation was immediately commenced.
ir proceedings were not promulgated for some days; and, in the
n time, rumour continued to travel through all the Highlands,
nifying each mysterious incident the farther it got from home.
·as said, that when the goodwife put her potato-pot on the fire,
ı potato, as the water boiled, changed into a demon, and grinned
·ibly at her as she lifted the lid; that not only chairs and tables,
carrots and turnips, skipped along the floor in the merriest man-
imaginable; that shoes and boots went through all the evolutions
he Highland fling without any visible wearers directing their
ions; and that a piece of meat detached itself from the hook on
ch it hung in the pantry, and placed itself before the fire, whence
the efforts of the people of the house were unable to remove it
il it was thoroughly roasted; and that it then flew up the chim-
with a tremendous bang. At Baldarroch itself the belief was not
·e so extravagant; but the farmer was so convinced that the devil
his imps were alone the cause of all the disturbance, that he tra-
ed a distance of forty miles to an old conjuror, named Willie Fore-
ı, to induce him, for a handsome fee, to remove the enchantment
n his property. There were, of course, some sensible and edu-
·d people, who, after stripping the stories circulated of their exag-
ıtion, attributed all the rest to one or other of two causes: first,
t some gipsies, or strolling mendicants, hidden in the neighbour-
plantation, were amusing themselves by working on the credulity
he country people; or, secondly, that the inmates of Baldarroch
·ied on this deception themselves, for some reason or other, which
not very clear to any body. The last opinion gained but few
evers, as the farmer and his family were much respected; and so
ıy persons had, in the most open manner, expressed their belief in
supernatural agency, that they did not like to stultify themselves
confessing that they had been deceived.

At last, after a fortnight's continuance of the noises, the whole
k was discovered. The two servant lasses were strictly examined,
. then committed to prison. It appeared that they were alone at
bottom of the whole affair, and that the extraordinary alarm and
lulity of their master and mistress, in the first instance, and of
neighbours and country people afterwards, made their task com-
atively easy. A little common dexterity was all they had used;
l, being themselves unsuspected, they swelled the alarm by the

POPULAR FOLLIES OF GREAT CITIES.

La faridondaine—la faridondon,
Vive la faridondaine !—*Beranger.*

HE popular humours of a great city are a never-failing source of amusement to the man whose sympathies are hospitable enough to embrace all his kind, and who, refined though he may be himself, will not sneer at the humble wit or grotesque peculiarities of the boozing mechanic, the squalid beggar, the vicious urchin, and all the motley group of the idle, the reckless, and the imitative that swarm in the alleys and broadways of a metropolis. He who walks through a great city to find subjects for weeping, may find plenty at every corner to wring his heart; but let such a man walk on his course, and enjoy his grief alone—we are not of e who would accompany him. The miseries of us poor earthllers gain no alleviation from the sympathy of those who merely t them out to be pathetic over them. The weeping philosopher often impairs his eyesight by his woe, and becomes unable from tears to see the remedies for the evils which he deplores. Thus ill often be found that the man of no tears is the truest philanpist, as he is the best physician who wears a cheerful face, even 1e worst of cases.

So many pens have been employed to point out the miseries, and 1any to condemn the crimes and vices, and more serious follies of multitude, that ours shall not increase the number, at least in chapter. Our present task shall be less ungracious, and wanderthrough the busy haunts of great cities, we shall seek only for sement, and note as we pass a few of the harmless follies and msies of the poor.

gns, however slight, of ancient service. Immediately the cry
and, like the war-whoop of the Indians, was repeated by a
ed discordant throats. He was a wise man who, finding him-
ider these circumstances "the observed of all observers," bore
nours meekly. He who shewed symptoms of ill-feeling at the
itions cast upon his hat, only brought upon himself redoubled
. The mob soon perceive whether a man is irritable, and, if
r own class, they love to make sport of him. When such a man,
.th such a hat, passed in those days through a crowded neigh-
.od, he might think himself fortunate if his annoyances were
ed to the shouts and cries of the populace. The obnoxious hat
:en snatched from his head and thrown into the gutter by some
al joker, and then raised, covered with mud, upon the end of
, for the admiration of the spectators, who held their sides with
er, and exclaimed in the pauses of their mirth, " *Oh, what a
g bad hat !*" " *What a shocking bad hat !*" Many a nervous
ian, whose purse could but ill spare the outlay, doubtless pur-
a new hat before the time, in order to avoid exposure in this
r.

: origin of this singular saying, which made fun for the metro-
r months, is not involved in the same obscurity as that which
s the origin of *Quoz* and some others. There had been a hotly
ed election for the borough of Southwark, and one of the can-
: was an eminent hatter. This gentleman, in canvassing the
s, adopted a somewhat professional mode of conciliating their
ill, and of bribing them without letting them perceive that
ere bribed. Whenever he called upon or met a voter whose
s not of the best material, or, being so, had seen its best
e invariably said, " *What a shocking bad hat you have got;
my warehouse, and you shall have a new one !*" Upon the
election this circumstance was remembered, and his oppo-
nade the most of it, by inciting the crowd to keep up an
nt cry of " *What a shocking bad hat !*" all the time the honour-
ndidate was addressing them. From Southwark the phrase
over all London, and reigned for a time the supreme slang of
son.

key *Walker*, derived from the chorus of a popular ballad, was
;h in favour at one time, and served, like its predecessor *Quoz*,
er all questions. In the course of time the latter word alone
the favourite, and was uttered with a peculiar drawl upon the
lable, and a sharp turn upon the last. If a lively servant girl
portuned for a kiss by a fellow she did not care about, she
her little nose, and cried " *Walker !*" If a dustman asked his

II.   R

paid visits too repeated to the gin-shop, and got damaged in conse-
ce, had *flared up*. To put one's self into a passion; to stroll
on a nocturnal frolic, and alarm a neighbourhood, or to create a
rbance in any shape, was to *flare up*. A lover's quarrel was a
up; so was a boxing-match between two blackguards in the
ts; and the preachers of sedition and revolution recommended
English nation to *flare up*, like the French. So great a favourite
the word, that people loved to repeat it for its very sound. They
ghted apparently in hearing their own organs articulate it; and
uring men, when none who could respond to the call were with-
earing, would often startle the aristocratic echoes of the West by
well-known slang phrase of the East. Even in the dead hours
e night, the ears of those who watched late, or who could not
, were saluted with the same sound. The drunkard reeling
e shewed that he was still a man and a citizen by calling "*flare*
' in the pauses of his hiccough. Drink had deprived him of the
r of arranging all other ideas; his intellect was sunk to the
of the brute's; but he clung to humanity by the one last link
ie popular cry. While he could vociferate that sound, he had
s as an Englishman, and would not sleep in a gutter, like a
Onwards he went, disturbing quiet streets and comfortable
le by his whoop, till exhausted nature could support him no
, and he rolled powerless into the road. When, in due time
wards, the policeman stumbled upon him as he lay, that guar-
of the peace turned the full light of his lantern on his face, and
imed, " Here's a poor devil who has been *flaring up !*" Then
the stretcher, on which the victim of deep potations was carried
ie watch-house, and pitched into a dirty cell, among a score of
shes about as far gone as himself, who saluted their new com-
by a loud, long shout of "*flare up !*"
o universal was this phrase, and so enduring seemed its popula-
that a speculator, who knew not the evanescence of slang, estab-
l a weekly newspaper under its name. But he was like the man
built his house upon the sand; his foundation gave way under
and the phrase and the newspaper were washed into the mighty
f the things that were. The people grew at last weary of
nonotony, and "*flare up*" became vulgar even among them.
ially it was left to little boys who did not know the world,
in process of time sank altogether into neglect. It is now
no more as a piece of popular slang; but the words are still
to signify any sudden outburst either of fire, disturbance, or ill-
e.
ie next phrase that enjoyed the favour of the million was less

pplicable to almost every variety of circumstance. The lovers
lain answer to a plain question did not like it at all. Insolence
use of it to give offence; ignorance to avoid exposing itself;
aggery to create laughter. Every new comer into an alehouse
om was asked unceremoniously, " *Who are you ?*" and if he
d foolish, scratched his head, and did not know what to reply,
s of boisterous merriment resounded on every side. An autho-
ve disputant was not unfrequently put down, and presumption
ry kind checked by the same query. When its popularity was
height, a gentleman, feeling the hand of a thief in his pocket,
d suddenly round and caught him in the act, exclaiming, " *Who*
u ?" The mob which gathered round applauded to the very echo,
hought it the most capital joke they had ever heard, the very
of wit, the very essence of humour. Another circumstance of
ilar kind gave an additional fillip to the phrase, and infused new
nd vigour into it just as it was dying away. The scene occurred
e chief criminal court in the kingdom. A prisoner stood at the
the offence with which he had been charged was clearly proved
1st him; his counsel had been heard, not in his defence, but in
1uation, insisting upon his previous good life and character as
ns for the lenity of the court. " And where are your witnesses ?"
ired the learned judge who presided. " Please you, my lord, I
vs the prisoner at the bar, and a more honester feller never
thed," said a rough voice in the gallery. The officers of the court
ed aghast, and the strangers tittered with ill-suppressed laughter.
ho are you ?" said the judge, looking suddenly up, but with im-
irable gravity. The court was convulsed; the titter broke out
a laugh; and it was several minutes before silence and decorum
d be restored. When the ushers recovered their self-possession,
made diligent search for the profane transgressor; but he was
to be found. Nobody knew him; nobody had seen him. After
ile the business of the court again proceeded. The next prisoner
ght up for trial augured favourably of his prospects when he
ned that the solemn lips of the representative of justice had ut-
d the popular phrase, as if he felt and appreciated it. There was
ear that such a judge would use undue severity. His heart was
1 the people; he understood their language and their manners,
would make allowances for the temptations which drove them
crime. So thought many of the prisoners, if we may infer it
n the fact that the learned judge suddenly acquired an immense
ease of popularity. The praise of his wit was in every mouth,
" *Who are you ?*" renewed its lease, and remained in possession
1ublic favour for another term in consequence.

)ut sixteen years ago, London became again most preposterously
l. The *vox populi* wore itself hoarse by singing the praises of
3ea, the Sea!" If a stranger (and a philosopher) had walked
h London, and listened to the universal chorus, he might have
.cted a very pretty theory upon the love of the English for the
rice, and our acknowledged superiority over all other nations
iat element. "No wonder," he might have said, "that this
is invincible upon the ocean. The love of it mixes with their
ioughts; they celebrate it even in the market-place; their
iinstrels excite charity by it; and high and low, young and
.le and female, chant *Io pœans* in its praise. Love is not
:d in the national songs of this warlike race—Bacchus is no
hem; they are men of sterner mould, and think only of ' the
: Sea!' and the means of conquéring upon it."
i would, doubtless, have been his impression if he had taken
ence only of his ears. Alas, in those days for the refined ears
'e musical! great was their torture when discord, with its
l diversities of tone, struck up this appalling anthem—there
:scape from it. The migratory minstrels of Savoy caught the
nd pealed it down the long vistas of quiet streets, till their
st and snuggest apartments re-echoed with the sound. Men
.iged to endure this crying evil for full six months, wearied
ration, and made *sea*-sick on the dry land.
·al other songs sprang up in due succession afterwards, but
them, with the exception of one, entitled "All round my
joyed any extraordinary share of favour, until an American
roduced a vile song called "Jim Crow." The singer sang his
. appropriate costume, with grotesque gesticulations, and a
rhirl of his body at the close of each verse. It took the taste
wn immediately, and for months the ears of orderly people
ined by the senseless chorus—

> " Turn about and wheel about,
>   And do just so—
> Turn about and wheel about,
>   And jump, Jim Crow!"

nstrels blackened their faces in order to give proper effect to
i; and fatherless urchins, who had to choose between thiev-
.nging for their livelihood, took the latter course, as likely
more profitable, as long as the public taste remained in that
The uncouth dance, its accompaniment, might be seen in
rfection on market nights in any great thoroughfare; and
of the song might be heard, piercing above all the din and

SHERWOOD FOREST.

ꟼULAR ADMIRATION OF GREAT THIEVES.

. Where shall we find such another set of practical philosophers, who,
n, are above the fear of death!
. Sound men and true!
n. Of tried courage and indefatigable industry!
 Who is there here that would not die for his friend?
·y. Who is there here that would betray him for his interest?
 Shew me a gang of courtiers that could say as much!

Dialogue of Thieves in the Beggar's Opera.

ι it be that the multitude, feeling the pangs of poverty,
se with the daring and ingenious depredators who take away
ιan's superfluity, or whether it be the interest that mankind
l feel for the records of perilous adventure, it is certain that
ace of all countries look with admiration upon great and
. thieves.   Perhaps both these causes combine to invest
er with charms in the popular eye.   Almost every country

.ude Duval, Dick Turpin, Jonathan Wild, and Jack Sheppard,
ise knights of the road and of the town, whose peculiar chivalry
med at once the dread and the delight of England during the
iteenth century ?   Turpin's fame is unknown to no portion of the
e population of England after they have attained the age of ten.
wondrous ride from London to York has endeared him to the im-
iation of millions; his cruelty in placing an old woman upon a fire,
orce her to tell him where she had hidden her money, is regarded
. good joke; and his proud bearing upon the scaffold is looked
i as a virtuous action.   The Abbé le Blanc, writing in 1737, says
ias continually entertained with stories of Turpin — how, when
obbed gentlemen, he would generously leave them enough to con-
e their journey, and exact a pledge from them never to inform
ist him, and how scrupulous such gentlemen were in keeping
word.   He was one day told a story with which the relator was
e highest degree delighted.   Turpin, or some other noted robber,
ed a man whom he knew to be very rich, with the usual saluta-
-" Your money or your life!" but not finding more than five
: guineas about him, he took the liberty of entreating him, in
iost affable manner, never to come out so ill-provided; adding
if he fell in with him, and he had no more than such a paltry
he would give him a good licking.   Another story, told by one
rpin's admirers, was of a robbery he had committed upon a
. near Cambridge.   He took from this gentleman his watch,
iff-box, and all his money but two shillings, and, before he left
equired his word of honour that he would not cause him to be
d or brought before a justice.   The promise being given, they
iarted very courteously.   They afterwards met at Newmarket,
iewed their acquaintance.   Mr. C. kept his word religiously;
only refrained from giving Turpin into custody, but made a
hat he had fairly won some of his money back again in an
way.   Turpin offered to bet with him on some favourite horse,
. C. accepted the wager with as good a grace as he could have
im the best gentleman in England.   Turpin lost his bet and
mmediately, and was so smitten with the generous behaviour
!., that he told him how deeply he regretted that the trifling
hich had happened between them did not permit them to
zether.   The narrator of this anecdote was quite proud that
was the birthplace of such a highwayman.*

.bbé, in the second volume, in the letter No. 79, addressed to Monsieur de
es the following curious particulars of the robbers of 1737, which are not
erest at this day, if it were only to shew the vast improvement which has
since that period.   "It is usual in travelling to put ten or a dozen guineas
e pocket, as a tribute to the first that comes to demand them; the right of

eatre. All the scenes were painted from nature, including the
blic-house that the robber frequented in Clare Market, and the
idemned cell from which he had made his escape in Newgate.*
The Rev. Mr. Villette, the editor of the *Annals of Newgate*, pub-
ied in 1754, relates a curious sermon, which he says a friend of
heard delivered by a street-preacher about the time of Jack's exe-
ion. The orator, after animadverting on the great care men took
:heir bodies, and the little care they bestowed upon their souls,
tinued as follows, by way of exemplifying the position :—" We
e a remarkable instance of this in a notorious malefactor, well

Since the publication of the first edition of this volume, Jack Sheppard's adventures
been revived. A novel upon the real or fabulous history of the burglar has afforded,
I extraordinary popularity, a further exemplification of the allegations in the text.
Sixth Report of the Inspector of Prisons for the Northern Districts of England contains
ss of information upon the pernicious effect of such romances, and of the dramas
ed upon them. The Inspector examined several boys attending the prison school
New Bailey at Manchester, from whose evidence the following passages bearing
the subject are extracted :
. L. (aged 14). The first time I was ever at the theatre was to see *Jack Sheppard.*
were two or three boys near to the house who were going, and they asked me.
sixpence from the money I used to lay up weekly for clothes. The next time I
which was the week after, I borrowed the money from a boy; I returned it to him
turday after. I then went many times. I took the money from my mother out of
cket as she was sitting down, and I beside her. There was more than sixpence in
:ket. I got a great love for the theatre, and stole from people often to get there. *I*
: this Jack Sheppard was a clever fellow for making his escape and robbing his master.
ild get out of gaol, I think I should be as clever as him : but, after all his exploits, he
ie at last. I have had the book out of a library at Dole Field. I had paid two-
. book for three volumes. I also got *Richard Turpin,* in two volumes, and paid the
I have seen *Oliver Twist,* and think the Artful Dodger is very like some of the
re. I am here for picking a pocket of 25*l.*
C. (aged 15). When we came to Manchester, I went to the play, and saw *Jack*
d the first night it came out. There were pictures of him about the streets on
ind on the walls; one of them was his picking a pocket in the church. I liked
ppard much. I had not been in prison there. I was employed in a warehouse
. a week, and was allowed 6*d.* out of it for myself, and with that I went regularly
ay. I saw *Jack Sheppard* afterwards four times in one week. I got the money
/ money-bag by stealth, and without my master's knowledge. I once borrowed
y mother's name from Mrs. ——, a shopkeeper, with whom she used to deal ;
. the play with it.
f'D. (aged 15). I have heard of *Jack Sheppard:* a lad whom I know told me of it,
seen it, and said it was *rare fun* to see him break out of prison.
. (aged 11). Has been to the play twice, and seen *Jack Sheppard.* Went with his
ie first time, and by himself the second. I took the money to go a second time
ther's house, off the chimney-piece, where she had left a sixpence. It was the
: *Jack Sheppard* was played. There was great talk about it, and there were nice
bout it all over the walls. I thought him a very clever fellow ; but Blueskin
most fun. I first went to the markets, and begun by stealing apples. I also
d, ——, who has been transported, and went with him two or three times.
I ever got was 10*s.* out of a till."
aspector's *Report on Juvenile Delinquency at Liverpool* contains much matter of
:ind ; but sufficient has been already quoted to shew the injurious effects of the
of great thieves by thoughtless novelists.

ırk in four-and-twenty hours—to be mangled by the rude hands of mannerly surgeons.

The death of Claude Duval would appear to have been no less ımphant. Claude was a gentlemanly thief. According to Butler, the famous ode to his memory, he

> " Taught the wild Arabs of the road
> To rob in a more gentle mode;
> Take prizes more obligingly than those
> Who never had been bred *filous;*
> And how to hang in a more graceful fashion
> Than e'er was known before to the dull English nation."

àct, he was the pink of politeness, and his gallantry to the fair was proverbial. When he was caught at last, pent in " stone s and chains and iron grates," their grief was in proportion to are merits and his great fame. Butler says, that to his dungeon

> " Came ladies from all parts,
> To offer up close prisoners their hearts,
> Which he received as tribute due—
> *　　*　　*　　*
> Never did bold knight to relieve
> Distress'd dames, such dreadful feats achieve,
> As feeble damsels for his sake
> Would have been proud to undertake,
> And, bravely ambitious to redeem
> The world's loss and their own,
> Strove who should have the honour to lay down,
> And change a life with him."

ıong the noted thieves of France, there is none to compare with nous Aimerigot Têtenoire, who flourished in the reign of Charles .'his fellow was at the head of four or five hundred men, and ed two very strong castles in Limousin and Auvergne. There ood deal of the feudal baron about him, although he possessed ınues but such as the road afforded him. At his death he left lar will. " I give and bequeath," said the robber, " one thou-'e hundred francs to St. George's Chapel, for such repairs as it ed; to my sweet girl, who so loyally loved me, I give two ıd five hundred; and the surplus I give to my companions. I ey will all live as brothers, and divide it amicably among If they cannot agree, and the devil of contention gets among is no fault of mine; and I advise them to get a good strong ɾe, and break open my strong-box. Let them scramble for contains, and the devil seize the hindmost." The people of e still recount with admiration the daring feats of this brigand.

There is another robber-hero, of whose character and exploits the
ple of Germany speak admiringly.   Mausch Nadel was captain of
onsiderable band that infested the Rhine, Switzerland, Alsatia,
l Lorraine, during the years 1824, 5, and 6.   Like Jack Sheppard,
endeared himself to the populace by his most hazardous escape
n prison.   Being confined at Bremen, in a dungeon on the third
y of the prison of that town, he contrived to let himself down
out exciting the vigilance of the sentinels, and to swim across
Weser, though heavily laden with irons.   When about half-way
, he was espied by a sentinel, who fired at him, and shot him in
calf of the leg; but the undaunted robber struck out manfully,
ied the shore, and was out of sight before the officers of justice
l get ready their boats to follow him.   He was captured again
26, tried at Mayence, and sentenced to death.   He was a tall,
g, handsome man, and his fate, villain as he was, excited much
thy all over Germany.   The ladies especially were loud in their
  that nothing could be done to save a hero so good-looking,
f adventures so romantic, from the knife of the headsman.
. Charles Macfarlane, in speaking of Italian banditti, remarks,
e abuses of the Catholic religion, with its confessions and abso-
, have tended to promote crime of this description.   But he adds
ruly, that priests and monks have not done half the mischief
as been perpetrated by ballad-mongers and story-tellers.   If he
l playwrights also, the list would have been complete.   In fact,
atre, which can only expect to prosper, in a pecuniary sense,
ering to the tastes of the people, continually recurs to the
f thieves and banditti for its most favourite heroes.   These
al robbers, with their picturesque attire, wild haunts, jolly,
  devil-may-care manners, take a wonderful hold upon the
ion, and whatever their advocates may say to the contrary,
a very pernicious influence upon public morals.   In the Me-
the Duke of Guise upon the Revolution of Naples in 1647
, it is stated, that the manners, dress, and mode of life of
olitan banditti were rendered so captivating upon the stage,
uthorities found it absolutely necessary to forbid the repre-
of dramas in which they figured, and even to prohibit their
t the masquerades.   So numerous were the banditti at this
the duke found no difficulty in raising an army of them,
in his endeavours to seize on the throne of Naples.   He
bes them :* "They were three thousand five hundred men,
e oldest came short of five-and-forty years, and the youngest
twenty.   They were all tall and well made, with long black

* See also *Foreign Quarterly Review*, vol. iv. p. 898.

s

.e already vicious to imitate it. Besides, there is the weighty
ity of Sir John Fielding, the chief magistrate of Bow Street,
serted positively, and proved his assertion by the records of his
that the number of thieves was greatly increased at the time
hat opera was so popular.

have another instance of the same result much nearer our own
Schiller's *Räuber*, that wonderful play, written by a green
perverted the taste and imagination of all the young men in
ay. An accomplished critic of our own country (Hazlitt),
g of this play, says it was the first he ever read, and such was
ct it produced on him, that it " stunned him, like a blow."
ne lapse of five-and-twenty years, he could not forget it; it
l, to use his own words, " an old dweller in the chambers of
a," and he had not even then recovered enough from it to de-
ow it was. The high-minded, metaphysical thief, its hero,
varmly admired, that several raw students, longing to imitate
ter they thought so noble, actually abandoned their homes
r colleges, and betook themselves to the forests and the wilds
ontributions upon travellers. They thought they would, like
under the rich, and deliver eloquent soliloquies to the setting
ne rising moon; relieve the poor when they met them, and
sks of Rhenish with their free companions in rugged mountain-
r in tents in the thicknesses of the forests. But a little ex-
wonderfully cooled their courage; they found that real, every-
rs were very unlike the conventional banditti of the stage, and
e months in prison, with bread and water for their fare, and
aw to lie upon, was very well to read about by their own fire-
; not very agreeable to undergo in their own proper persons.
Byron, with his soliloquising, high-souled thieves, has, in a
gree, perverted the taste of the juvenile rhymers of his
As yet, however, they have shewn more good sense than
ws of Germany, and have not taken to the woods or the
Much as they admire Conrad the Corsair, they will not
and hoist the black flag for him. By words only, and not
they testify their admiration, and deluge the periodicals
-shops of the land with verses describing pirates' and ban-
s, and robber adventures of every kind.
is the playwright who does most harm; and Byron has
of this nature to answer for than Gay or Schiller. With
scenery, fine dresses, and music, and the very false notions
y, they vitiate the public taste, not knowing,

" Vulgaires rimeurs !
Quelle force ont les arts pour demolir les mœurs."

FIGHT BETWEEN DU GUESCLIN AND TROUSSEL.

DUELS AND ORDEALS.

There was an ancient sage philosopher,
Who swore the world, as he could prove,
Was mad of fighting.—*Hudibras.*

·iters, in accounting for the origin of duelling, derive it from
ike habits of those barbarous nations who overran Europe in
ϒ centuries of the Christian era, and who knew no mode so
for settling their differences as the point of the sword.   In
lling, taken in its primitive and broadest sense, means no-
ɔre than combating, and is the universal resort of all wild
including man, to gain or defend their possessions, or avenge
ɪlts.   Two dogs who tear each other for a bone, or two ban-
ːing on a dunghill for the love of some beautiful hen, or two
Vimbledon Common, shooting at each other to satisfy the
ffended honour, stand on the same footing in this respect,
·ach and all mere duellists.   As civilisation advanced, the
·ned men naturally grew ashamed of such a mode of adjust-
·es, and the promulgation of some sort of laws for obtaining
· injuries was the consequence.   Still there were many cases

ectators, declaring the custom to be hellish and detestable, and
uced by the devil for the destruction both of body and soul.
added also, that princes who connived at duels should be de-
of all temporal power, jurisdiction, and dominion over the
where they had permitted them to be fought.   It will be seen
er that this clause only encouraged the practice which it was
ed to prevent.

t it was the blasphemous error of these early ages to expect
ie Almighty, whenever he was called upon, would work a
in favour of a person unjustly accused.   The priesthood, in
ining the duel, did not condemn the principle on which it was
i.   They still encouraged the popular belief of divine inter-
in all the disputes or differences that might arise among
or individuals.   It was the very same principle that regulated
eals, which with all their influence they supported against the
By the former, the power of deciding the guilt or innocence
ted wholly in their hands; while by the latter they enjoyed
er or privilege at all.   It is not to be wondered at that, for
son, if for no other, they should have endeavoured to settle
erences by the peaceful mode.   While that prevailed, they
they wished to be, the first party in the state; but while the
arm of individual prowess was allowed to be the judge in all
l cases, their power and influence became secondary to those
obility.

it was not the mere hatred of bloodshed which induced them
ch the thunderbolts of excommunication against the com-
: it was a desire to retain the power, which, to do them jus-
y were in those times the persons best qualified to wield.   The
f knowledge and civilisation lay within the bounds of their
or they were the representatives of the intellectual, as the
were of the physical power of man.   To centralise this power
hurch, and make it the judge of the last resort in all appeals,
civil and criminal cases, they instituted five modes of trial,
agement of which lay wholly in their hands.   These were,
upon the evangelists; the ordeal of the cross and the fire-
or persons in the higher ranks; the water-ordeal, for the
classes; and, lastly, the *corsned*, or bread and cheese ordeal,
bers of their own body.
ath upon the evangelists was taken in the following manner.
sed who was received to this proof, says Paul Hay, Count du
, in his *Memoirs of Bertrand du Guesclin*, swore upon a copy
ew Testament, and on the relics of the holy martyrs, or on
tbs, that he was innocent of the crime imputed to him.   He

. If he stepped regularly in the vacant spaces, avoiding the fire,
as adjudged innocent; if he burned himself, he was declared
y. As none but the clergy interfered with the arrangement of
loughshares, they could always calculate beforehand the result
e ordeal. To find a person guilty, they had only to place them
egular distances, and the accused was sure to tread upon one of
. When Emma, the wife of King Ethelréd, and mother of Ed-
the Confessor, was accused of a guilty familiarity with Alwyn
p of Winchester, she cleared her character in this manner. The
ition, not only of their order, but of a queen, being at stake, a
t of guilty was not to be apprehended from any ploughshares
priests had the heating of. This ordeal was called the *Judi-
Dei*, and sometimes the *Vulgaris Purgatio*, and might also be
oy several other methods. One was to hold in the hand, unhurt,
e of red-hot iron, of the weight of one, two, or three pounds.
we read not only that men with hard hands, but women of
and more delicate skin, could do this with impunity, we must
vinced that the hands were previously rubbed with some pre-
.ve, or that the apparently hot iron was merely cold iron painted
Another mode was to plunge the naked arm into a caldron of
; water. The priests then enveloped it in several folds of linen
unnel, and kept the patient confined within the church, and
their exclusive care, for three days. If, at the end of that
he arm appeared without a scar, the innocence of the accused
was firmly established.*
regards the water-ordeal, the same trouble was not taken. It
rial only for the poor and humble, and, whether they sank or

y similar to this is the fire-ordeal of the modern Hindoos, which is thus
in Forbes's *Oriental Memoirs*, vol. i. ch. xi.:—"When a man, accused of a
ime, chooses to undergo the ordeal trial, he is closely confined for several days,
hand and arm are covered with thick wax-cloth, tied up and sealed, in the
of proper officers, to prevent deceit. In the English districts the covering was
ealed with the Company's arms, and the prisoner placed under a European
.t the time fixed for the ordeal, a caldron of oil is placed over a fire; when it
iece of money is dropped into the vessel; the prisoner's arm is unsealed and
i the presence of his judges and accusers. During this part of the ceremony
lant Brahmins supplicate the Deity. On receiving their benediction, the
lunges his hand into the boiling fluid, and takes out the coin. The arm is
s again sealed up until the time appointed for a re-examination. The seal is
an: if no blemish appears, the prisoner is declared innocent; if the contrary,
the punishment due to his crime." . . . . . On this trial the accused thus
the element before plunging his hand into the boiling oil:—"Thou, O fire! per-
things. O cause of purity! who givest evidence of virtue and of sin, declare
n this my hand!" If no juggling were practised, the decisions by this ordeal
.ll the same way; but as some are by this means declared guilty, and others
t is clear that the Brahmins, like the Christian priests of the middle ages,
me deception in saving those whom they wish to be thought guiltless.

e slightest degree.   The flames had not even warmed it.· Upon
.t was resolved, that both were alike agreeable to God, and that
should be used by turns in all the churches of Seville.*
the ordeals had been confined to questions like this, the laity
i have had little or no objection to them ; but when they
introduced as decisive in all the disputes that might arise be-
1 man and man, the opposition of all those whose prime virtue
ersonal bravery, was necessarily excited.   In fact, the nobility,
a very early period, began to look with jealous eyes upon them.
were not slow to perceive their true purport, which was no
than to make the Church the last court of appeal in all cases,
civil and criminal; and not only did the nobility prefer the
it mode of single combat from this cause, in itself a sufficient
ut they clung to it because an acquittal gained by those dis-
of courage and address which the battle afforded, was more
able in the eyes of their compeers than one which it required
tle or none of either to accomplish.   To these causes may be
another, which was perhaps more potent than either in rais-
e credit of the judicial combat at the expense of the ordeal.
oble institution of chivalry was beginning to take root, and,
hstanding the clamours of the clergy, war was made the sole
ss of life, and the only elegant pursuit of the aristocracy.   The
irit of honour was introduced, any attack upon which was only
venged in the lists, within sight of applauding crowds, whose
of approbation was far more gratifying than the cold and-
acquittal of the ordeal.   Lothaire, the son of Louis I., abo-
that by fire and the trial of the cross within his dominions ;
England they were allowed so late as the time of Henry III.,
early part of whose reign they were prohibited by an order of
.   In the mean time, the Crusades had brought the institu-
chivalry to the full height of perfection.   The chivalric spirit
hieved the downfall of the ordeal system, and established the
combat on a basis too firm to be shaken.   It is true that with
of chivalry, as an institution, fell the tournament and the
er in the lists; but the duel, their offspring, has survived to
, defying the efforts of sages and philosophers to eradicate it.
all the errors bequeathed to us by a barbarous age, it has proved
it pertinacious.   It has put variance between men's reason
r honour; put the man of sense on a level with the fool, and
ousands who condemn it submit to it or practise it.
e who are curious to see the manner in which these combats
gulated, may consult the learned Montesquieu, where they
e de Messire Bertrand du Guesclin, par Paul Hay du Chastelet, liv. l. ch. xix.

espair, when a champion suddenly appeared in the person of Ingel-
rius count of Anjou, a boy of sixteen years of age, who had been
ld by the countess on the baptismal font, and received her husband's
me. He tenderly loved his godmother, and offered to do battle in
r cause against any and every opponent. The king endeavoured
persuade the generous boy from his enterprise, urging the great
ength, tried skill, and invincible courage of the challenger; but

DUEL BETWEEN INGELGERIUS AND GONTRAN.

sisted in his resolution, to the great sorrow of all the court,
d it was a cruel thing to permit so brave and beautiful a child
to such butchery and death.

r, should share equally with their uncles in the property of their lfather, at the death of the latter. The difficulty of this ques-was found so insurmountable, that none of the lawyers of that ould resolve it. It was at last decreed that it should be decided ngle combat. Two champions were accordingly chosen; one nd the other against, the claims of the little ones. After a long ʒle, the champion of the uncles was unhorsed and slain; and it herefore decided that the right of the grandchildren was esta-d, and that they should enjoy the same portion of their grand-'s possessions that their father would have done had he been alive.)on pretexts just as strange, and often more frivolous than these, continued to be fought in most of the countries of Europe, dur-e whole of the fourteenth and fifteenth centuries. A memorable ce of the slightness of the pretext on which a man could be to fight a duel to the death, occurs in the memoirs of the brave ˌble, Du Guesclin. The advantage he had obtained, in a skirmish Rennes, against William Brembre, an English captain, so preyed spirits of William Troussel, the chosen friend and companion latter, that nothing would satisfy him but a mortal combat ιe Constable. The Duke of Lancaster, to whom Troussel ap-ɔr permission to fight the great Frenchman, forbade the battle, warranted by the circumstances. Troussel nevertheless burned fierce desire to cross his weapon with Du Guesclin, and sought ccasion to pick a quarrel with him. Having so good a will for ιurse he found a way. A relative of his had been taken pri-y the Constable, in whose hands he remained till he was able his ransom. Troussel resolved to make a quarrel out of this, patched a messenger to Du Guesclin, demanding the release risoner, and offering a bond, at a distant date, for the payment ɹansom. Du Guesclin, who had received intimation of the ɔurposes of the Englishman, sent back word that he would ɘpt his bond, neither would he release his prisoner until the ɔunt of his ransom was paid. As soon as this answer was , Troussel sent a challenge to the Constable, demanding repa-ɹr the injury he had done his honour, by refusing his bond, ring a mortal combat, to be fought three strokes with the ιree with the sword, and three with the dagger. Du Guesclin, ι ill in bed with the ague, accepted the challenge, and gave the Marshal d'Andreghem, the king's lieutenant-general in ɔrmandy, that he might fix the day and the place of combat. ιhal made all necessary arrangements, upon condition that ɹas beaten should pay a hundred florins of gold to feast the ιd gentlemen who were witnesses of the encounter.

. as he had denied his guilt by asserting that the lady was a will-
arty. The lady's asseverations of innocence were held to be no
nce by the parliament, and the duel was commanded, with all
eremonies. "On the day appointed," says Brantôme,* "the
ame to witness the spectacle in her chariot; but the king made
escend, judging her unworthy, because she was criminal in his
ill her innocence was proved, and caused her to stand upon a
d to await the mercy of God and this judgment by the battle.
a short struggle, the Sieur de Carrouges overthrew his enemy,
ade him confess both the rape and the slander. He was then
to the gallows and hanged in the presence of the multitude;
the innocence of the lady was proclaimed by the heralds, and
ised by her husband, the king, and all the spectators."

merous battles of a similar description constantly took place,
he unfortunate issue of one encounter of the kind led the
king, Henry II., to declare solemnly that he would never
ermit any such encounter, whether it related to a civil or cri-
ase, or the honour of a gentleman.

s memorable combat was fought in the year 1547. François
nne, lord of La Chataigneraie, and Guy de Chabot, lord of
had been friends from their early youth, and were noted at
rt of Francis I. for the gallantry of their bearing and the mag-
e of their retinue. Chataigneraie, who knew that his friend's
ere not very ample, asked him one day in confidence how it
t he contrived to be so well provided? Jarnac replied, that
r had married a young and beautiful woman, who, loving the
etter than the sire, supplied him with as much money as he

La Chataigneraie betrayed the base secret to the dauphin,
hin to the king, the king to his courtiers, and the courtiers
ir acquaintance. In a short time it reached the ears of the
de Jarnac, who immediately sent for his son, and demanded
in what manner the report had originated, and whether he
. vile enough not only to carry on such a connexion but to
t? De Jarnac indignantly denied that he had ever said so,
reason to the world to say so, and requested his father to
y him to court and confront him with his accuser, that he
the manner in which he would confound him. They went
ly; and the younger de Jarnac, entering a room where the
La Chataigneraie, and several courtiers were present, ex-
loud, "That whoever had asserted that he maintained a
onnexion with his mother-in-law was a liar and a coward!"
was turned to the dauphin and La Chataigneraie, when the

* *Mémoires de Brantôme touchant les Duels.*

1 prepared at the extremity of the lists. De Jarnac was not so
ent, though perhaps more desperate. At noon, on the day ap-
:d, the combatants met, and each took the customary oath that
re no charms or amulets about him, or made use of any magic,
him against his antagonist. They then attacked each other,
in hand. La Chataigneraie was a strong robust man, and over
:nt ; De Jarnac was nimble, supple, and prepared for the worst.
>mbat lasted for some time doubtful, until De Jarnac, over-
·d by the heavy blows of his opponent, covered his head with
eld, and stooping down, endeavoured to make amends by his
for his deficiency of strength. In this crouching posture he
two blows at the left thigh of La Chataigneraie, who had
uncovered, that the motion of his leg might not be impeded.
·low was successful, and, amid the astonishment of all the
>rs, and to the great regret of the king, La Chataigneraie
>ver upon the sand. He seized his dagger, and made a last
> strike De Jarnac : but he was unable to support himself,
powerless into the arms of the assistants. The officers now
ed, and De Jarnac being declared the victor, fell down upon
es, uncovered his head, and, clasping his hands together,
ed : *" O Domine, non sum dignus !"* La Chataigneraie was
itied by the result of the encounter, that he resolutely re-
have his wounds dressed. He tore off the bandages which
·eons applied, and expired two days afterwards. Ever since
ie, any sly and unforeseen attack has been called by the
ι *coup de Jarnac.* Henry was so grieved at the loss of his
, that he made the solemn oath already alluded to, that he
·ver again, so long as he lived, permit a duel. Some writers
erted, and among others, Mezerai, that he issued a royal
bidding them. This has been doubted by others, and as
>ears no registry of the edict in any of the courts, it seems
>able that it was never issued. This opinion is strengthened
ct, that, two years afterwards, the council ordered another
ιe fought with similar forms, but with less magnificence,
ιt of the inferior rank of the combatants. It is not any
·ted that Henry interfered to prevent it, notwithstanding
ι oath ; but that, on the contrary, he encouraged it, and
the Marshal de la Marque to see that it was conducted
to the rules of chivalry. The disputants were Fendille
ιerre, two gentlemen of the household, who, quarrelling in
chamber, had proceeded from words to blows. The coun-
informed of the matter, decreed that it could only be de-
he lists. Marshal de la Marque, with the king's permis-

he combat were forthwith appointed. When the hour had come,
. all were ready, Marolles turned to his second, and asked whether
opponent had a casque or helmet only, or whether he wore a
ide, or headpiece. Being answered a helmet only, he said gaily,
) much the better; for, sir my second, you shall repute me the
:edest man in all the world, if I do not thrust my lance right
ugh the middle of his head and kill him." Truth to say, he did
t the very first onset,' and the unhappy L'Isle-Marivaut expired
out a groan. Brantôme, who relates this story, adds, that the
r might have done as he pleased with the body, cut off the
, dragged it out of the camp, or exposed it upon an ass; but
being a wise and very courteous gentleman, he left it to the re-
:s of the deceased to be honourably buried, contenting himself
the glory of his triumph, by which he gained ro little renown
onour among the ladies of Paris.
ι the accession of Henry IV., that monarch determined to set his
ʒainst duelling; but such was the influence of early education
ιe prejudices of society upon him, that he never could find it in
art to punish a man for this of-

He thought it tended to foster
·like spirit among his people.
the chivalrous Créqui demanded
·mission to fight Don Philippe
ɔire, he is reported to have said,
ιnd if I were not a king, I would
ιr second." It is no wonder
hen such was known to be the
disposition, his edicts attracted
ιall attention. A calculation
.de by M. de Lomenie, in the
07, that since the accession of
in 1589, no less than four
d French gentlemen had lost

HENRY IV.

·es in these conflicts; which, for the eighteen years, would
en at the rate of four or five in a week, or eighteen per

Sully, who reports this fact in his Memoirs, does not
ιe slightest doubt upon its exactness; and adds, that it
fly owing to the facility and ill-advised good-nature of his
ster that the bad example had so empoisoned the court, the
the whole country. This wise minister devoted much of his
attention to the subject; for the rage, he says, was such as
him a thousand pangs, and the king also. There was hardly
oving in what was called good society, who had not been

that the king turned towards him, and said—" Great master!
our face I conjecture that you know more of this matter than
would have us believe.   I pray you, and indeed I command, that
tell us what you think, and what you know."   The coy minister
ied, as he says, out of mere politeness to his more ignorant col-
les; but, being again pressed by the king, he entered into a his-
of duelling both in ancient and modern times.   He has not pre-
d this history in his Memoirs; and, as none of the ministers or
cillors present thought proper to do so, the world is deprived
discourse which was, no doubt, a learned and remarkable one.
result was, that a royal edict was issued, which Sully lost no
in transmitting to the most distant provinces, with a distinct
cation to all parties concerned that the king was in earnest, and
l exert the full rigour of the law in punishment of the offenders.
himself does not inform us what were the provisions of the new
but Father Matthias has been more explicit, and from him we
that the marshals of France were created judges of a court of
ry, for the hearing of all causes wherein the honour of a noble
tleman was concerned, and that such as resorted to duelling
be punished by death and confiscation of property, and that
conds and assistants should lose their rank, dignity, or offices,
banished from the court of their sovereign.*
t so strong a hold had the education and prejudice of his age
he mind of the king, that though his reason condemned, his
hies approved the duel.   Notwithstanding this threatened
v, the number of duels did not diminish, and the wise Sully
ll to lament the prevalence of an evil which menaced society
ter disorganisation.   In the succeeding reign the practice pre-
if possible, to a still greater extent, until the Cardinal de
u, better able to grapple with it than Sully had been, made
vere examples in the very highest classes.   Lord Herbert, the
ambassador at the court of Louis XIII., repeats, in his let-
observation that had been previously made in the reign of
V., that it was rare to find a Frenchman moving in good
vho had not killed his man in a duel.   The Abbé Millot says
eriod, that the duel madness made the most terrible ravages.
l actually a frenzy for combating.   Caprice and vanity, as
he excitement of passion, imposed the necessity of fighting.
were obliged to enter into the quarrels of their friends, or be
es called out for their refusal, and revenge became hereditary
families.   It was reckoned that in twenty years eight thou-

* Le Père Matthias, tome ii. livre iv.

bined to make him detest it, and when his power in France was
ly established, he set vigorously about repressing it. In his *Tes-
nt Politique*, he has collected his thoughts upon the subject, in
:hapter entitled " Des moyens d'arrêter les Duels." In spite of
:dicts that he published, the members of the nobility persisted in
ing upon the most trivial and absurd pretences. At last Richelieu
: a terrible example. The infamous De Bouteville challenged
fought the Marquis de Beuvron; and although the duel itself
1ot fatal to either, its consequences were fatal to both. High as
were, Richelieu resolved that the law should reach them both,
:hey were both tried, found guilty, and beheaded. Thus did
:y get rid of one of the most bloodthirsty scoundrels that ever
:ed it.

1632 two noblemen fought a duel in which they were both
. The officers of justice had notice of the breach of the law,
rrived at the scene of combat before the friends of the parties
ime to remove the bodies. In conformity with the cardinal's

SULLY.

: code upon the subject, the
: were ignominiously stripped
ianged upon a gallows with
heads downwards, for several
within sight of all the people.*
everity sobered the frenzy of
ition for a time; but it was
orgotten. Men's minds were
:ply imbued with a false notion
our to be brought to a right
thinking : by such examples,
:r striking, Richelieu was un-
persuade them to walk in the
ath, though he could punish
r choosing the wrong one. He
:h all his acuteness, miscalculated the spirit of duelling. It was
th that a duellist feared; it was shame, and the contempt of
)ws. As Addison remarked more than eighty years afterwards,
1 was not sufficient to deter men who made it their glory to
it; but if every one who fought a duel were to stand in the
it would quickly diminish the number of those imaginary men
ır, and put an end to so absurd a practice." Richelieu never
of this.

r says, that in his time the Germans were also much addicted
ing. There were three places where it was legal to fight;

* *Mercure de France*, vol. xiii.

replied Bussy, "and, since you wish to put me in my uncle's
э, I answer, that whoever asserted that he called you a drunkard,
a lie!" "My brother said so," replied Bruc, "and he is a child."
эrsewhip him, then, for his falsehood," returned De Bussy. " I
not have my brother called a liar," returned Bruc, determined
ларrel with him ; "so draw, and defend yourself !" They both
their swords in the public street, but were separated by the spec-
·s. They agreed, however, to fight on a future occasion, and with
ле regular forms of the duello. A few days afterwards, a gentle-
whom De Bussy had never before seen, and whom he did not
· even by name, called upon him and asked if he might have
эrivilege of serving as his second. He added, that he neither
him nor Bruc, except by reputation, but having made up his
to be second of one of them, he had decided upon accompany-
'e Bussy as the braver man of the two. De Bussy thanked him
incerely for his politeness, but begged to be excused, as he had
ly engaged four seconds to accompany him, and he was afraid
f he took any more the affair would become a battle instead of
l.

hen such quarrels as these were looked upon as mere matters of
·, the state of society must have been indeed awful. Louis XIV.
arly saw the evil, and as early determined to remedy it. It was
owever, till the year 1679, when he instituted the "Chambre
te," for the trial of the slow poisoners and pretenders to sorcery,
e published any edict against duelling. In that year his famous
was promulgated, in which he reiterated and confirmed the
enactments of his predecessors Henry IV. and Louis XIII., and
sed his determination never to pardon any offender. By this
ıted ordinance, a supreme court of honour was established, com-
of the marshals of France. They were bound, on taking the
to give to every one who brought a well-founded complaint be-
ıem, such reparation as would satisfy the justice of the case.
any gentleman against whom complaint was made refuse to
ıe mandate of the court of honour, he might be punished by
ıd imprisonment; and when that was not possible, by reason
ıbsenting himself from the kingdom, his estates might be con-
l till his return.
·ry man who sent a challenge, be the cause of offence what it
was deprived of all redress from the court of honour—sus-
three years from the exercise of any office in the state—was
imprisoned for two years, and sentenced to pay a fine of half
·ly income.
who accepted a challenge was subject to the same punishment.

ιce in Elizabeth's reign, which is curious, perhaps the more so when ə consider that it was perfectly legal, and that similar combats reιined so till the year 1819. A proceeding having been instituted the Court of Common Pleas for the recovery of certain manorial ɟhts in the county of Kent, the defendant offered to prove by single mbat his right to retain possession. The plaintiff accepted the ιllenge, and the Court having no power to stay the proceedings, reed to the champions who were to fight in lieu of the principals. ιe queen commanded the parties to compromise; but it being reprented to her majesty that they were justified by law in the course ey were pursuing, she allowed them to proceed. On the day apinted, the justices of the Common Pleas, and all the counsel gaged in the cause, appeared as umpires of the combat, at a place Tothill-fields, where the lists had been prepared. The champions ɔre ready for the encounter, and the plaintiff and defendant were ιblicly called to come forward and acknowledge them. The defend-t answered to his name, and recognised his champion with the due rmalities, but the plaintiff did not appear. Without his presence d authority the combat could not take place; and his absence being nsidered an abandonment of his claim, he was declared to be non-ited, and barred for ever from renewing his suit before any other ιbunal whatever.

The queen appears to have disapproved personally of this mode of ttling a disputed claim, but her judges and legal advisers made no tempt to alter the barbarous law. The practice of private duelling cited more indignation, from its being of every-day occurrence. In e time of James I. the English were so infected with the French ιdness, that Bacon, when he was attorney-general, lent the aid of ɜ powerful eloquence to effect a reformation of the evil. Informa-ɔns were exhibited in the Star Chamber against two persons, named iest and Wright, for being engaged, as principal and second, in a ιel, on which occasion he delivered a charge that was so highly proved of by the Lords of the Council, that they ordered it to be inted and circulated over the country, as a thing "very meet and ɔrthy to be remembered and made known unto the world." He gan by considering the nature and greatness of the mischief of ιelling. "It troubleth peace—it disfurnisheth war—it bringeth lamity upon private men, peril upon the state, and contempt upon e law. Touching the cause of it," he observed, "that the first ɔtive of it, no doubt, is a false and erroneous imagination of honour d credit; but then, the seed of this mischief being such, it is ιurished by vain discourses and green and unripe conceits. Here-ιto may be added, that men have almost lost the true notion and

days, and then surrendered to take his trial, in the hope (happily
e) that Justice would belie her name, and be lenient to a murderer
ause he was a nobleman, who on a false point of honour had
ught fit to take revenge into his own hands. The most powerful
rcessions were employed in his favour, but James, to his credit,
deaf to them all. Bacon, in his character of attorney-general,
secuted the prisoner to conviction; and he died the felon's death
the 29th of June, 1612, on a gibbet erected in front of the gate of
stminster Hall.

With regard to the public duel, or trial by battle, demanded under
sanction of the law, to terminate a quarrel which the ordinary
se of justice could with difficulty decide, Bacon was equally op-
d to it, and thought that in no case should it be granted. He
gested that there should be declared a constant and settled resolu-
in the state to abolish it altogether; that care should be taken
the evil be no more cockered, nor the humour of it fed, but that
persons found guilty should be rigorously punished by the Star
mber, and those of eminent quality banished from the court.

n the succeeding reign, when Donald Mackay, the first Lord
y, accused David Ramsay of treason, in being concerned with the
quis of Hamilton in a design upon the crown of Scotland, he was
lenged by the latter to make good his assertion by single combat.*
d been at first the intention of the government to try the case
he common law, but Ramsay thought he would stand a better
ice of escape by recurring to the old and almost exploded custom,
which was still the right of every man in appeals of treason.
Reay readily accepted the challenge, and both were confined in
Tower until they found security that they would appear on a
in day appointed by the court to determine the question. The
gement of the affair was delegated to the Marischal Court of
minster, and the Earl of Lindsay was created Lord Constable of
and for the purpose. Shortly before the day appointed, Ramsay
ssed in substance all that Lord Reay had laid to his charge, upon
h Charles I. put a stop to the proceedings.

ut in England, about this period, sterner disputes arose among
than those mere individual matters which generate duels. The
of the Commonwealth encouraged no practice of the kind, and
bdued aristocracy carried their habits and prejudices elsewhere,
fought their duels at foreign courts. Cromwell's parliament,
ver—although the evil at that time was not so crying—pub-
l an order in 1654 for the prevention of duels, and the punish-
of all concerned in them. Charles II., on his restoration, also

* See *History of the House and Clan of Mackay.*

! upon the subject in the following impressive words :—" A Chris-
ι and a gentleman are made inconsistent appellations of the same
ion.   You are not to expect eternal life if you do not forgive in-
es, and your mortal life is rendered uncomfortable if you are not
!y to commit a murder in resentment of an affront ; for good sense,
'ell as religion, is so utterly banished the world, that men glory
ιeir very passions, and pursue trifles with the utmost vengeance,
ttle do they know that to forgive is the most arduous pitch human
re can arrive at.   A coward has often fought, a coward has often
uered; but a coward never forgave." Steele also published a
ιhlet, in which he gave a detailed account of the edict of Louis
, and the measures taken by that monarch to cure his subjects
eir murderous folly.

n the 8th of May, 1711, Sir Cholmely Deering, M.P. for the
:y of Kent, was slain in a duel by Mr. Richard Thornhill, also a
ιer of the House of Commons.   Three days afterwards Sir Peter
brought the subject under the notice of the legislature ; and
Iwelling at considerable length on the alarming increase of the
ce, obtained leave to bring in a bill for the prevention and
ιment of duelling.   It was read a first time that day, and or-
for a second reading in the ensuing week.

out the same time, the attention of the Upper House of Parlia-
vas also drawn to the subject in the most painful manner.   Two
most noted members would have fought had it not been that
Anne received notice of their intention, and exacted a pledge
.ey would desist ; while a few months afterwards two other of
ιbers lost their lives in one of the most remarkable duels upon

The first affair, which happily terminated without a meet-
s between the Duke of Marlborough and the Earl Pawlet ; the
.nd fatal encounter was between the Duke of Hamilton and
ohun.

first arose out of a debate in the Lords upon the conduct of
:e of Ormond in refusing to hazard a general engagement with
my, in which Earl Pawlet remarked that nobody could doubt
rage of the Duke of Ormond.   "He was not like a .certain
who led troops to the slaughter, to cause great numbers of
:o be knocked on the head in a battle, or against stone walls,
to fill his pockets by disposing of their commissions." Every
that the remark was aimed at the Duke of Marlborough, but
ned silent, though evidently suffering in mind. Soon after
ιe broke up, the Earl Pawlet received a visit from Lord Mo-
o told him that the Duke of Marlborough was anxious to
ιn explanation with him relative to some expressions he had

ι.   •   ᴜ

he event be what it will." Lord Mohun did not wish that the
nds should engage, but the duke insisted that *" Macartney should
a share in the dance."* All being ready, the two principals took
heir positions, and fought with swords so desperately, that after
ort time they both fell down mortally wounded. The Lord
un expired upon the spot, and the Duke of Hamilton in the arms
s servants as they were carrying him to his coach.

his unhappy termination caused the greatest excitement not only
e metropolis, but all over the country. The Tories, grieved at
oss of the Duke of Hamilton, charged the fatal combat on the
party, whose leader, the Duke of Marlborough, had so recently
ie example of political duels. They called Lord Mohun the bully
Whig faction (he had already killed three men in duels, and
twice tried for murder), and asserted openly that the quarrel was
cted between him and General Macartney to rob the country of
rvices of the Duke of Hamilton by murdering him. It was also
ed that the wound of which the duke died was not inflicted by
Mohun, but by Macartney; and every means was used to pro-
this belief. Colonel Hamilton, against whom and Macartney
roner's jury had returned a verdict of wilful murder, surrendered
days afterwards, and was examined before a privy council sit-
t the house of Lord Dartmouth. He then deposed, that seeing
Mohun fall, and the duke upon him, he ran to the duke's assist-
and that he might with the more ease help him, he flung down
heir swords, and as he was raising the duke up, *he saw Macart-
ike a push at him.* Upon this deposition, a royal proclamation
imediately issued, offering a reward of 500*l.* for the apprehen-
Macartney, to which the Duchess of Hamilton afterwards
reward of 300*l.*

n the further examination of Colonel Hamilton, it was found
iance could not be placed on all his statements, and that he
icted himself in several important particulars. He was ar-
at the Old Bailey for the murder of Lord Mohun, the whole
l circles of London being in a fever of excitement for the re-
ll the Tory party prayed for his acquittal, and a Tory mob
ied the doors and all the avenues leading to the court of
for many hours before the trial began. The examination
esses lasted seven hours. The criminal still persisted in
General Macartney of the murder of the Duke of Hamil-
in other respects, say the newspapers of the day, prevari-
illy. He was found guilty of manslaughter. This favour-
lict was received with universal applause, "not only from
and all the gentlemen present, but the common people

saction, in the course of which Du Barri contradicted an asser-
of the other, by saying "That is not true!" Count Rice im-
iately asked him if he knew the very disagreeable meaning of
words he had employed. Du Barri said he was perfectly well
e of their meaning, and that Rice might interpret them just
e pleased. A challenge was immediately given and accepted.
nds were sent for, who, arriving with but little delay, the whole
r, though it was not long after midnight, proceeded to a place
d Claverton Down, where they remained with a surgeon until
ght. They then prepared for the encounter, each being armed
two pistols and a sword. The ground having been marked out
e seconds, Du Barri fired first, and wounded his opponent in the
. Count Rice then levelled his pistol, and shot Du Barri mor-
in the breast. So angry were the combatants, that they refused
sist; both stepped back a few paces, and then rushing forward,
irged their second pistols at each other. Neither shot took effect,
oth throwing away their pistols, prepared to finish the sangui-
struggle by the sword. They took their places, and were ad-
ng towards each other, when the Vicomte du Barri suddenly
red, grew pale, and, falling on the ground, exclaimed, "Je
'emande ma vie." His opponent had but just time to answer
e granted it, when the unfortunate Du Barri turned upon the
and expired with a heavy groan. The survivor of this savage
t was then removed to his lodgings, where he lay for some
in a dangerous state. The coroner's jury, in the mean while,
on the body of Du Barri, and disgraced themselves by return-
'erdict of manslaughter only. Count Rice, upon his recovery,
dicted for the murder notwithstanding this verdict. On his
e entered into a long defence of his conduct, pleading the
s of the duel, and its unpremeditated nature; and, at the
ime, expressing his deep regret for the unfortunate death
Barri, with whom for many years he had been bound in ties
strictest friendship. These considerations appear to have
l with the jury, and this fierce duellist was again found
of manslaughter only, and escaped with a merely nominal
nent.
iel, less remarkable from its circumstances, but more so from
c of the parties, took place in 1789. The combatants on this
were the Duke of York and Colonel Lenox, the nephew and
he Duke of Richmond. The cause of offence was given by the
York, who had said in presence of several officers of the Guards,
'ds had been used to Colonel Lenox at Daubigny's to which
eman ought to have submitted. Colonel Lenox went up

example to the Irish that such murders were not to be committed
th impunity. A dispute arose, in the month of June 1807, be-
een Major Campbell and Captain Boyd, officers of the 21st regi-
nt, stationed in Ireland, about the proper manner of giving the
rd of command on parade. Hot words ensued on this slight oc-
tion, and the result was a challenge from Campbell to Boyd. They
ired into the mess-room shortly afterwards, and each stationed him-
f at a corner, the distance obliquely being but seven paces. Here,
hout friends or seconds being present, they fired at each other,
l Captain Boyd fell mortally wounded between the fourth and fifth
s. A surgeon, who came in shortly, found him sitting in a chair,
niting and suffering great agony. He was led into another room,
jor Campbell following, in great distress and perturbation of mind.
d survived but eighteen hours, and just before his death, said, in
y to a question from his opponent, that the duel was not fair,
 added, " You hurried me, Campbell—you're a bad man."—
od God!" replied Campbell, " will you mention before these
lemen, was not every thing fair ? Did you not say that you
 ready ?" Boyd answered faintly, " Oh, no! you know I wanted
to wait and have friends." On being again asked whether all
fair, the dying man faintly murmured, " Yes :" but in a minute
, he said, " You're a bad man!" Campbell was now in great
tion, and wringing his hands convulsively, he exclaimed, " Oh,
l! you are the happiest man of the two! Do you forgive me?"
 replied, " I forgive you—I feel for you, as I know you do for
    He shortly afterwards expired, and Major Campbell made
scape from Ireland, and lived for some months with his family
: an assumed name, in the neighbourhood of Chelsea. He was,
ver, apprehended, and brought to trial at Armagh, in August
    He said   e in prison, that, if found guilty of murder, he
l suffer as an example to duellists in Ireland ; but he endea-
d to buoy himself up with the hope that the jury would only con-
im of manslaughter. It was proved in evidence upon the trial,
he duel was not fought immediately after the offence was given,
iat Major Campbell went home and drank tea with his family
he sought Boyd for the fatal encounter. The jury returned a
t of wilful murder against him, but recommended him to mercy
 ground that the duel had been a fair one. He was condemned
in the Monday following, but was afterwards respited for a few
nger. In the mean time the greatest exertions were made in
talf. His unfortunate wife went upon her knees before the
 of Wales, to move him to use his influence with the king
ur of her unhappy husband. Every thing a fond wife and a

* Scores of duels (many of them fatal) have been fought from
utes at cards, or a place at a theatre; while hundreds of chal-
es, given and accepted over-night in a fit of drunkenness, have
i fought out the next morning to the death of one or both of the
gonists.

Two of the most notorious duels of modern times had their origin
uses no more worthy than the quarrel of a dog and the favour of
estitute: that between Macnamara and Montgomery arising from
former; and that between Best and Lord Camelford from the
r. The dog of Montgomery attacked a dog belonging to Mac-
ira, and each master interfering in behalf of his own animal, high
s ensued. The result was the giving and accepting a challenge
iortal combat. The parties met on the following day, when
gomery was shot dead, and his antagonist severely wounded.
affair created a great sensation at the time, and Heaviside, the
on who attended at the fatal field to render his assistance if
sary, was arrested as an accessory to the murder, and committed
wgate.

t the duel between Best and Lord Camelford, two pistols were
which were considered to be the best in England. One of them
hought slightly superior to the other, and it was agreed that
lligerents should toss up a piece of money to decide the choice
ipons. Best gained it, and at the first discharge, Lord Camel-
ell mortally wounded. But little sympathy was expressed for
te; he was a confirmed duellist, had been engaged in many
igs of the kind, and the blood of more than one fellow-creature
his door. As he had sowed, so did he reap; and the violent
iet an appropriate death.

now only remains to notice the means that have been taken to
ie prevalence of this madness of false honour in the various
ies of the civilised world. The efforts of the governments of
and England have already been mentioned, and their want of

eigh at one period of his life appeared to be an inveterate duellist, and it was
im that he had been engaged in more encounters of the kind than any man of
ing his contemporaries. More than one fellow-creature he had deprived of life;
ived long enough to be convinced of the sinfulness of his conduct, and made a
ow never to fight another duel. The following anecdote of his forbearance is
wn, but it will bear repetition:
iute arose in a coffee-house between him and a young man on some trivial point,
latter, losing his temper, impertinently spat in the face of the veteran. Sir
instead of running him through the body, as many would have done, or chal-
im to mortal combat, coolly took out his handkerchief, wiped his face, and said,
nan, if I could as easily wipe from my conscience the stain of killing you, as I
spittle from my face, you should not live another minute." The young man
ely begged his pardon.

)rive me of one-half of my officers. There are still men who know
v to unite the character of a hero with that of a good subject; and
)nly can be so who respects the laws. ·

"*August*, 1771. JOSEPH."*

In the United States of America the code varies considerably. In
or two of the still wild and simple states of the far west, where
luel has yet been fought, there is no specific law upon the subject
)nd that in the Decalogue, which says, "Thou shalt do no mur-
" but duelling every where follows the steps of modern civilisa-
; and by the time the backwoodsman is transformed into the
en, he has imbibed the false notions of honour which are preva-
in Europe and around him, and is ready, like his progenitors, to
e his differences with the pistol. In the majority of the States
)unishment for challenging, fighting, or acting as second, is soli-
imprisonment and hard labour for any period less than a year,
disqualification for serving any public office for twenty years.
ermont the punishment is total disqualification for office, depri-
n of the rights of citizenship, and a fine; in fatal cases the same
;hment as that of murderers. In Rhode Island, the combatant,
ğh death does not ensue, is liable to be carted to the gallows,
a rope about his neck, and to sit in this trim for an hour exposed
e peltings of the mob. He may be further imprisoned for a year,
e option of the magistrate. In Connecticut the punishment is
disqualification for office or employ, and a fine varying from one
red to a thousand dollars. The laws of Illinois require certain
:s of the state to make oath, previous to their instalment, that
have never been, nor ever will be, concerned in a duel.†
nongst the edicts against duelling promulgated at various times
.rope, may be mentioned that of Augustus king of Poland, in
which decreed the punishment of death against principals and
ls, and minor punishments against the bearers of a challenge.
lict was also published at Munich in 1773, according to which
)rincipals and seconds, even in duels where no one was either
or wounded, should be hanged, and their bodies buried at the
f the gallows.
e king of Naples issued an ordinance against duelling in 1738,
.ch the punishment of death is decreed against all concerned in

le the Letters of Joseph II. to distinguished Princes and Statesmen, published
irst time in England in *The Pamphleteer* for 1821. They were originally pub-
. Germany a few years previously, and throw a great light upon the character of
iarch and the events of his reign.
yclopedia Americana, art. Duelling.

wever severe the laws may be. Men must have redress for injuries
licted ; and when those injuries are of such a nature that no tri-
nal will take cognisance of them, the injured will take the law into
ir own hands, and right themselves in the opinion of their fellows,
the hazard of their lives. Much as the sage may affect to despise
? opinion of the world, there are few who would not rather expose
ir lives a hundred times than be condemned to live on in society,
t not of it—a by-word of reproach to all who know their history,
l a mark for scorn to point his finger at.

The only practicable means for diminishing the force of a custom
ich is the disgrace of civilisation, seems to be the establishment of
ourt of honour, which should take cognisance of all those delicate
l almost intangible offences which yet wound so deeply. The court
ablished by Louis XIV. might be taken as a model. No man now
hts a duel when a fit apology has been offered ; and it should be
? duty of this court to weigh dispassionately the complaint of every
n injured in his honour, either by word or deed, and to force the
ender to make a public apology. If he refused the apology, he
uld be the breaker of a second law ; an offender against a high
irt, as well as against the man he had injured, and might be
iished with fine and imprisonment, the latter to last until he saw
 error of his conduct, and made the concession which the court
nanded.

If, after the establishment of this tribunal, men should be found
a nature so bloodthirsty as not to be satisfied with its peaceful
isions, and should resort to the old and barbarous mode of an
eal to the pistol, some means might be found of dealing with
m. To hang them as murderers would be of no avail.; for to such
n death would have few terrors. Shame alone would bring them
reason. Transportation, the tread-wheel, or a public whipping,
uld perhaps be sufficient.

v of William Tell—the swords of Wallace or of Hampden—or
3ible whose leaves were turned by some stern old father of the
 ?

'hus the principle of reliquism is hallowed and enshrined by love.
from this germ of purity how numerous the progeny of errors and
rstitions! Men, in their admiration of the great, and of all that
rtained to them, have forgotten that goodness is a component
of true greatness, and have made fools of themselves for the jaw-
 of a saint, the toe-nail of an apostle, the handkerchief a king
his nose in, or the rope that hanged a criminal. Desiring to
ιe some slight token from the graves of their predecessors, they
confounded the famous and the infamous, the renowned and
ιotorious. Great saints, great sinners; great philosophers, great
ks; great conquerors, great murderers; great ministers, great
·es; each and all have had their admirers, ready to ransack earth,
the equator to either pole, to find a relic of them.

'he reliquism of modern times dates its origin from the centuries
ediately preceding the Crusades. The first pilgrims to the Holy
ι brought back to Europe thousands of apocryphal relics, in the
hase of which they had expended all their store. The greatest
ιrite was the wood of the true cross, which, like the oil of the
ιw, never diminished. It is generally asserted, in the traditions
ιe Romish Church, that the Empress Helen, the mother of Con-
tine the Great, first discovered the veritable " *true cross*" in her
·image to Jerusalem. The Emperor Theodosius made a present
ιe greater part of it to St. Ambrose, Bishop of Milan, by whom
ιs studded with precious stones, and deposited in the principal
·ch of that city. It was carried away by the Huns, by whom it
burnt, after they had extracted the valuable jewels it contained.
;ments, purporting to have been cut from it, were, in the eleventh
twelfth centuries, to be found in almost every church in Europe,
would, if collected together in one place, have been almost suf-
ιt to have built a cathedral. Happy was the sinner who could
ι sight of one of them; happier he who possessed one! To ob-
them the greatest dangers were cheerfully braved. They were
ιght to preserve from all evils, and to cure the most inveterate
ιses. Annual pilgrimages were made to the shrines that contained
ι, and considerable revenues collected from the devotees.

ἴext in renown were those precious relics, the tears of the Saviour.
ϝhom and in what manner they were preserved, the pilgrims did
inquire. Their genuineness was vouched by the Christians of the
r Land, and that was sufficient. Tears of the Virgin Mary, and
ι of St. Peter, were also to be had, carefully enclosed in little

Spain has seven or eight, all said to be undoubted relics.
s at one time preserved, and perhaps does now, the teeth of
dule. The faithful, who suffered from the toothache, had
pray, look at them, and be cured. Some of these holy bones
en buried in different parts of the Continent. After a certain
f time, water is said to ooze from them, which soon forms a
and cures all the diseases of the faithful.

curious to remark the avidity manifested in all ages, and in
ntries, to obtain possession of some relic of any persons who
en much spoken of, even for their crimes. When William
ard, leader of the populace of London in the reign of Richard I.,
ged at Smithfield, the utmost eagerness was shewn to obtain
rom his head, or a shred from his garments. Women came
sex, Kent, Suffolk, Sussex, and all the surrounding counties,
ct the mould at the foot of his gallows. A hair of his beard
ieved to preserve from evil spirits, and a piece of his clothes
hes and pains.

nore modern days, a similar avidity was shewn to obtain a
the luckless Masaniello, the fisherman of Naples. After he
n raised by mob favour to a height of power more despotic
narch ever wielded, he was shot by the same populace in the
as if he had been a mad dog. His headless trunk was dragged
the mire for several hours, and cast at night-fall into the
h. On the morrow the tide of popular feeling turned once
his favour. His corpse was sought, arrayed in royal robes,
ied magnificently by torch-light in the cathedral, ten thousand
en, and as many mourners, attending at the ceremony. The
n's dress which he had worn was rent into shreds by the
o be preserved as relics; the door of his hut was pulled off
es by a mob of women, and eagerly cut up into small pieces,
ade into images, caskets, and other mementos. The scanty
e of his poor abode became of more value than the adorn-
f a palace; the ground he had walked upon was considered
nd, being collected in small phials, was sold at its weight in
d worn in the bosom as an amulet.

st as extraordinary was the frenzy manifested by the popu-
Paris on the execution of the atrocious Marchioness de Brin-
There were grounds for the popular wonder in the case of
llo, who was unstained with personal crimes. But the career
me de Brinvilliers was of a nature to excite no other feelings
gust and abhorrence. She was convicted of poisoning several
and sentenced to be burned in the Place de Grève, and to
ashes scattered to the winds. On the day of her execution,

rers, but among the more wealthy inhabitants of Canterbury and neighbourhood. The tree against which he fell when he was shot, s stripped of all its bark by the curious; while a letter, with his nature to it, was paid for in gold coins; and his favourite horse ;ame as celebrated as its master. Parties of ladies and gentlemen nt to Boughton from a distance of a hundred and fifty miles, to it the scene of that fatal affray, and stroke on the back the horse the "mad knight of Malta." If a strict watch had not been kept er his grave for months, the body would have been disinterred, and bones carried away as memorials.

Among the Chinese no relics are more valued than the *boots* which ve been worn by an upright magistrate. In Davis's interesting scription of the empire of China, we are informed, that whenever udge of unusual integrity resigns his situation, the people all congate to do him honour. If he leaves the city where he has pre-ed, the crowd accompany him from his residence to the gates, ere his boots are drawn off with great ceremony, to be preserved the hall of justice. Their place is immediately supplied by a w pair, which, in their turn, are drawn off to make room for hers before he has worn them five minutes, it being considered fficient to consecrate them that he should have merely drawn them .

Among the most favourite relics of modern times, in Europe, are akspeare's mulberry-tree, Napoleon's willow, and the table at Warloo on which the emperor wrote his despatches. Snuff-boxes of akspeare's mulberry-tree are comparatively rare, though there are ubtless more of them in the market than were ever made of the ood planted by the great bard. Many a piece of alien wood passes der this name. The same may be said of Napoleon's table at Warloo. The original has long since been destroyed, and a round ozen of counterfeits along with it. Many preserve the simple stick wood; others have them cut into brooches and every variety of nament; but by far the greater number prefer them as snuff-boxes. France they are made into *bonbonnières*, and are much esteemed the many thousands whose cheeks still glow and whose eyes still arkle at the name of Napoleon.

Bullets from the field of Waterloo, and buttons from the coats of e soldiers who fell in the fight, are still favourite relics in Europe. ut the same ingenuity which found new tables after the old one was stroyed, has cast new bullets for the curious. Many a one who inks himself the possessor of a bullet which aided in giving peace the world on that memorable day, is the owner of a dump, first tracted from the ore a dozen years afterwards. Let all lovers of

INDEX.

smer, Anthony, the founder of animal
magnetism, his history and theory, i.
75; his theory and practice, 276; ele-
ance of his house at Paris, 278; infatua-
on of his disciples, 282.
als, transmutation of. (See Alchy-
ists.)
eoric phenomena, their effect in incit-
g to the Crusades, ii. 3, 11.
ors regarded as omens, i. 223.
n, plague of 1630 prophesied, i. 225;
ir of poisoners, Mora and others exe-
ed, 226; appearance of the devil, 227.
nium, the, universally expected at
end of the tenth century, ii. 3.
ISSIPPI SCHEME, the, its history, i.
t; financial difficulties in France,
edients of the Regent Orleans, i. 6;
cial peculation and corruption, 7;
n Law's propositions; his French cog-
nen, "Lass;" his bank established,
his notes at a premium; branch
ks established; Mississippi trading
pany established; bank made a pub-
nstitution; extensive issue of notes,
opposition of the Parliament, 11;
Regent uses coercion; Mississippi
es rise, 12; the Company of the
es formed; magnificent promises;
ense excitement and applications for
es; Law's house in the Rue de Quin-
oix (engraving), 13; hunchback used
writing-desk (engraving), 15; enor-
gains of individuals, 14, 16, 19, 20,
Law's removal to the Place Ven-
, 14; continued excitement, 15;
val to the Hotel de Soissons (en-
g), 15; noble and fashionable spe-
rs, 17; ingenious schemes to ob-
hares (engraving), 18; avarice and
ion of the speculators; robberies
urders, 20; a broker murdered by
d'Horn, and robbed of shares (en-
g), 21; temporary stimulus to
and illusive prosperity; Law
ses estates, and turns Catholic.
s charity and modesty, 25; cari-
i of him, as Atlas, 25; " Lucifer's
w barge," 29, in a car drawn by
40; increase of luxury in Paris,
Regent purchases the great dia-
27; symptoms of distrust; coin
depreciated, 28; use of specie
en, at Law's suggestion, 29; po-
tred excited, 30; fall of shares,
scription for the Mississippi gold
engraving), 31; further issue of
nd increased distrust and dis-
?; payment stopped, and Law
d from the ministry, 33; his
rom the populace, 33, 35, 38;
seau's measures to restore cre-
ait), 34; run on the Bank, 34;
idents in the crowd, 34; the
pi and India companies de-
f their privileges, 39; Law
rance, 40; D'Argenson's dis-
nd unpopularity, 42; Law's
nt history and death, 43; cari-
the scheme in its success and
, 29, 37, 40, 44.

Modern prophecies, i. 222-241.
Mohra, in Sweden, absurd charges of witch-
craft, and numerous executions, ii. 177.
Mohun, Lord, his duel with the Duke of
Hamilton, ii. 290.
Mompesson, Mr., his "haunted house" at
Tedworth, ii. 224.
Money Mania. (See the Mississippi Scheme
and South-Sea Bubble.)
Montesquieu "Esprit des Loix," ii. 262-267.
Montgomery and Macnamara, frivolous
cause of their fatal duel, ii. 297.
More, Hannah, on animal magnetism, i.
287.
Mormius, the alchymist, memoir of, i. 178.
Mortlake, Dr. Dee's house at, i. 153, 162.
Moses cited by alchymists as an adept, i. 95;
claimed as a Rosicrucian, 175.
Moustaches, fashion of wearing, i. 302.
Mummies, an ingredient in charms and
nostrums, i. 271.
Munting's history of the tulip mania, i. 87.

Nadel, Mausch, a German robber, ii. 257.
Naiades. (See the Rosicrucians.)
Nantwich, Nixon's prophecy of its fate,
i. 240.
Naples, arrest and execution of La Topha-
nia, the slow poisoner, ii, 207.
Napoleon's willow at St. Helena and other
relics, ii. 307.
Naudé, Gabriel, his exposure of the Rosi-
crucians, i. 173.
Necromancy, its connexion with alchymy,
i. 129; danger of its practice, 250.
New England, women, a child, and a dog,
executed as witches, ii. 180.
Nice besieged by the Crusaders, ii. 26.
Nixon, Robert, the Cheshire prophet, i.
238.
Noah, the patriarch, a successful alchymist
i. 95.
Noises. (See Haunted Houses.)
Normandy, witches in, ii. 172.
Nostradamus, the astrologer; his prophe-
cies (portrait), i. 246.

Oath on the Evangelists and holy relics, a
test of innocence, ii. 264.
Odomare, a French alchymist, i. 136.
Official peculation in France under the
Regent Orleans, i. 7.
Omens: winding-sheets, howling dogs,
death-watch, "coffins," shivering, walking under ladders, upsetting salt, thirteen at table, piebald horses, sneezing,
dogs, cats, bees, itching; Oriental belief
in omens, 255. (See Comets, Falling Stars,
and Meteors.)
Oneiro-criticism; interpreting dreams. (See
Dreams.)
Ordeals. (See Duels and Ordeals.)
Orleans, Duke of. (Regent of France) por-
trait of; his patronage of the Mississippi
Scheme, i. 5; his financial errors, 10, 12,
33, 41; enforces the execution of Count
D'Horn for murder, 23; his purchase of
the celebrated diamond, 27; his ill-treatment of Law, 33.
Orleans, Duchess of, her remarks on the
Mississippi scheme, i. 5, 19, 24, 35, 36.

Ingram Content Group UK Ltd.
Milton Keynes UK
UKHW021115180423
420361UK00006B/610